T0182011

Communications
in Computer and Information Science **1444**

More information about this series at http://www.springer.com/series/7899

Marcelo Naiouf · Enzo Rucci ·
Franco Chichizola · Laura De Giusti (Eds.)

Cloud Computing, Big Data & Emerging Topics

9th Conference, JCC-BD&ET
La Plata, Argentina, June 22–25, 2021
Proceedings

 Springer

Editors
Marcelo Naiouf ⓘ
III-LIDI, Facultad de Informática
Universidad Nacional de La Plata
La Plata, Argentina

Enzo Rucci ⓘ
III-LIDI, Facultad de Informática
Universidad Nacional de La Plata and CIC
La Plata, Argentina

Franco Chichizola ⓘ
III-LIDI, Facultad de Informática
Universidad Nacional de La Plata
La Plata, Argentina

Laura De Giusti ⓘ
III-LIDI, Facultad de Informática
Universidad Nacional de La Plata and CIC
La Plata, Argentina

ISSN 1865-0929   ISSN 1865-0937 (electronic)
Communications in Computer and Information Science
ISBN 978-3-030-84824-8   ISBN 978-3-030-84825-5 (eBook)
https://doi.org/10.1007/978-3-030-84825-5

This Springer imprint is published by the registered company Springer Nature Switzerland AG
The registered company address is: Gewerbestrasse 11, 6330 Cham, Switzerland

Preface

Welcome to the proceedings of the 9th Conference on Cloud Computing, Big Data & Emerging Topics (JCC-BD&ET 2021), held in an interactive, live online setting due to the COVID-19 situation. JCC-BD&ET 2021 was organized by III-LIDI and the Postgraduate Office both from School of Computer Science of the National University of La Plata.

Since 2013, this event has been an annual meeting where ideas, projects, scientific results, and applications in cloud computing, big data, and other related areas are exchanged and disseminated. The conference focuses on the topics that allow interaction between academia, industry, and other interested parties.

JCC-BD&ET 2021 covered the following topics: cloud, edge, fog, accelerator, green and mobile computing; big data; data analytics, data intelligence, and data visualization; machine and deep learning; and special topics related to emerging technologies. In addition, special activities were also arranged, including a plenary lecture and a discussion panel.

In this edition, the conference received 37 submissions. The authors of these submissions came from the following 9 countries: Argentina, Brazil, Chile, Ecuador, France, Portugal, Spain, Switzerland, and Uruguay. Moreover, 7 of the 37 submissions are international collaborations.

All the accepted papers were peer-reviewed by at least three referees (single-blind review) and evaluated on the basis of technical quality, relevance, significance, and clarity. To achieve this, JCC-BD&ET 2021 was supported by 50 Program Committee (PC) members and 70 additional external reviewers. According to the recommendations of the referees, 14 papers were selected for this book (37% acceptance rate). We hope readers will find these contributions useful and inspiring for their future research.

Special thanks to all the people who contributed to the conference's success: the PC and organizing committee members, authors, reviewers, speakers, and all conference attendees. Finally, we want to thank Springer for its support in publishing this book.

June 2021

Marcelo Naiouf
Franco Chichizola
Laura De Giusti
Enzo Rucci

Organization

General Chair

Armando De Giusti — Universidad Nacional de La Plata and CONICET, Argentina

Program Committee Chairs

Marcelo Naiouf — Universidad Nacional de La Plata, Argentina
Franco Chichizola — Universidad Nacional de La Plata, Argentina
Laura De Giusti — Universidad Nacional de La Plata and CIC, Argentina
Enzo Rucci — Universidad Nacional de La Plata and CIC, Argentina

Program Committee

María José Abásolo — Universidad Nacional de La Plata and CIC, Argentina
José Aguilar — Universidad de Los Andes, Venezuela
Jorge Ardenghi — Universidad Nacional del Sur, Argentina
Javier Balladini — Universidad Nacional del Comahue, Argentina
Oscar Bria — Universidad Nacional de La Plata and INVAP, Argentina
Silvia Castro — Universidad Nacional del Sur, Argentina
Mónica Denham — Universidad Nacional de Río Negro and CONICET, Argentina
Javier Diaz — Universidad Nacional de La Plata, Argentina
Ramón Doallo — Universidade da Coruña, Spain
Marcelo Errecalde — Universidad Nacional de San Luis, Argentina
Elsa Estevez — Universidad Nacional del Sur and CONICET, Argentina
Aurelio Fernandez Bariviera — Universitat Rovira i Virgili, Spain
Héctor Florez Fernández — Universidad Distrital Francisco José de Caldas, Colombia
Fernando Emmanuel Frati — Universidad Nacional de Chilecito, Argentina
Carlos Garcia Garino — Universidad Nacional de Cuyo, Argentina
Carlos García Sánchez — Universidad Complutense de Madrid, Spain
Adriana Angélica Gaudiani — Universidad Nacional de General Sarmiento, Argentina
Graciela Verónica Gil Costa — Universidad Nacional de San Luis and CONICET, Argentina
Roberto Guerrero — Universidad Nacional de San Luis, Argentina
Waldo Hasperué — Universidad Nacional de La Plata and CIC, Argentina
Francisco Daniel Igual Peña — Universidad Complutense de Madrid, Spain
Tomasz Janowski — Gdansk University of Technolgy, Poland

Laura Lanzarini	Universidad Nacional de La Plata, Argentina
Guillermo Leguizamón	Universidad Nacional de San Luis, Argentina
Edimara Luciano	Pontificia Universidade Católica do Rio Grande do Sul, Brazil
Emilio Luque Fadón	Universidad Autónoma de Barcelona, Spain
Mauricio Marín	Universidad de Santiago de Chile, Chile
Luis Marrone	Universidad Nacional de La Plata, Argentina
Katzalin Olcoz Herrero	Universidad Complutense de Madrid, Spain
José Angel Olivas Varela	Universidad de Castilla-La Mancha, Spain
Xoan Pardo	Universidade da Coruña, Spain
María Fabiana Piccoli	Universidad Nacional de San Luis, Argentina
Luis Piñuel	Universidad Complutense de Madrid, Spain
Adrian Pousa	Universidad Nacional de La Plata, Argentina
Marcela Printista	Universidad Nacional de San Luis, Argentina
Dolores Isabel Rexachs del Rosario	Universidad Autónoma de Barcelona, Spain
Nelson Rodríguez	Universidad Nacional de San Juan, Argentina
Juan Carlos Saez Alcaide	Universidad Complutense de Madrid, Spain
Aurora Sánchez	Universidad Católica del Norte, Chile
Victoria Sanz	Universidad Nacional de La Plata UNLP and CIC, Argentina
Remo Suppi	Universidad Autónoma de Barcelona, Spain
Francisco Tirado Fernández	Universidad Complutense de Madrid, Spain
Juan Touriño Dominguez	Universidade da Coruña, Spain
Gabriela Viale Pereira	Danube University Krems, Austria
Gonzalo Zarza	Globant, Argentina

Additional Reviewers

Nelson Acosta
Hugo Alfonso
Pedro Alvarez
Analía Amandi
Leandro Antonelli
Rubén Apolloni
Sandra Baldasarri
Ricardo Barrientos
Javier Bazzocco
Germán Braun
Agustina Buccella
Alejandra Cechich
Cecilia Challiol
Teresa Coma-Rosello
Leonardo Corbalán
Marisa De Giusti
Marcelo De Vicenzi

Lisandro Delía
Mario José Diván
Saúl Domínguez-Isidro
Diego Encinas
Silvia Esponda
César Estrebou
Guillermo Feierherd
Alejandro Fernandez
Alberto Fernández
Pablo Fillottrani
María Luján Ganuza
Mario Alejandro García
Christian García Bauza
Gorkem Giray
Susana Herrera
Jorge Ierache
Ramiro Jordan

Martín Larrea
Ariel Maiorano
Cristina Manresa-Yee
Ariel Maiorano
Ramón Más-Sansó
Sandra Méndez
Diego Montezanti
Regina Motz
Antonio Navarro Martín
Manuel Ortega Cantero
Ariel Pasini
Pilar Peral-García
Claudia F. Pons
Manuel Prieto-Matías
Facundo Quiroga
Hugo Ramón
Daniel Riesco
Franco Ronchetti

Alejandro Rosete-Suárez
Gustavo Rossi
Alejandro Sánchez
Cecilia Sanz
José Daniel Texier
Pablo J. Thomas
Fernando G. Tinetti
Cristian Tissera
Juan Toloza
Diego Torres
Marcelo Vénere
Paula Venosa
Pablo J. Vidal
Augusto Villa Monte
Gonzalo Luján Villarreal
Álvaro Wong
Marcos Zárate
Alejandro Zunino

Sponsors

COMISIÓN DE
INVESTIGACIONES CIENTÍFICAS

CONICET

Ministerio de Ciencia,
Tecnología e Innovación Productiva
Presidencia de la Nación

Sistema Nacional
de Computación
de Alto
Desempeño

AGENCIA

Agencia Nacional de Promoción
Científica y Tecnológica

RedUNCI

Red de Universidades Nacionales
con Carreras de Informática

Contents

Parallel and Distributed Computing

Analyzing the I/O Patterns of Deep Learning Applications

Edixon Párraga[1]([✉]), Betzabeth León[1], Román Bond[2], Diego Encinas[2,3],
Aprigio Bezerra[4], Sandra Mendez[5], Dolores Rexachs[1], and Emilio Luque[1]

[1] Computer Architecture and Operating Systems Department,
Universitat Autònoma de Barcelona, Campus UAB, Edifici Q,
Bellaterra, 08193 Barcelona, Spain
{edixon.parraga,betzabeth.leon,dolores.rexachs,emilio.luque}@uab.es

[2] SimHPC-TICAPPS, Universidad Nacional Arturo Jauretche,
1888 Florencio Varela, Argentina
{rbond,dencinas}@unaj.edu.ar

[3] Informatics Research Institute LIDI, CIC's Associated Research Center,
Universidad Nacional de La Plata, 1900 La Plata, Argentina

[4] Departamento de Ciências Exatas e Tecnológicas,
Universidade Estadual de Santa Cruz, Ilhéus, Bahia, Brazil
aalbezerra@uesc.br

[5] Computer Sciences Department, Barcelona Supercomputing Center (BSC),
08034 Barcelona, Spain
sandra.mendez@bsc.es

Abstract. A traditional HPC storage system is designed to manage an I/O workload dominated by write operation bursts, mainly for applications carrying out simulations and checkpointing partial results. Currently, this context is more diverse because of artificial intelligence applications' workload, such as machine learning and deep learning. As ML/DL applications are becoming more compute-intensive, they require the power of HPC systems. However, the HPC I/O system could be a bottleneck to scaling these kind of applications, mainly in the training stage. In this paper, we present a methodology for analyzing the I/O patterns of deep learning applications that allows us to understand the DL applications' I/O in HPC systems. We have applied our approach to serial and distributed DL codes by using the TensorFlow2 and PyTorch framework for the MNIST and CIFAR-10 datasets.

Keywords: Deep learning · I/O HPC · I/O Patterns · Distributed DL

1 Introduction

A traditional HPC storage system is designed to manage an Input/Output (I/O) workload dominated by write operation bursts, mainly for applications carrying out simulations and checkpointing partial results. Currently, this context is more diverse because of the artificial intelligence (AI) applications' workload, such as

M. Naiouf et al. (Eds.): JCC-BD&ET 2021, CCIS 1444, pp. 3–16, 2021.
https://doi.org/10.1007/978-3-030-84825-5_1

machine learning (ML) and deep learning (DL). Deep learning has been applied to a wide range of areas such as image recognition, natural language processing, computer vision, autonomous driving, and so on. As ML/DL models become more complex and I/O data becomes larger, ML/DL is becoming a compute-intensive application that requires the power of HPC systems [1]. Therefore, DL applications are more common in HPC systems and represent the kinds of applications that require different I/O systems to manage file data on an large scale. However, the HPC I/O system could be a bottleneck to scaling these kinds of applications. The ML/DL applications are characterized by read-intensive and randomly access from a larger number of small files during the training phase. Furthermore, for large scaling ML/DL modeling, the checkpointing techniques are needed to be able to use a pre-trained model for inference without having to retrain or to resume the training process.

Most DL applications are implemented by using framework that relies on the Python programming language. HPC tools have been adding support to these kinds of applications for performance evaluation. However, I/O tools still need some additional configuration to detect and extract the DL I/O patterns.

Unlike the traditional HPC I/O subsystem, the I/O software stack and I/O patterns differ from the classical software and tools for scientific applications. This is not only a challenge for the developer and administrator, but also for the users who need to analyze the DL I/O performance. The evaluation of the I/O performance requires to analyze the DL I/O patterns to understand their I/O behavior on the underlying HPC I/O systems.

In this paper, we present a methodology to analyze the I/O patterns of DL applications focused on the training stage of DL codes. Our approach is composed by three mains steps: characterization of the DL application, analysis of the trace, and description of the I/O behavior. We have analyzed the file I/O for serial and distributed DL codes executed in HPC systems. Furthermore, in order to evaluate how the framework can impact on the I/O pattern, we have evaluated the example codes for TensorFlow2 and PyTorch for the MNIST and CIFAR-10 datasets.

This paper is organized as follows: Sect. 2 presents a background of file I/O for DL applications, Sect. 3 describes the proposed methodology and Sect. 4 presents and discusses the experimental results. Finally, in Sect. 5, we explain our conclusions and future work.

2 Background

In this section, we briefly describe the main concepts related to Deep Learning and the file I/O for a better understanding of our methodology for analyzing the file I/O patterns.

2.1 File I/O in DL Applications

The ability of intelligent systems to learn and improve through experience gained from historical data is known as machine learning [2]. Machine learning requires an appropriate representation of input data in order to predict accurately. Every representation of the project characteristics that enables the system to reach a decision is known as a feature. The challenge of feature extraction, which often involves abstract features critical to a prediction system's decision in real-world applications is addressed by DL. DL builds complex representations from simpler ones and has multiple layers of abstraction. The algorithm allows models consisting of several processing layers to be operated on and thus learn data representations using multiple levels of abstraction [3].

From the point of view of I/O, training is the step where datasets are read. Depending on the problem size, this could be a bottleneck for running applications at scale. This bottleneck could mainly occur in learning frameworks running on GPU clusters with very high computational performance. DL applications must repeatedly read entire sets of data at random. If the datasets are small, the system cache or local node storage, such as an SSD, could hold the whole dataset and not impact performance. But, if they are substantial datasets that do not fit in the file system cache or local node storage, they could affect the learning workload's performance due to the bottleneck [4,5]. Another I/O source in the deep learning training phase corresponds to the checkpoint. As deep learning training jobs can take days, it is important to use a strategy that can avoid losing progress using checkpoints. The checkpoints can be configured to save the information after each epoch or save only the best weights. So by saving the model it would allow us to have a copy of the progress in a determined epoch and it can be used without having to return to the beginning of the training.

2.2 I/O Software Stack

Unlike the traditional I/O software stack in HPC (See Fig. 1), the software for the computations for training and predictions is performed by a framework. A framework for DL is typically written in Python, i.e. Caffe [6], Tensorflow[7] and PyTorch[8]. As can be seen in Fig. 1, the Deep Learning I/O software stack is still unclear at I/O middleware level. Although DL frameworks provide different file data formats and methods for dataset manipulation, there is still not a common middleware at high and low level for parallel I/O in DL.

In general, we can find two kinds of I/O bottleneck source: 1) thousands of small files that can overload the metadata server of the underlying file system (metadata issues) and 2) large amounts of data that needs to be read from storage because there is not enough cache/memory for the whole file (data-server issues). Both cases have access patterns of random reads and writes. This access pattern can have less impact on the I/O performance by using two levels of storage (fast and slow). These kinds of storage infrastructures can be managed by modern technology like the Distributed Application Object Storage (DAOS)[9]. DAOS is a forward-thinking open-source next step in HPC file-systems that utilizes objects rather than files. This enables next-generation data-centric workflows which combine simulation, data analytics and AI.

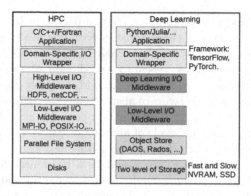

Fig. 1. Traditional HPC I/O SW stack vs expected DL I/O SW stack (adapted from source [10])

3   Proposed Methodology

To analyze the I/O behavior of a DL application, we focus our study on the most common DL stages: training, evaluation and prediction (left picture in Fig. 2). DL training is a stage that begins with the loading of the dataset (data read from the I/O system). During a long-term training process, snapshots of the weight variables can be taken periodically through checkpoints. The checkpoint permits the subsequent restart of the training in case of system failure [11], as well as in those systems that use a system of jobs in queues. In these systems, the execution must stop due to queue waiting time. They could use checkpoints to return to the queue, starting from the last image stored and not lose all the previous processing carried out. The file size of these checkpoints depends on the DL network in use, and each checkpoint can easily reach hundreds of megabytes in the case of most modern architectures [12]. After having the trained model, an evaluation is carried out to verify its accuracy. This can be loaded from the checkpoint that was saved in the training stage. Once obtaining the evaluated model, a prediction can then be made. In this paper, we select the training stage that presents the main interactions with the I/O system.

We propose a methodology composed of three main steps: characterization of the DL application, analysis of the trace and description of the file I/O behavior (depicted in right picture of Fig. 2).

To explain the different steps, we apply the methodology to a simple example (`FirstNetworkWithPrediction` download from [13]). We select the CIFAR-10 dataset with TensorFlow 2.0 and the Keras API. The example shows the trained and saved model from predicting image classes. It initially loads the model from the checkpoint for training, the provided values are 4-dimensional and they allow predicting multiple images in one go.

1. **Characterization of the DL application:** For this step, we use the Darshan profiling tool [14] that allows us to trace I/O operations carried out by

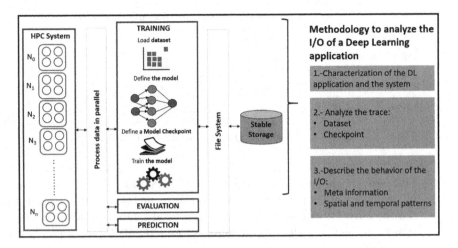

Fig. 2. Methodology to analyze the I/O of a deep learning application

Python codes. The CIFAR-10 dataset is divided into five training batches and a test batch, each containing 10,000 images, for a total of 50,000 training images and 10,000 test images. This test batch has 10,000 randomly selected images from each class. Thus, this dataset contains 60,000 32 × 32 color images in 10 categories, with 6,000 images per class. All this dataset information is organized as shown in Table 1:

Table 1. CIFAR-10 dataset information distribution by files

Number of files	Sizes of each file (MiB)	Total sizes of all files (MiB)
6	29.59	177.59

2. **Analysis of the trace:** The DL's application's I/O operations for each file are extracted by using the DTX utility of Darshan Tool. A snippet of the DTX's output is shown in Fig. 3. This is composed of a header for each file and a row for each I/O operation carried out in such a file. Each row presents the module type, the rank identifier (Rank), the type of I/O operation (Wt/Rd), the Offset, the size (Length), Start(s) and End(s) of the operation. Additionally, as this example reads from a Lustre file system, the Object Storage Target (OST) identifier where the operation is performed can also be observed. In a Lustre file system, user file data is stored in one or more objects, each object on a separate OST. A total of seven files were filtered as application files that correspond to the dataset and checkpointing.

```
# DXT, file_id:                174254740860852 file_name:  /mnt/lustre/scratch/TDarshan/cifar-10-batches-py/data_batch_1
# DXT, rank:                   0,               hostname:  c7257
# DXT, write_count:            0,               read_count:        3
# DXT, mnt_pt:                 /mnt/lustre/scratch , fs_type:   lustre
# DXT, Lustre stripe_size:     1048576,         Lustre stripe      1
# DXT, Lustre OST obdidx:                  40
# Module        Rank    Wt/Rd   Segment  Offset      Length     Start(s)  End(s)   [OST]
X_POSIX         0       read    0               0   4194304    4.6421    4.6933   [ 40]
X_POSIX         0       read    1         4194304  25165824    4.6964    4.7904   [ 40]
X_POSIX         0       read    2        29360128   1675576    4.7904    4.8123   [ 40]
```

Fig. 3. Output for the Darshan Tool's DXT utility

- **Dataset:** In our example, each file of the dataset is read three times following a similar pattern to the one shown in Fig. 3. Table 2 presents the total read operations, their sizes and total I/O made in the dataset that corresponds to the total amount of the CIFAR-10 files' data shown in Table 1.

Table 2. Total reads in the CIFAR-10 dataset

Number of reads	Sizes of each Read (MiB)	Total sizes of all reads (MiB)
6	24.00	144.00
6	4.00	24.00
6	1.60	9.60
Total size read from dataset		177.60

Table 3. Checkpoint write and read operations

#Operation	Size write (MiB)	#Operation	Size read (MiB)
0	0.00009155	0	0.00000763
1	0.00247192	1	0.00000763
2	0.00009155	:	:
3	12.00	125	12.00
:	:	126	0.00048828
33	0.00009155	128	0.00003815

- **Checkpoint files:** The checkpoint file is generated when the application is executed, and it has a size of 36.05 MiB. Table 3 shows the number of operations for each type and their size in one epoch. Most reads and writes are small in size, except for some that reach 12 MiB in both types of operations. In the case of writes, it needs to perform 33 operations to complete the 36.05 MiB, and 128 read operations to complete the 36.07 MiB, which is approximately the size of the checkpoint file.

3. **Description of the I/O behavior:** From the previous analysis, we represent the spatial and temporal I/O behavior. For performance issues, the I/O behavior of the DL application could be influenced by some hyper-parameters like the number of epochs or the batch size, among others. This example is run for a different number of epochs starting from one to forty.

   – **Dataset I/O Pattern:** To show the temporal order of I/O events, we present the different files in the same timeline. Figure 4 depicts the temporal pattern for this serial execution, where the x-axis represents the order of I/O events and y-axis the operation size. Each point represents a read operation with its corresponding request size. We can observe data_batch files are read in order from data_batch_1 to data_batch_5 and finally the test_batch. The I/O operations are for each epoch. As can be seen in Fig. 4, each file (data_batch) performs three readings, the first of 4 MiB, the second 24 MiB and the third 1.60 MiB.

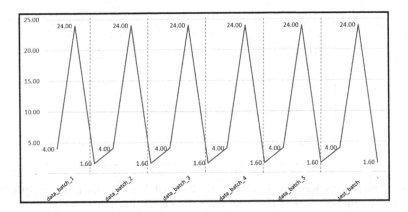

Fig. 4. Temporal pattern for CIFAR-10's dataset by epoch. I/O operations are in MiB. The x-axis represents the order of the events and the y-axis the operation size.

   – **Checkpoint I/O Pattern:** The temporal pattern for the checkpoint file is shown in Fig. 5. Several runs with different epoch numbers were performed to observe the interaction with the I/O system. Figure 5 shows a pattern only for writes, where many small write accesses occur, and every certain amount of writes forms a large one of 12 MiB. In this example, we execute from one to forty epochs; in each epoch 33 writes are carried out with the previously described pattern. Figure 6 depicts the read operations for the checkpoint file. In this case, 128 reading operations are performed regardless of the number of epochs.

   – **I/O latency:** in the temporal pattern, the time consumed by each I/O operation can be useful to explain some issues related to the access order. In the trace, in Fig. 3, two times can be observed: the start and the end of the operation. If we subtract these values, we get the operation

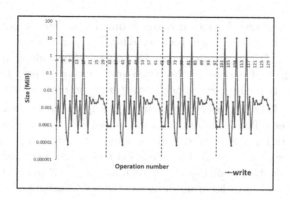

Fig. 5. Temporal pattern for the checkpoint file (only writes). Writes are in MiB. The x-axis represents the order of the events and the y-axis the operation size.

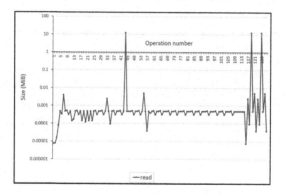

Fig. 6. Temporal pattern for the checkpoint file (only reads). Reads are in MiB. The x-axis represents the order of the events and the y-axis the operation size.

latency time, which is how much an I/O takes from request to completion. Figure 7 shows the time and size of the operations performed. This time corresponds to the I/O operation latency. Therefore a relationship between the size of the operation and its duration can be observed. In this case, we can observe an expected behavior, while the write and read size increases, the latency also increases.

We can summarize the observed I/O pattern, as shown in Table 4.

By using this methodology, we can analyze the trace and focus on the relevant aspects that can give us information on the behavior of the I/O in order to propose strategies that help reduce its impact on DL applications.

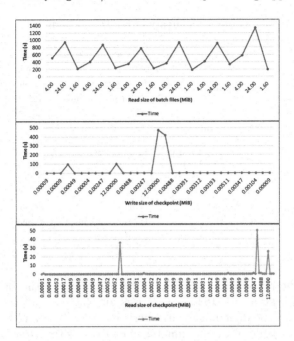

Fig. 7. I/O operation latency for the data_batch's files and the checkpoint file. The x-axis represents the request size and the y-axis its duration in seconds.

4   Experimental Results

Two different experimental environments are used. Serial and distributed experiments have been analyzed by using our methodology. As distributed DL, we select Horovod [15], which is a distributed deep learning training framework for TensorFlow, Keras, PyTorch, and Apache MXNet.

The technical description of experimental environments is as follows:

- **Experimental Environment 1:** Compute nodes - Processor Haswell 2680v3, Intel(R) Xeon(R) CPU E5-2680 v3 @ 2.50GHz, 24 CORES, 128 GB of RAM.
- GPU: NVIDIA Tesla K80
- I/O system: LUSTRE
- Software: Tensorflow 2.0 [7], Keras [16], Python 3.7, Dataset: CIFAR-10 [17].
- **Experimental Environment 2:** Compute nodes - Processor Intel(R) Xeon-(R) Gold 6148 CPU @ 2.40 GHz, 24 CORES, 512 GB of RAM.
- GPU: NVIDIA A100 GPUs
- I/O system: GPFS
- Software: Horovod, Tensorflow 2.0, Keras, Python 3.7, Dataset: MNIST [18].

4.1   Serial DL

In this section, we applied the methodology to the same example and framework used in Sect. 3, but with the MNIST (National Modified Institute of Standards and Technology) dataset.

Table 4. Summary of the I/O pattern

I/O features	Dataset	Checkpoint	
	Read	Write	Read
Number of epoch	From 1 to 40	From 1 to 40	From 1 to 40
Number of operations	18	33 * Epoch number	128
Total size (MiB)	177.6	36.05	36.07
Pattern description	Perform this sequence six times: a 4 MiB, a 24 Mib, and a 1.60 MiB reading	Three 12 MiB writes and 30 small writes	Three 12 MiB reads and 125 small reads
Number of files	6	1	1
File size (MiB)	6 * 29.60 MiB	36.05	36.05
Access type	sequential	Pseudo-random	Pseudo-random
Access mode	Only read	Read/rewrite	

Applying the proposed methodology, the first phase is the characterization of the DL application: MNIST is a dataset of 60,000 small square 28 × 28 pixel grayscale single-digit images handwritten between 0 and 9. This data is distributed in a single file, approximately 11 MiB in size. Later the analysis of the trace and description of I/O behavior were performed. Table 5 shows the summary of the I/O pattern for this case.

Table 5. Summary of the I/O pattern for the Serial DL example

I/O Features	Dataset	Checkpoint	
	Read	Write	Read
Number of epoch	From 1 to 200	From 1 to 200	From 1 to 200
Number of operations	10	25 * Epoch number	97
Total size (MiB)	17.4	1.18	1.2
Pattern description	Make ten accesses four 4MiB operations one of 1.39 MiB and the rest small	25 accesses are small the biggest are three of 392KiB	97 accesses are small the biggest are three of 392KiB
Number of files	1	1	1
File size (MiB)	11	1.2	1.2
Access type	Sequential	Pseudo-random	Pseudo-random
Access mode	Only read	Read/rewrite	

As can seen in Table 5, the experiments were run from 1 to 200 epochs. Dataset files are fully loaded, ten reads are carried out regardless of the number of epochs executed. The checkpoint file presents 25 writes per epoch. Ttherefore, as the number of epochs increases, the checkpoint file grows. For 200 epochs the number of writes is 200×25, meanwhile reads are 97 regardless of the number of epochs. Regarding the latency, this has the same behavior as shown in the methodology; the larger the size, the longer the time, but given the small sizes, the times were also small. This behavior could change when carrying out large-scale runs.

Discussion of Observed I/O Behavior - Serial DL. Regarding the I/O patterns obtained from serial experiments, the readings made from the dataset in both cases showed a similar I/O pattern, because the pattern was repetitive, regardless of the number of epochs. In this case, the dataset is read in the first epoch only, because the total datasets are loaded in the cache/memory. Therefore the epoch has no impact on the pattern observed. The regularity was observed both in CIFAR-10, for its five files and test file, and for the MINIST in its single file. In the checkpoint case, concerning the writings, both maintained a regular behavior that was repeated for each epoch executed.

4.2   Distributed DL

In this section, we applied our methodology to the Horovod framework for TensorFlow2 and PyTorch by using the MNIST dataset.

Tensorlow MNIST [19]: For the first experiment, the `tensorflow2_mnist.py` script was used, with different mappings of four processes in 1 node, eight processes in 2 nodes, 16 processes in 4 nodes and 32 processes in 8 nodes, to maintain the workload in 4 processes per node. In this paper, the I/O analysis for 32 processes in eight nodes are presented. The I/O strategy observed is one file per process, in this case the dataset file is needed for each parallel process. In Fig. 8, the left plot shows spatial pattern for this application. The y-axis represents the offset file, x-axis the MPI process and the colorbar represents the request size in a specific offset. As can be observed in the left plot of Fig. 8, three main sizes are depicted that represent the reading of the whole file. However, by analyzing the temporal pattern (right plot of Fig. 8), we can observe more operations. In this case, each process performs ten readings in the following order: two operations of approximately 10 MiB in the same offset (in dark purple), small reads in different offset (in yellow), one operation of 9.8 MiB (light purple) in a different offset and finally a read of 10 MiB in the same offset of the two first operations. This behavior is similar for the other experiments by using different numbers of processes and mapping.

Pytorch MNIST [20]: For the second experiment we used the `pytorch_mnist-.py` script from the Horovod benchmark by using 32 processes in 8 nodes and a mapping of four processes per node. In this example, we have 1 file for training and a file for testing. Both files are opened as shared files for all the processes.

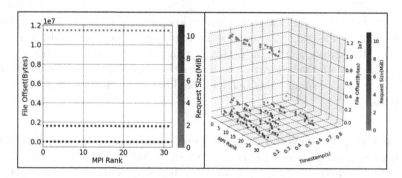

Fig. 8. Spatial and temporal pattern (tensorflow2_mnist.py) (Color figure online)

Figure 9 shows the spatial pattern for both files: training.pt and test.pt. Regarding the spatial behavior of the patterns in the training.pt file, all the processes perform eleven readings, of which three readings are 16 MiB, and one is approximately 28.86 MiB. The rest of the readings are very small. In the case of the test.pt file that is also shared by each process, it performed eight readings, of which three are approximately 7.5 MiB; the rest are small in size. Figure 10 presents the temporal pattern for both files. For shared training files each process performs eleven operations in the following order: 2 read operations of 16 MiB at file offset 0 (blue-green), small reads at the end of the file (yellow), one operation of 16 MiB at file offset 0 (blue-green), one operation of 30 MiB at the offset file 16 MiB (dark purple) and, finally, a small operation at end of the file (yellow). The temporal pattern for the testing file is more simple and is composed of the following operations: two read operations of 7 MiB at file offset 0 (dark purple), five small operations at the end of the file (yellow) and finally an operation of 7 MiB at file offset 0 (dark purple).

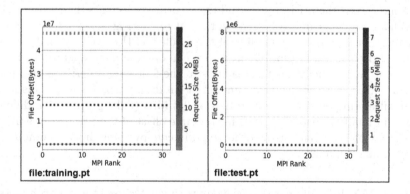

Fig. 9. Spatial pattern, pytorch_mnist.py (Color figure online)

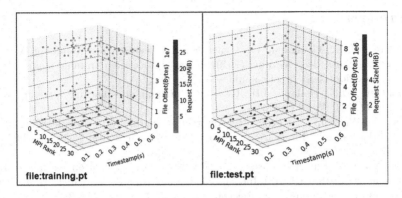

Fig. 10. Temporal pattern, pytorch_mnist.py (Color figure online)

Discussion of Observed I/O Behavior - Distributed DL. In this case, two different types of applications were analyzed, which were selected because they present different I/O strategies for reading datasets. In the case of TensorFlow2, the I/O strategy is one file per MPI process; where each process reads its own file. As in traditional HPC, these kinds of patterns represent a problem for scaling the application. In the case of PyTorch, all processes accessed a single shared file, but each one reads the whole file. As can be seen in Fig. 10, a serialization of the I/O operations is observed in both files that can be more significant due to a larger number of processes.

5   Conclusions

A methodology has been proposed to analyze the I/O behavior of Deep Learning applications. We have focused on the training phase, where most of the I/O is done; because it is here where the dataset is loaded and the checkpoint is generated. In this way, experiments were carried out for serial and distributed frameworks, and the methodology was applied to analyze the I/O patterns of each case. This work presents a first approximation with relatively small datasets and workloads in order to observe in more detail the execution of Deep Learning applications and thus be able to apply it on a larger scale later. The mainly I/O limitation observed for the Horovod DL framework is primarily related to parallel I/O approaches. As future work, it is intended to analyze another type of framework and find aspects of the system that could influence the I/O in order to reduce its impact on the execution of DL applications.

Acknowledgments. This research has been supported by the Agencia Estatal de Investigación (AEI), Spain and the Fondo Europeo de Desarrollo Regional (FEDER) UE, under contract TIN2017-84875-P and partially funded by the Fundacion Escuelas Universitarias Gimbernat (EUG).

References

1. Podareanu, D., Codreanu, V., Aigner, S., van Leeuwen, C., Weinberg, V.: Best practice guide - deep learning (2019). https://prace-ri.eu/training-support/best-practice-guides/best-practice-guide-deep-learning/
2. Goldberg, D.E., Holland, J.H.: Genetic algorithms and machine learning. Mach. Learn. **3**(2–3), 95–99 (1988)
3. Ilin, R., Watson, T., Kozma, R.: Abstraction hierarchy in deep learning neural networks. In: 2017 International Joint Conference on Neural Networks (IJCNN), pp. 768–774 (2017)
4. Zhu, Y., et al.: Entropy-aware I/O pipelining for large-scale deep learning on HPC systems. In: 2018 IEEE 26th International Symposium on Modeling, Analysis, and Simulation of Computer and Telecommunication Systems (MASCOTS), pp. 145–156 (2018)
5. Brinkmann, A., et al.: Ad hoc file systems for high-performance computing. J. Comput. Sci. Technol **35** (2020)
6. Jia, Y., et al.: Caffe: convolutional architecture for fast feature embedding. arXiv preprint arXiv:1408.5093 (2014)
7. Abadi, M., et al.: TensorFlow: large-scale machine learning on heterogeneous systems (2015). https://www.tensorflow.org/
8. Pytorch. https://pytorch.org/docs/stable/index.html/. Accessed 24 Mar 2021
9. Intel: DAOS - Distributed Application Object Storage. Intel, Technical report (2019). https://www.intel.com/content/dam/www/public/us/en/documents/solution-briefs/high-performance-storage-brief.pdf
10. Koziol, Q.: I/O for deep learning at scale. NERSC, Technical report (2019). https://storageconference.us/2019/Invited/Koziol.slides.pdf
11. Rojas, E., Kahira, A.N., Meneses, E., Gomez, L.B., Badia, R.M.: A study of checkpointing in large scale training of deep neural networks. arXiv preprint arXiv:2012.00825 (2020)
12. Chien, S.W.D., et al.: Characterizing deep-learning i/o workloads in tensorflow. In: 2018 IEEE/ACM 3rd International Workshop on Parallel Data Storage Data Intensive Scalable Computing Systems (PDSW-DISCS), pp. 54–63 (2018)
13. arconsis IT-Solutions GmbH: Firstnetworkwithprediction. Technical report. https://github.com/arconsis/cifar-10-with-tensorflow2
14. Carns, P., et al.: Understanding and improving computational science storage access through continuous characterization. ACM Trans. Storage (TOS) **7**(3), 1–26 (2011)
15. Sergeev, A., Balso, M. D.: Horovod: fast and easy distributed deep learning in TensorFlow. arXiv preprint arXiv:1802.05799 (2018)
16. Chollet, F., et al.: Keras (2015). https://github.com/fchollet/keras
17. Krizhevsky, A.: Learning multiple layers of features from tiny images. Technical report (2009)
18. LeCun, Y., Cortes, C., Burges, C.: MNIST. http://yann.lecun.com/exdb/mnist/. Accessed 24 Mar 2021
19. Horovod - tensorflow2_mnist.py. https://github.com/horovod/horovod/tree/master/examples/tensorflow2. Accessed 26 Mar 2021
20. LeCun, Y., Cortes, C., Burges, C.: Horovod - pytorch_mnist.py. https://github.com/horovod/horovod/tree/master/examples/pytorch. Accessed 26 Mar 2021

HESS-IM: A Uncertainty Reduction Method that Integrates Remote Sensing Data Applied to Forest Fire Behavior Prediction

Miguel Méndez-Garabetti[1,2](✉) ⓘ, Germán Bianchini[1] ⓘ,
and Paola Caymes-Scutari[1,2] ⓘ

[1] Laboratorio de Investigación en Cómputo Paralelo/Distribuido (LICPaD),
Departamento de Ingeniería en Sistemas de Información Facultad Regional Mendoza,
Universidad Tecnológica Nacional, Mendoza, Argentina
mmendez@mendoza-conicet.gob.ar,
{gbianchini,pcaymesscutari}@frm.utn.edu.ar
[2] Consejo Nacional de Investigaciones Científicas y Técnicas (CONICET),
Buenos Aires, Argentina

Abstract. Natural disasters alter the stability and living conditions in the environment. Natural disasters are caused by different types of hazards, which can be of natural or man-made origin, the latter in turn can be intentional or unintentional. Forest fires cause great losses and harms every year, some of which are often irreparable. Among the different strategies and technologies available to mitigate the effects of fire, the forest fire behavior prediction may be a promising strategy. This approach allows for identifying areas at greatest risk of being burned, thereby permitting to take decisions in advance to reduce losses and damages. In this work, we present a Hybrid Evolutionary-Statistical System with Island Model (HESS-IM), a new approach of the uncertainty reduction method that integrates remote sensing data applied to forest fire behavior prediction. HESS-IM uses hybrid metaheuristics under a collaborative approach as an optimization technique, satellite images for application to real cases, statistical analysis, and heterogeneous high-performance computing to generate predictions in the shortest time possible.

Keywords: Remote sensing · Satellite information · Forest fire prediction · Uncertainty reduction · HPC

1 Introduction

Natural disasters alter the stability and living conditions in the environment. Natural disasters are caused by different types of hazards, which can be of natural or man-made origin, the latter in turn can be intentional or unintentional [1]. Natural disasters have caused the loss of millions of lives in recent decades,

© Springer Nature Switzerland AG 2021
M. Naiouf et al. (Eds.): JCC-BD&ET 2021, CCIS 1444, pp. 17–30, 2021.
https://doi.org/10.1007/978-3-030-84825-5_2

displacing some 26 million people each year into poverty. Also causing economic damage in the order of 520 million dollars annually [2].

The risk of natural disasters not only depends on the occurrence of them possibility, but also on the existing vulnerability conditions that facilitates disasters unleash. According to [3] *"vulnerability is closely linked to the social processes that take place in prone areas and usually has to do with the fragility, susceptibility, or lack of resilience of the population to threats of different nature"*. It also mentions that, *"disasters are events with an environmental component, but also a social (socio-environmental) whose materialization is the result of the social construction of risk"*.

Due to this, it is considered important to work to reduce the conditions that allow the occurrence of natural phenomena. Such actions involve socio-economic aspects, such as land-use planning. Development of integrated risk management systems, increased funds for research in early warning and response systems, improvement of the conservation of natural spaces, environmental education, development of prediction systems, among others.

In Argentina, one of the natural phenomena that occur most frequently are forest fires. Year after year, forest fires affect millions of hectares making one of the main agents of disturbance of the planet's ecosystems. In addition, forest fires occur more frequently in the summer season, where dryness, temperatures, and/or wind increase, this facilitates the spread of fire thus reaching large areas. Due to this, different areas of science are constantly working on the development of: tools, systems, strategies, among others, that allow reducing the adverse effects they cause. Among those can be found: evacuation strategies, technologies for fire suppression, firebreaks, fire simulators, prediction systems, etc. These tools are usually used in different stages of the fire fighting process, being the same: prevention, prediction, detection, and monitoring.

In this work, we present the Hybrid Evolutionary-Statistical System with Island Model (HESS-IM) [4,5]. HESS-IM is a new approach of an uncertainty reduction method that integrates remote sensing data applied to forest fire behavior prediction. It is proposed as a framework that can operate with different optimization techniques and can apply to different propagation-based prediction problems. HESS-IM uses hybrid metaheuristics under a collaborative approach as an optimization technique, satellite images for application to real cases, statistical analysis, and heterogeneous high-performance computing to generate predictions in the shortest time possible.

In this paper, in Sect. 2 the problematic of forest fire prediction with classical approaches is described. Next, in Sect. 3 the concept of uncertainty in prediction systems is presented. The approach, implementation and methodology of Hybrid Evolutionary-Statistical System with Island Model (HESS-IM) and the operation of the automatic map generation module are explained in Sect. 4. Finally, the experimental results and comparison are shown in Sect. 5, and conclusions are provided in Sect. 6.

2   Forest Fire Prediction

In the literature, the term *Forest Fire Prediction* can refer to two similar but very different concepts. One of them consists of being able to predict the *occurrence* of a forest fire in a given area under evaluation. The other, on the other hand, refers to the *behavior* prediction of a forest fire that has already started.

In this work, we refer to forest fire behavior prediction, a process that consists of trying to forecast the spreading behavior of a forest fire that has already started, identifying the areas that present the highest risk of being hit by fire.

This kind of simulation implies a high level of complexity, both due to the models used, the software implementations, as well for the uncertainty that affects this process. This uncertainty comes from different sources such as: inaccurate or missing data, incomplete scientific understanding of the ecological response to fire and the response of fire behavior to mitigation treatments, among others [6].

2.1   Classical Prediction

The Classical Prediction method consists in evaluating the position of the fire after a certain initial period of time, using any existing fire simulator behavior. In Fig. 1 we present a general scheme of this kind of methodology. As can be seen, the simulator **FS** is fed by two sets of data: a) the real fire line of the wildfire at time t_0 (RFL_0), generally represented by a map that shows the burned area where the fire started, and b), the information that describes the environment on which the fire spreads, such as weather data, vegetation, terrain description, among others (all these data are called input parameters). Each input parameter has a value assigned, and this set of values, along with RFL_0, is used by **FS** to make the Prediction of the Fire Line (**PFL**) for the next time instant (t_1) through a single simulation. This approach is also known as one-step prediction [7]. In any prediction method it is expected that the estimated prediction carried out by the simulator coincides in the best possible way with reality. However, due to the uncertainty in the input parameters, the model complexity and since the prediction is based on a unique simulation, this prediction methodology provides generally far from reality predictions. Examples of classical prediction in wildfires are [8–13]. Due to the limitations of classical prediction, has been necessary the development of methods that allow for reducing the uncertainty in order to improve the prediction quality.

In addition, since these systems tend to work with large data sets and since they must perform complex operations, these systems often need to be implemented on high-performance computing platforms. Which allows reducing processing time by using multiple computing units simultaneously.

3   Uncertainty Reduction

The uncertainty concept itself has different meanings that can refer to the lack of knowledge, the lack of certainty, lack of comprehension, among others. In this

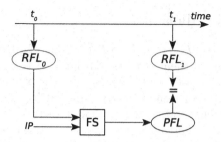

Fig. 1. Classical prediction: diagram of wildfire propagation (**FS:** Fire Simulator; **PFL:** Predicted Fire Line; **IP:** Input Parameters; **RFL**$_x$**:** Real Fire Line on time x)

work, we refer mainly to the lack of knowledge of the parameters that determine the behavior of the model, and secondly, to the lack of detailed understanding of the phenomenon. Mainly, this kind of uncertainty is usually observed in those variables that present a dynamic behavior. Some examples of this kind of variables are wind speed, wind direction, humidity content in vegetation, etc. These variables strongly affect wildfire behavior and should be measured in real-time. To do this, devices such as wireless sensor networks (WSNs) or internet of Things (IoT) approaches could be of great help [14,15]. By using this type of sensors in areas affected by fires, we can obtain temperature measurements, wind speed and direction, etc. It is important to note that although the WSN/IoT can be a promising tool to reduce uncertainty in the input parameters, this technology can only be used in protected areas where the installation of a sensor network is economically possible. In our work, we consider that there is no exact set of input parameters to feed the propagation model because it is not possible to know the exact value of each parameter when the fire begins and along the time. Furthermore, in most cases these models cannot be analytically solved and must be solved by applying numerical methods that are only an approximation to reality. Therefore, make a forest fire behavior prediction with estimated values cannot be considered as reliable.

At this point, we could say that in any prediction system we are going to have to work to reduce the existing uncertainty. When this imprecision is present, the prediction capacity of the method is considerably affected, since this is equivalent to feed the simulator with incorrect values, which usually will produce wrong predictions.

Due to the imprecision of the parameters and the difficulty to measure them in real-time, it is necessary to use some technique to enable the uncertainty reduction, such as the Data-Driven Methods (DDM). The DDM considers a large number of values for each parameter, instead of a single value for each parameter. Consequently, these methods perform a search to find a set of parameters that describes in the best possible way the previous fire behavior that will be used to predict the near future behavior, basing on some kind of time and space locality. In other words, the DDM perform a calibration to obtain these "optimal" values of input parameters. Nevertheless, these methods obtain a single set of values, and for those dynamic parameters, the found value is not generally useful to correctly describe the model behavior. This category of methods is called Data-Driven Methods of Unique Solution [16,17].

There is another classification of DDM that works with overlapping cases and combinations of parameters to make predictions. This category is called Data-Driven Methods with Multiple Overlapping Solutions (DDM-MOS). Statistical System for Forest Fire Management (S^2F^2M) [18,19], Evolutionary Statistical System (ESS) [20], Evolutionary Statistical System with Island Model (ESS-IM) [21], Evolutionary Statistical System with Island Model and Differential Evolution (ESS-IM-DE) [22] and Hybrid Evolutionary-Statistical System with Island Model (HESS-IM) [4,5] are included in this category. Specifically in this work, with the architecture proposed in HESS-IM, it is possible to increase two of the main characteristics of this type of methodologies, which are: a) the quality of prediction, and b) the response time.

DDMs are strongly related to Data Assimilation Methods (DAM), which are characterized by the incorporation of data into a running model [23]. From this point of view, we can say that HESS-IM belongs to both classifications: DDM-MOS and DAM, because its objective is to find a set of values that allows improving the final result and incorporating data at the execution time. Another approach that is particularly related to DDM-MOS is that of Dynamic Data Driven Application Systems (DDDAS). The DDDAS concept is to dynamically incorporate data and provide applications with the ability to dynamically direct measurement processes. Some data inputs can be acquired in real-time (on-line) or can be obtained through local storage. The DDDAS approach can allow an improvement in the modeling methods, increasing the prediction and analysis capabilities and increasing the efficiency of the simulation [24].

4   Hybrid Evolutionary-Statistical System with Island Model – HESS-IM

As mentioned in the previous section, data-driven methodologies provide a successful approach when it comes to developing prediction systems for phenomena under conditions of uncertainty and high dynamicity. In this context, HESS-IM focuses its efforts on minimizing the problem of uncertainty in the input parameters using techniques of: simulation [25], statistical analysis [26], high-performance computing [27], metaheuristic optimization [28] and remote sensing data [29]. It is important to note that HESS-IM has been proposed as the core of a larger project. Specifically, we talk about an Integrated System of Detection, Early warning, and Forest Fire Behavior Prediction, in Fig. 2 we can see a general scheme of this proposal. As can be seen, HESS-IM is integrated into two subsystems: 1) a module for the automatic map generation (AMG), and 2) a data injection module based on a network (WSN/IoT) for early detection of forest fires. In this work we present the integration of HESS-IM with the automatic map generation module.

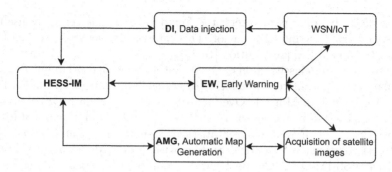

Fig. 2. General scheme of the integrated system of detection, early warning, and forest fire behavior prediction.

4.1   Metodology of HESS-IM

HESS-IM is a general-purpose parallel uncertainty reduction method that can be applied to different propagation models with propagation characteristics. In this work, it has been used as a parallel uncertainty reduction method for forest fire spread prediction. ESS-IM uses a Hybrid Metaheuristic (HM) based on a collaborative scheme of three evolutionary population-based metaheuristics: Evolutionary Algorithms (EA) [30], Differential Evolution (DE) [31] and Particle Swarm Optimization (PSO) [32], to optimize the parameters search that feed the model. In HESS-IM, the input parameter sets are represented by scenarios, according to each metaheuristic these can be: individuals, particles or vectors, for simplicity we will refer to any of these as individuals. Each individual contains a value for each input parameters which are grouped into populations. These parameters represent the input variables (e.g., vegetation type, moisture content, speed and wind direction, slope, and so on) which determine the behavior of a wildfire. Besides the use of HM to guide the search, HESS-IM uses statistical analysis to calibrate the results.

A general scheme of the HESS-IM operation is presented in Fig. 3. As we can see, there are three types of processes: a) *monitor* process, b) *master* process, and c) *worker* process. In a HESS-IM instance where j islands are operating, and w workers per island, a total of $1 + j + w * j$ processes will occur in parallel, that is to say 1 monitor process, j master processes (one for each island), and $w * j$ worker processes.

The prediction methodology start in the *monitor* process, which is responsible for sending to the *masters* of each island, the initial information of the fire (i.e., real fire map, time intervals to be considered, parameters, etc.). Previously, the monitor process will receive from the AMG module –through the communication module (CM)– the maps of the fire to be evaluated.

Each master (in each island) executes the Optimization Stage (OS_{master}), initiating its assigned metaheuristic (i.e., EA, DE or PSO). As can be observed, the metaheuristic stage is divided into two sub-stages: on the one hand, the metaheuristic sub-stage of the master process (M_M), and on the other hand, the metaheuristic sub-stage of the worker processes (M_W). The M_M stage is in charge of the fitness evaluation of the individuals, and the M_W stage is in charge of the rest of the operations involved in each metaheuristic. The workers of each island evaluate the individuals' fitness using a Fire Simulator (FS). FS is based on the model defined by Rothermel [33] and implemented using the fireLib library [34]. In order to perform the fitness assessment in t_i, it is necessary to have the actual Real Fire Line (RFL) in t_{i-1} (i.e., RFL_{i-1}) and the input parameters values, which are stored in the Parameter Vectors (VP). When the individuals are evaluated, they are sent with their fitness value to the stage M_M. M_M, in addition to performing the rest of the operations of each metaheuristic (i.e., alteration of individuals, evolution of the population, etc.), is responsible for the individuals migration to the neighboring islands. The migration process consists of selecting, sending/receiving and replacing individuals between the different islands. The metaheuristics hybridization of HESS-IM considers the different speeds of each algorithm, with the objective that all metaheuristics advance at the same time.

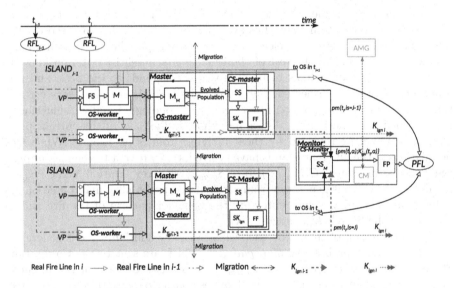

Fig. 3. Hybrid evolutionary-statistical system with island model: **FS:** Fire Simulator; **PEA:** Parallel Evolutionary Algorithm; **M_M:** Metaheuristic sub-stage in master; **M_W:** Metaheuristic sub-stage in worker; **OS:** Optimization Stage; **SS:** Statistical Stage; **SK:** Search K_{ign}; **K_{ign}:** key value used to make the prediction model; **FF:** Fitness Function; **CS:** Calibration Stage; **SS_M:** monitor Statistical Stage; **MK_{ign}:** monitor $K_{ign} value$; **FP:** Fire Prediction; **PFL:** Predicted Fire Line; **RFL_x:** Real Fire Line on time x; **PV:** Parameters Vectors; **pm:** probability map; **CM:** Communication Module; **AMG:** Automatic Map Generation.

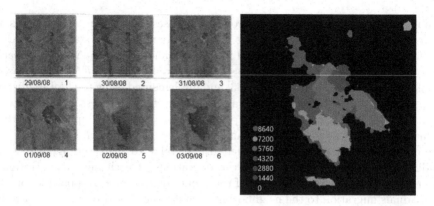

Fig. 4. Case study: At letf, forest fire that occurred in the town of Capilla del Monte, Córdoba Province, Argentina, 2008. Sequence of satellite images of the evolution of the fire (MODIS). At right, final fire map automatically generated by the AMG module.

Although in the same way the exchanges of individuals between the islands are carried out asynchronously, thus avoiding any problem due to speed decoupling. The migration process select, from the current population, those individuals who will be sent to the rest of the islands. A semi-elitist criterion is used, where 50% of the individuals to be migrated corresponds to the best, and the other 50% is randomly selected. The selected individuals are sent every certain time (i.e., migration frequency) following a ring topology. Finally, replacement is performed, this mechanism determines those individuals of the current population that will be replaced by those arriving from other islands. When the populations of the different islands have evolved, they are sent to the master process Calibration Stage (CS_{master}). In CS_{master} the Key Ignition Value (K_{ign}) is calculated, which is generated from a calculated probability map based on all individuals. The K_{ign} value represents the behavior pattern of the fire and is obtained in the Search K_{ign} stage (SK_{ign}).

At every instant of time i, on each island j, a key ignition value is generated $K_{ign}(t_i, is)$ and a probability map $pm(t_i, j)$, which are sent to the Calibration Stage of the *monitor* process $CS_{monitor}$. The Statistical Stage of the monitor process (SS_M) generates in t_i a pair of values $\{pm(t_i, \alpha); K_{ign}(t_i, \alpha)\}$ composed of a probability map and a key ignition value. Where α indicates the number of island that has obtained the best fitness value. Finally these values are entered in the Fire Prediction stage (FP). FP calculates the Predicted Fire Line for the next time instant $i + 1$, i.e., PFL_{i+1}.

4.2   Automatic Map Generation

In [5] HESS-IM was applied to controlled burns on reduced scenarios for validation of results. In order to apply this type of method to forest fires in real situations, it is necessary to have tools to generate maps of the perimeters of the initial burned area. The satellite images can allow, in near real time, to feed the prediction systems with the required information.

In the literature, there are several antecedents of the use of satellite images for the detection of thermal anomalies such as heat sources, active fire fronts, characterization of fires [35]. Each of these using different satellite platforms such as MODIS (Moderate-Resolution Imaging Spectroradiometer) [36], GOES (Geostationary Operational Environmental Satellite) [37], NOAA-AVHRR (National Oceanic and Atmospheric Administration - Advanced Very High Resolution Radiometer) [38], VIIRS (Visible Infrared Imaging Radiometer Suite) [39–41].

MODIS images have been used in this work. Bands 1 and 2 are usually applied to detect burned areas and smoke, moreover, bands 1, 2, 6, 7, 20–25, 31 and 32, are normally used for active fire detection. Among them, band number 7 is sensitive to high temperatures, which makes it proper for verifying the intensity of the fire [42]. The combination used in this work corresponds to 7-2-1, better known as MODIS (Terra/Aqua) Corrected Reflectance [43]. The development of this module has been written in Python making use of Worldview API calls for the automated download of fire maps in TIFF format. It is only necessary to provide the days and places where the fire has occurred or is occurring (limited by data availability).

HESS-IM, due to limitations of the simulator used, is not capable of processing satellite images directly, so they must be adapted to the raster format (ASCII). This is achieved through the GDAL library [44], this library allows decomposing each of the RGB bands as an independent map. Putting these maps together allows you to see the burned area, the fire, and the smoke from the fire. Subsequently, each map must be transformed into ASCII format. Where the value of each cell corresponds to its value in RGB for each band (i.e., between 0 and 255), such values are used to distinguish between the burned and unburned area at each instant of time.

Then a comparison of maps is done, the result is another map containing the burned and unburned cells with burning moments. The objective of this stage is to determine those cells that have been burned in the current image (instant of time x). The cells that are identified as burned at the current instant, be marked (in the output map) with the time value of the current time (x). And the cells that are not identified as burned, in the new map, will have a value equal to zero, implying that the flames did not reach said cell at the current moment. This is achieved by comparing the value of R in each, if it is greater than the values of G and B at the time evaluated, the cell will be marked as burned, otherwise, it will not. Once this process is finished, the totality of the output maps is obtained, that is, a new set of maps with the delimitation of the burned area in its specific time interval. Finally, a combination of the set of these maps obtained is made. Once the process is finished, the output is a map with the burn time values in each cell. Allowing to identify the direction of fire spread over time, the burned area, and the fire front.

5   Experimental Results

In this section, we present the results obtained after applying HESS-IM to a forest fire that occurred in the town of Capilla del Monte, Córdoba Province, Argentina in 2008 (see Fig. 4) with an approximate area of 51.852 hectares. In order to verify whether the hybridization of metaheuristics in HESS-IM offers improvements in the prediction quality, the results of the HESS-IM were compared with those produced by ESS-IM and a previous implementation of HESS-IM that only implemented two metaheuristics (EA and DE). In Fig. 5, we represent time (x axis) and quality of prediction achieved by each method (y axis). It is important to recall that a fitness value equal to 1 indicates a perfect prediction and a value close to 0 indicates a very poor prediction. In this figure, we can see three curves, one for ESS-IM, another for HESS-IM with EA and DE, named as HESS-IM (a), and the third for HESS-IM with EA, DE, and PSO called HESS-IM (b). The time values correspond to intervals of 1440 min, equivalent to one day. It can be observed that the prediction quality of HESS-IM(b) completely surpasses the rest of the evaluations. In Table 1, it can be seen that the best prediction value is obtained at the first prediction instant (value 0.740158) for HESS-IM (b). Another aspect to consider is that the prediction quality has been decreasing since the beginning of the experimentation, this may be related to the complexity of the morphology of the burned area for each instant of time. It can be seen in Fig. 4, that the burned area at minutes 2880 and 4320, where the prediction values are higher, the shape of the burned area presents greater homogeneity.

Moreover, the executions were carried out on a cluster with 36 cores distributed in 9 computers with Intel-Q9550 Quad Core 2.83 GHz processors and RAM memory of 4 GB DDR3 1333 MHz. All the nodes are connected by Gigabit Ethernet network. Base software on the cluster includes a 64 bits Debian 5 Lenny Operating System. In the codification we use the MPICH library [45] for message passing communication between participating nodes.

Table 1. Case study: Prediction quality obtained by ESS-IM, HESS-IM (a), and HESS-IM (b) for each time interval. In bold: the best values reached by an instant of time, and with an asterisk (*): the highest prediction reached.

Interval (min.)	ESS-IM	HESS-IM (a)	HESS-IM (b)
0 a 1440	–	–	–
1440 a 2880	0,24054	0,630584	**0,740158***
2880 a 4320	0,61584	0,56058	**0,633215**
4320 a 5760	0,319806	0,365882	**0,50546**
5760 a 7200	0,401589	0,42015	**0,460235**
7200 a 8640	0,23985	0,30365	**0,40235**
Average	0,363525	0,4561692	**0,500315**

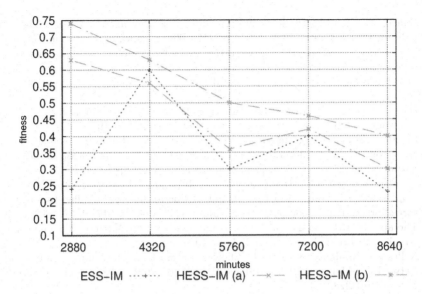

Fig. 5. Prediction quality assessment: comparison between ESS-IM, HESS-IM (a: EA and DE), HESS-IM (b: EA, DE and PSO).

6   Conclusions

This work has addressed the treatment of uncertainty reduction in relation to the prediction and prevention of natural disaster methods. Specifically, the problem of forest fires has been approached as a case study, one of the biggest problems that affect large regions throughout the world.

HESS-IM uses a hybrid-parallel metaheuristic based on a collaborative scheme using Evolutionary Algorithms, Differential Evolution and Particle Swarm Optimization, under a parallel strategy based on islands. The evaluation of the method was carried out by its application to one forest fire of more than 50,000 hectares that occurred in Córdoba, Argentina, where the quality of prediction of the method were evaluated. The results obtained were compared with the ESS-IM method and a previous version of HESS-IM with two metaheuristics EA and DE. In addition, these results prove that the hybridization technique used and the selected metaheuristics improve the search mechanism of the method, allowing for more accurate and reliable predictions. Finally, as future work, we plan to carry out calibration studies to optimize HESS-IM operation in large fires.

References

1. Hyndman, D.W., Hyndman, D.W.: Natural Hazards and Disasters. Brooks/Cole, Cengage Learning (2014)

2. Banco, M.: Los desastres naturales empujan a 26 millones de personas a la pobreza y provocan pérdidas por USD 520 000 millones al año, según un nuevo análisis del Banco Mundial (2016). http://www.bancomundial.org/es/news/press-release/2016/11/14/natural-disasters-force-26-million-people-into-poverty-and-cos t-520bn-in-losses-every-year-new-world-bank-analysis-finds. Accessed 30 Apr 2018

3. BID: Indicadores de Riesgo de Desastres Naturales y de Gestión de Riesgos. Technical report, BID, Banco Interamericano de Desarrollo (2010)

4. Méndez-Garabetti, M.: Método de Reducción de incertidumbre basado en algoritmos evolutivos y paralelismo orientado a la predicción y prevención de desastres naturales. Ph.D. thesis, Universidad Nacional de San Luis (2020)

5. Méndez-Garabetti, M., Bianchini, G., Tardivo, M.L., Caymes Scutari, P.G., Gil Costa, G. V.: Hybrid-parallel uncertainty reduction method applied to forest fire spread prediction. J. Comput. Sci. Technol. **17**(1), 12–19 (2017). ISSN-e 1666–6038

6. Thompson, M.P., Calkin, D.E.: Uncertainty and risk in wildland fire management: a review. J. Environ. Manage. **92**, 1895–1909 (2011)

7. Nelles, O.: Nonlinear System Identification: From Classical Approaches to Neural Networks and Fuzzy Models. Springer, Heidelberg (2001). https://doi.org/10.1007/978-3-662-04323-3

8. Wallace, G.: A numerical fire simulation-model. Int. J. Wildland Fire **3**(2), 111 (1993)

9. Finney, M.A.: FARSITE: fire area simulator—model development and evaluation. USDA Forest Service Research Paper, no. February, p. 47 (1998)

10. Andrews, P.L., Bevins, C.D., Seli, R.C., Andrews, A., Bevins, P.L., Seli, C.D.: BehavePlus fire modeling system, version 4.0: User's Guide Revised (2008)

11. Heinsch, F.A., Andrews, P.L.: BehavePlus fire modeling system, version 5.0: design and features. Technical report 249 (2010)

12. Lopes, A., Cruz, M., Viegas, D.: FireStation—an integrated software system for the numerical simulation of fire spread on complex topography. Environ. Modell. Softw. **17**, 269–285 (2002)

13. Ribeiro, L., Viegas, D., Lopes, A., Mangana, P., Moura, P.: Operational application of a decision support tool in fire management in Portugal. For. Ecol. Manage. **234**(Supplement 1), 243 (2006)

14. Iyengar, S.S., Brooks, R.R: Distributed Sensor Networks: Sensor Networking and Applications, 2 edn. Chapman and Hall/CRC, Florida (2013)

15. Dubey, V., Kumar, P., Chauhan, N.: Forest fire detection system using IoT and artificial neural network. In: Bhattacharyya, S., Hassanien, A.E., Gupta, D., Khanna, A., Pan, I. (eds.) International Conference on Innovative Computing and Communications. LNNS, vol. 55, pp. 323–337. Springer, Singapore (2019). https://doi.org/10.1007/978-981-13-2324-9_33

16. Beven, K., Binley, A.: The future of distributed models: model calibration and uncertainty prediction. Hydrol. Process. **6**, 279–298 (1992)

17. Abdalhaq, B.: A Methodology to enhance the prediction of forest fire propagation. Universitat Autonoma de Barcelona, November 2004

18. Bianchini, G.: Wildland fire prediction based on statistical analysis of multiple solutions. Ph. d thesis, Universidad Autonoma de Barcelona, July 2006

19. Bianchini, G., Denham, M., Cortés, A., Margalef, T., Luque, E.: Wildland fire growth prediction method based on multiple overlapping solution. J. Comput. Sci. **1**, 229–237 (2010)

20. Bianchini, G., Caymes-Scutari, P., Méndez-Garabetti, M.: Evolutionary-statistical system: a parallel method for improving forest fire spread prediction. J. Comput. Sci. **6**, 58–66 (2015)
21. Méndez-Garabetti, M., Bianchini, G., Caymes-Scutari, P., Tardivo, M.L.: Increase in the quality of the prediction of a computational wildfire behavior method through the improvement of the internal metaheuristic. Fire Saf. J. **82**, 49–62 (2016)
22. Tardivo, M.L., Caymes-Scutari, P., Bianchini, G., Méndez-Garabetti, M., Cencerrado, A., Cortés, A.: A comparative study of evolutionary statistical methods for uncertainty reduction in forest fire propagation prediction. Proc. Comput. Sci. **108**, 2018–2027 (2017)
23. Bouttier, F., Courtier, P.: Data assimilation concepts and methods (2002)
24. Darema, F.: Introduction to the ICCS 2007 workshop on dynamic data driven applications systems. In: Shi, Y., van Albada, G.D., Dongarra, J., Sloot, P.M.A. (eds.) ICCS 2007, Part I. LNCS, vol. 4487, pp. 955–962. Springer, Heidelberg (2007). https://doi.org/10.1007/978-3-540-72584-8_125
25. Arahal, M.R., Berenguel Soria, M., Rodríguez Días, F.: Técnicas de predicción con aplicaciones en ingeniería. Secretariado de Publicaciones, Universidad de Sevilla, Sevilla (2006)
26. Montgomery, D., Runger, G.: Applied Statistics and Probability for Engineers, 6th edn. Limusa Wiley & Sons, New Jersey (2014)
27. Buyya, R.: High Performance Cluster Computing: Architectures and Systems. Prentice Hall, PTR, NJ (1999)
28. Talbi, E.-G.: Metaheuristics: From Design to Implementation. Wiley, Hoboken (2009)
29. Chuvieco, E.: Wildland Fire Danger Estimation and Mapping. Series in Remote Sensing, vol. 4. World Scientific (2003)
30. Eiben, A.E., Smith, J.E.: Introduction to Evolutionary Computing. Natural Computing Series, Springer, Heidelberg (2003). https://doi.org/10.1007/978-3-662-05094-1
31. Storn, R., Price, K.: Differential evolution - a simple and efficient adaptive scheme for global optimization over continuous spaces. Technical report, TR- 95–012, ICSI, Berkeley, CA (1995)
32. Kennedy, J., Eberhart, R.: Particle swarm optimization. In: Proceedings of ICNN'95 - International Conference on Neural Networks, vol. 4, pp. 1942–1948 (1995)
33. Rothermel, R.: A mathematical model for predicting fire spread in wildland fuels, vol. II. Research Paper INT-115, US Department of Agriculture, Forest Service, Intermountain Forest and Range Experiment Station (Ogden, UT) (1972)
34. Bevins, C.D.: fireLib user manual and technical reference. Technical report, Intermountain Research Station, Forest Service, U.S. Department of Agriculture (1996)
35. Fischer, M.A., Di Bella, C.M., Jobbágy, E.G.: Fire patterns in central semiarid Argentina. J. Arid Environ. **78**, 161–168 (2012)
36. Hmimina, G., et al.: Evaluation of the potential of MODIS satellite data to predict vegetation phenology in different biomes: an investigation using ground-based NDVI measurements. Remote Sens. Environ. (2013)
37. Xu, W., Wooster, M.J., Roberts, G., Freeborn, P.: New GOES imager algorithms for cloud and active fire detection and fire radiative power assessment across North, South and Central America. Remote Sens. Environ. (2010)

38. Van De Griend, A.A., Owe, M.: On the relationship between thermal emissivity and the normalized difference vegetation index for natural surfaces. Int. J. Remote Sens. (1993)
39. Schroeder, W., et al.: Validation of GOES and MODIS active fire detection products using ASTER and ETM+ data. Remote Sens. Environ. **112**, 2711–2726 (2008)
40. Waigl, C.F., Stuefer, M., Prakash, A., Ichoku, C.: Detecting high and low-intensity fires in Alaska using VIIRS I-band data: an improved operational approach for high latitudes. Remote Sens. Environ. **199**, 389–400 (2017)
41. Hawbaker, T.J., Radeloff, V.C., Syphard, A.D., Zhu, Z., Stewart, S.I.: Detection rates of the MODIS active fire product in the United States. Remote Sens. Environ. **112**, 2656–2664 (2008)
42. Zhang, J.H., Yao, F.M., Liu, C., Yang, L.M., Boken, V.K.: Detection, emission estimation and risk prediction of forest fires in China using satellite sensors and simulation models in the past three decades-an overview. Int. J. Environ. Res. Public Health **8**(8), 3156–3178 (2011)
43. Moderate Resolution Imaging Spectroradiometer (MODIS)—Earthdata
44. Warmerdam, F., Rouault, E.: GDAL—GDAL documentation (2019)
45. Amer, A., et al.: MPICH user's guide. Technical report (2015)

Detection of Crop Lines and Weeds in Corn Fields Based on Images Obtained from a Drone

Marco Pusdá-Chulde[1,2]([✉]) [iD], Adrian Robayo[1] [iD], Armando De Giusti[2] [iD], and Iván García-Santillán[1] [iD]

[1] Facultad de Ingeniería en Ciencias Aplicadas, Universidad Técnica del Norte, Ibarra, Ecuador
{mrpusda,arobayoo,idgarcia}@utn.edu.ec
[2] Facultad de Informática, Universidad Nacional de La Plata, La Plata, Argentina
degiusti@info.unlp.edu.ar

Abstract. Precision agriculture (PA) automates agriculture by collecting and analyzing agricultural data for decision-making and obtaining efficient farming productions. Weeds are one of the main factors affecting the yield and quality of farming products. The PA is one of the technological solutions to detect weeds in corn crops through the analysis of digital images to carry out different actions that allow reducing the risk of production in a traditional or automated way. In the present work, an alternative is proposed for the detection of weeds in corn crops in the first 4 weeks of growth using images acquired by a DJI Mavic 2 Pro drone (UAV- Unmanned Aerial Vehicle) with a resolution of 5472 × 3648. The images used are publicly available online. Matlab libraries (Image Processing Toolbox) for the implementation of the algorithm was used in 4 phases: vegetation detection, crop line detection, crop exclusion, weed detection, this allows separating the weed from the crop lines detected in the images captured at 5, 10, and 15 m in height. The results obtained show that the crop lines (85%) and weeds (34.61%) of the total vegetation can be better identified in the fourth week 15 m high. With the proposed algorithm, the processing times evaluated for the finding of weeds, on average, are 3.41 s per image that reaches an area between 20 and 114 m^2 at 5 and 15 m in height, respectively.

Keywords: Image analysis · Crop row detection · Weed detection · UAV

1 Introduction

Precision agriculture (PA) aims to use Information and Communication Technologies (ICT) resources and services in agricultural tasks for data collection and analysis to improve production crop productivity and reduce environmental pollution [1, 2]. UAV technology is a technological complement for capturing high-quality images at a low cost [3]. Currently, this type of vehicle uses in various fields of science. In PA, it has been used efficiently in different agricultural activities such as crop line detection, weed detection, crop monitoring, disease detection, detection of pests, plant counting, fumigations, detection of soil nutrients, among other activities [3–7].

© Springer Nature Switzerland AG 2021
M. Naiouf et al. (Eds.): JCC-BD&ET 2021, CCIS 1444, pp. 31–45, 2021.
https://doi.org/10.1007/978-3-030-84825-5_3

The harmful incidence of unpleasant plants (weeds) are the high obstacles in agricultural production; they compete with crops for nutrients, light, water, and other factors necessary for high-quality production. The economic damage of weeds in some developing countries is estimated annual losses of up to 125 million tons of food [8]. The detection of weeds in corn crops with large extensions requires time, financial resources, and personnel for adequate treatment, maintaining the quality and quantity of production. This problem would improve under the application and use of new technologies that allow the detection, identification, and elimination of weeds in the first days of their growth stage in corn crops [9–13], facilitating producers to make informed decisions to save inputs, reduce production costs and avoid environmental contamination [14].

The analysis of agricultural images obtained from drones has been used in different investigations of weed treatment using artificial vision and digital image processing in farming activities. In [15], a neural network applied to segment marigold crops from images cut into mosaics of 256×256 pixels, separating the land without weeds and the crop lines to discriminate the weed, obtaining a precision of 93.4% and image execution times 35.90 ms. [16] proposed a method for the discrimination of crops/weeds in images captured in cornfields, during the initial stages of growth, with images obtained under perspective projection with a camera installed in the front of a tractor to identify weeds both within and between rows of corn crops used image preprocessing techniques and algorithms for line and vegetation detection, such as the Hough transform (HT) and excess green (ExG) in order. The performance of the proposed approach was quantitatively compared with three existing strategies, achieving an accuracy of 91.8%, determined by pixels against manually constructed terrain truth images, with processing times ≤ 280 ms, which can be helpful for applications in real-time. [17] proposed a method in analyzing colors (CMA) in RGB images acquired by drones for estimating the fractional vegetation cover (FVC) in a field. For the measurement of the algorithm, it compared with three methods for the estimation of vegetation (FCLS SMA, HAGFVC, LAB2) using the set of images collected with a drone, the outcomes of the study determined an excellent efficiency of the algorithm in obtaining the FVC with short-range images, and at high resolutions. For the analysis and prediction of the yield in potato crops, [18] used a drone to capture RGB and hyperspectral images to measure and compare the precision of the predictive algorithm based on the vegetation index before and after 90 days after sowing. Techniques such as the excess green index (ExG) used to create a binary mask of the plants, the aerial biomass calculation (AGB) to estimate the average of potato crops in the samples, and the RReliefF algorithm to predict the Relative distance between two samplings, the results present an average estimate of the crop in 81% after 90 days, proving to be a good tool for crop management.

The rest of the document is structured as follows: In the materials and methods section, the implementation of the algorithm in Matlab for weed detection using images acquired with a drone is explained; The results section shows the main findings obtained and discussion with similar works, and finally in the conclusions section the main contribution of the study and future work.

2 Materials and Methods

The process used for the development of the proposed algorithm was divided into four stages: (i) image acquisition with the drone, (ii) image download from the drone, (iii) image labeling for each week and height, (iv) offline processing of images with a customized algorithm. Each of them is detailed below:

2.1 Acquired Images

The drone model used for this study was the DJi Mavic 2 Pro, equipped with a high-quality camera to capture original RGB images in JPG format. The images used are publicly available online at the following link: https://bit.ly/3gsAbpp. The software to control the flight of the drone was DJI GO 4 at an average speed of 15 m/s. The data were obtained on sunny and shady days in the morning. Due to the presence of direct sunlight, some images were faulty for this reason, new shots were taken until images with high-grade resolution were obtained. The technical specifications of the drone are detailed in Table 1.

Table 1. DJI Mavic 2 Pro drone technical specifications [19]

Characteristic	Detail
Weight	907 g (with battery)
Maximum speed	72 km/h (sport mode)
Ascent/descent speed	18/10.8 Km/h
Maximum flight distance (no wind)	8 km (at a constant speed of 50 km/h)
Maximum flight altitude	6 km
Camera - Sensor	CMOS 1 in. 20 MP
Camera - Lens	28 mm lens (77° angle)
Photo	20 MP (5472 × 3648) JPEG - RAW - Panoramas - Burst 3/5 frames
Gimbal	3 axis motorized
Drums	31 min long
Drone control	App (Android – IOS)
Positioning	GPS + GLONASS
Sensors	Omnidirectional - front, sides, rear, top and bottom

2.2 Details of Culture Samples

The land used for sampling is in Natabuela, Antonio Ante parish, Imbabura province in the "La Pradera" farm with an area of 300 m^2. The images were taken at a resolution of 5472 × 3648 from a height of 5, 10, and 15 m. The corn planting was carried out on November 18, 2020, while the monitoring and collection of samples began from November 28 to December 19, 2020, approximately four weeks after sowing, the crucial growth stage of corn plants. The images used for image processing, crop line, and weed recognition are detailed in Table 2.

Table 2. Details of the images captured from the drone

Characteristic	Measure
Length approx. row	40 m
Distance approx. between rows	0.8 m
Distance approx. between plants per row	0.4 m

Table 3 shows the data for the corn crop.

Table 3. Crop information during the first 4 weeks

Characteristics	First week 28-11-2020	Second week 5-12-2020	Third week 12-12-2020	Fourth week 19-12-2020
Plant width	9–12 cm	14–15 cm	18 cm	20–21 cm
Number of sheets	3	4.2	7	7.5
Plant height	8 cm	13 cm	29.5 cm	35.5 cm
Sheet size	5.2 cm	5.7 cm	11.43 cm	12.89 cm

2.3 Discrimination of Crops and Weeds

In this section, the images obtained in the fourth week were considered. The personalized algorithm used for weed detection set up four phases: detection of vegetation on the ground, detection of crop lines, exclusion of the crop, and recognition of weeds. The phases of the algorithm (Fig. 1) were implemented using the image processing toolbox included in Matlab R2020b (Image Processing Toolbox).

Vegetation Detection. This phase consists of the detection of the plants in the field, without classifying between crop and weed, through the ExG index, which allows highlighting merely the presence of vegetation in a digital image, extracting the values of the channels in red, green, and blue (RGB) [14] .

After applying ExG, the image was binarized using the Otsu method [20]. The result of applying the excess green and binarization to Fig. 2a is presented in Fig. 2b, which is a image of the collection acquired at 10m height. In some sectors of the crop, there were weeds of a similar size to that of the crop, therefore it was difficult to distinguish between

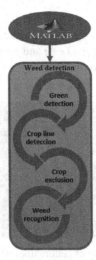

Fig. 1. Algorithm for weed detection

the two. Erosion and dilation processes were used to improve detection to significantly reduce both the regions of interest and the weeds and, consequently, that the detection of culture lines.

Fig. 2. (a) Image at 15 m height and (b) vegetation detection applying ExG and Otsu

Crop Line Detection. This phase consists of the detection of culture lines through the Hough Transform [21], from a binary image previously obtained. The parameters used for the calculation are: the image (BW) and the Theta range to establish the angle of the lines found almost vertically (−5.5). The obtained values are stored in the hough matrix (H), the theta value (theta), and the distance from the origin to the line (rho). The function "houghpeaks" [20] finds the peaks of the Hough matrix obtained from the previous function. The most important parameters are the matrix (H), the number of peaks representing the number of lines to find, and "*NHoodSize*" [20] which allows to exclude neighboring lines and avoid overlapping. Using the "*houghlines*" function

[20] line segments are extracted from the provided image to avoid uneven lines or lines that do not correspond to the crop. The indicated parameters were established by experimentation for each culture week (1−4) and each drone height (5, 10, and 15 m). The result for the detection of the culture lines is presented in Fig. 3.

Fig. 3. Detection and tracing of culture lines using the Hough transform

Crop Exclusion. This phase consists of creating a new image that excludes the corn plants located within the crop lines and shows only the weedy regions [7]. Each crop line in the image is marked with 2 additional lines 50 (15 m), 70 (10 m) and 150 (5 m) pixels depending on the height, the line drawn in red (see Fig. 4a - Image taken at 10m in the fourth week), represents the center of the area, to exclude crop plants two new lines were created at distances of 70 pixels, one to the left (blue) and another to the right (green) of the central one (red) to assign the area in the image where the crop is situated. All the white pixels set in this area (between blue and green lines) and representing the culture were changed from white to black, Fig. 4b.

(a)   (b)

Fig. 4. (a) Exclusion of crop lines to (b) identify the weed in the image (Color figure online)

Weed Detection. In this last phase of the algorithm, the focus is on detecting the white regions of the binary image resulting from the previous step and labeling them as weeds in the original image for better visualization. In the binary image Fig. 4b, some white pixels are slight and probably do not correspond to weeds but some noise. To avoid confusion with weeds, a morphological erosion operation was applied to the binary image using the *"imerode"* function [20] and remove certain small areas (white pixels) considered as noise. In Fig. 5a (image taken at 5m in the fourth week) the resulting image with the detection of weeds (in red) of the entire processed image is shown in Fig. 5b a section of the original image is shown zoomed to improve the visualize the labeling of the weed found.

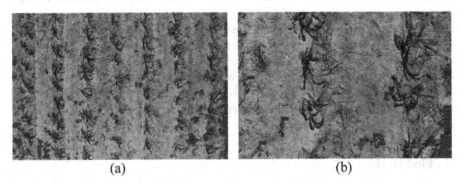

(a)   (b)

Fig. 5. Labeling, in red, of the weed detected in the image (Color figure online)

Calculation of the Percentage of Weeds. To establish the average percentage of weeds include in the image, a calculation was made through the count of white pixels in the original binary image Fig. 4a and the processed binary image Fig. 4b excluding the crop rows as explained before. Taking into account that the pixels of the original image represented in the matrix M, is the total vegetation (TV), the white regions resulting from the exclusion process are stored in the Matrix N of cultivation (MT), (m, n) represents the dimensions of the image (height, width) in Eq. 1 and Eq. 2. The average percentage calculation of weeds (PW) was carried out using a rule of three to obtain an average percentage represented in Eq. 3.

$$TV = \sum_{i=0,j=0}^{i=n,j=m} M_{ij}; \forall M_{ij} = 1 \tag{1}$$

$$MT = \sum_{i=0,j=0}^{i=n,j=m} N_{ij}; \forall N_{ij} = 1 \tag{2}$$

$$PW = \frac{MT * 100}{TV} \tag{3}$$

3   Results and Discussion

The collected images exhibit different properties and characteristics depending on the week (1–4) in which the captures were made, for this reason, the results were divided into four parts corresponding to the number of weeks of follow-up of the culture. During the four weeks of gathering images, there were frequent rains, therefore, the growth of the crop, as well as the weeds, was very fast, causing it to disperse throughout the land and in some sectors containing large amounts of weeds.

To set the algorithm accuracy, the count of detected crop lines and the value of the average percentage of weeds found in the corn crop images during the four weeks of follow-up. The processed images were 5 for each height selected randomly, avoiding factors such as blur, darkness, or little visibility of the crop with the naked eye. Despite having more crop monitoring images, only 5 images were considered because the amount of scrub was identified manually, which is a complicated and time-consuming process. Similarly, several images saturated by the direct presence of the sun to the drone camera were not considered. The metrics evaluated in the image processing were: number of crop rows in the image (CR), lines detected (LD) by the algorithm, percentage of weed found out (PW), and execution time (ET) in seconds. The computer used in the implementation of the algorithm was a Dell laptop, Intel Core i10, 10 generations with Windows 10, 16 GB RAM, GPU RTX 2060 6 GB.

3.1   First Week

In the first week of image collection (November 28, 2020), there were problems with the visualization of the crop in the acquired images due to the low growth of the plants, even at the slightest heights (5 m), so it was hard to distinguish it even to the human eye. In addition, the excessive lighting of that day made it almost imperceptible to see the presence of green in the images, however the illumination and contrast were configured to have a better quality image. These factors directly affect the detection of crop lines and weeds despite the filters and changes applied via software. In Fig. 6a the original image of the sample taken at 10 m high in the first week of the study is presented. Fig. 6b shows tiny points of vegetation that are difficult to consider as weeds or crop lines.

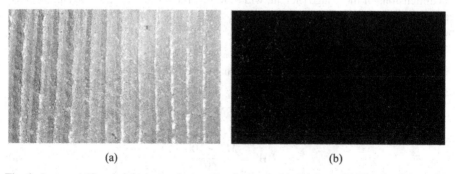

(a)   (b)

Fig. 6. Image at 10 m height in the first week of growth. (a) Original. (b) Binarized detecting vegetation

Despite the filters and changes applied to the images Fig. 6 and having modified the parameters of the algorithm functions such as the dilation of white regions, they were not enough to identify the cultivation rows, and the results obtained do not comply with the expectancy.

3.2 Second Week

This week (December 5), the crop grew enough to be visualized in images. However, the weed size was similar to the crop, so it was still difficult to distinguish between the two, especially at the time of the erosion process as both the regions of interest (crop) and the weeds were significantly reduced. In some sectors of the crop, the weed has greater volume concerning crop. Figure 7a shows the original image and the image processed in Fig. 7b captured in the second week of the study.

(a)   (b)

Fig. 7. Image at 10 m high. (a) Original. (b) Binarized detecting vegetation

In this week of study, Fig. 7, there are areas of the land where the vegetation is vast that no matter what morphological processes are applied, the algorithm presents failures in the identification of weeds when several white regions accumulate in the same place, causing lines to overlap. Table 4 shows the results obtained during the processing of the 5 processed images.

Table 4. Second week results

Image	5 m high				10 m high				15 m high			
	CR	LD	PW	ET	CR	LD	PW	ET	CR	LD	PW	ET
1	8	2	78.82	1.18	15	8	59.62	1.77	19	3	92.31	2.26
2	7	2	23.15	1.23	13	5	63.81	1.85	20	4	90.76	2.23
3	8	2	76.21	1.19	16	6	56.02	1.75	20	3	83.87	2.19
4	6	3	21.05	1.21	15	4	66.89	1.83	19	3	85.37	2.27
5	6	3	52.98	1.16	12	10	43.91	1.81	19	3	88.6	1.98

3.3 Third Week

In the third week **(December 12),** the results changed significantly. In the images, it is easy to visualize the crop in those images of 5, 10, and 15 m high, both for the human being and for the drone. In Fig. 8 the results obtained in the processing of the images for the identification of crop lines are shown Fig. 8a, 8c, 8e, and weeds Fig. 8b, 8d, 8f.

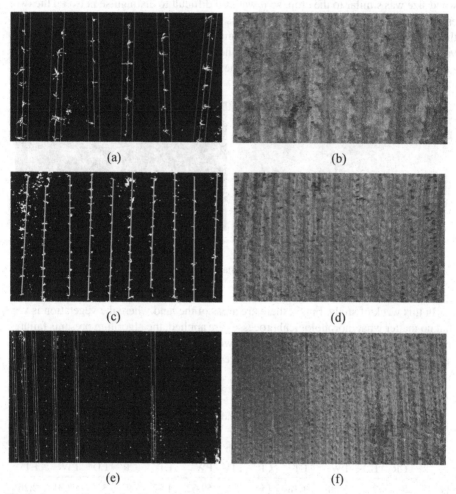

(a)   (b)

(c)   (d)

(e)   (f)

Fig. 8. Images taken in the third week detecting crop lines (a, c, e) and weeds (b, d, f) at 5, 10 and 15 m height, respectively.

In this week, Fig. 9, the precision in the detection of crop lines was better, almost infallible with images at 5 m high, while with 10 there were some errors in images in which there was excess weed because the white regions were agglomerated and various lines were drawn in a single part of the terrain. With the 15-m images, there were also some errors in the finding of crop lines and weeds because some areas had little vegetation (possibly the seed did not germinate). Table 5 details the results obtained during the processing of the 5 images in the third week

Table 5. Results table third week

Image	5 m height				10 m height				15 m height			
	CR	LD	PW	ET	CR	LD	PW	ET	CR	LD	PW	ET
1	6	6	31.06	4.94	13	12	33.68	9.36	20	14	56.64	3.84
2	6	6	20.15	5.71	13	12	27.68	8.62	20	13	36.06	4.54
3	6	6	7.69	6.63	13	12	43.21	9.04	20	13	46.18	3.93
4	6	5	8.70	3.15	13	12	21.98	12.10	19	8	32.07	4.43
5	6	6	6.33	4.91	13	12	23.94	12.16	20	13	51.79	3.32

3.4 Fourth Week

The last week (November 19) of culture follow-up was the one that presented the best results in the precision of the algorithm. By this date, the growth of the leaves was considerable, making the exclusion of crops and weeds treatable in the three heights (5, 10, and 15 m), Table 3. The image had the number of white regions needed to detect lines in the Hough spacing, therefore the images did not have to be heavily modified by applying pixel dilation and erosion. Figure 9 shows the results obtained in the processing of the images at 5, 10, and 15 m for the description of crop lines Fig. 9a, 9c, 9e and weeds Fig. 9b, 9d, 9f.

However, during the fourth week, the problems dealt with in the previous weeks persist, such as overlapping lines or ignoring rows present in the image. Table 6 details the results obtained during the processing of the 5 images in the fourth week.

The implementation of the algorithm during this week increases the area of recognition of crop lines and weeds, enabling significant processing related to coverage in square meters during the fourth week. Table 7 shows the increase in the recognition area according to the drone altitude in the fourth week:

The present work demonstrates an improvement in the detection of weeds in images that cover areas of approximately 114 m (fourth week) square, using images obtained with the drone at 15 m, facilitating the detection of an average of 17 crop lines that is equivalent to 85% of the total cultivation lines (20), and 34.61% of the whole weeds without considering the vegetation found between the corn crop plants (within the same row). The average image processing time is not very long regarding the crop area.

3.5 Discussion

Based on the results obtained from this study, it was determined that there is a better performance of the algorithm at 15 m height in the fourth week of growth. However, it

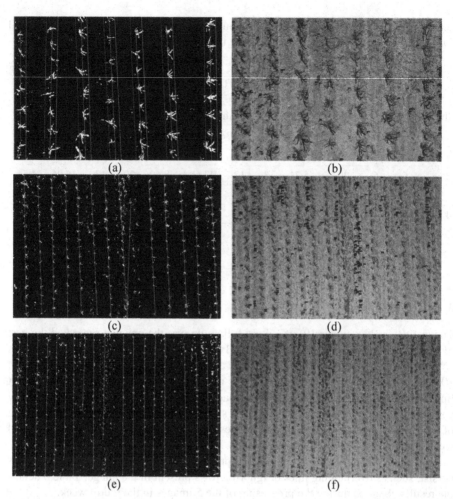

Fig. 9. Images of the fourth week (a, b) 5 m height, (c, d) 10 m height, (e, f) at 15 m height

Table 6. Fourth week results

Image	5 m height				10 m height				15 m height			
	CR	LD	PW	ET	CR	LD	PW	ET	CR	LD	PW	ET
1	7	7	13.59	6.62	14	13	13.69	8.35	20	17	25.05	3.09
2	7	7	5.2	7.21	14	14	26.61	8.82	21	19	25.70	3.43
3	7	7	6.84	9.55	14	11	58.28	7.22	20	16	34.37	4.06
4	7	7	4	8.75	13	9	35.84	7.89	20	14	25.05	3.16
5	7	6	5.6	5.29	13	11	20.57	8.12	21	19	34.61	3.33

Table 7. Crop lines and weeds processed in the fourth week

Height (meters)	Real crop lines (average)	Crop lines detected (average)	% crop lines detected	Execution time (Average)	Area (m^2) of vegetation detected (approximate)
5	7	7	100	7.05	20.16
10	14	12	85.71	8.08	61.44
15	20	17	85.00	3.41	114.24

is known from the work done by [5, 12], and [22] that multispectral cameras yield better results when using multiband (NIR, near infrared) to classify vegetation. However, the same studies yielded results varying from 5% to 10%, approximately, with an average accuracy of 80% when using RGB images. Unlike the work [16] perfomed on detection of weeds in corn crops with images, in perspective view using a camera installed on a tractor, covering an area of 5 m^2 with 4 crop lines, 87.9% is recognized weed on curved crop lines and 90.7 on straight crop lines; While in the present work, 85% (17 of crop lines) are recognized, using images in a zenith view acquired at a height of 15 m allowing coverage of approximately 114 m^2.

The proposed methodology can be adapted in any corn crop considering the intrinsic and extrinsic parameters of the drone chamber, the distance between crop lines, and plant height; the algorithm can be adapted with similar crops or new crops from the area or different countries that require more pre-processing. Additionally, it is significant to monitor the crop during the 4 weeks to monitor the growth of the weed in the first weeks so that it does not affect the corn plants; From the fourth week on, both the weeds and the corn plants are large, making it difficult to distinguish between crop lines and weeds

Regarding the limitations of the present study, the detection of the localized weed between the crop plants (intra-row) is mainly considered, as well as the reduction of the execution times of the proposed algorithm. These restrictions can be addressed in future work considering techniques to map crops using neural networks, with an image set greater than 5 images to improve the algorithm efficiency in multicore and GPU architectures.

4   Conclusions and Future Work

In the first week, the detection of crop lines and weeds at the 3 heights experienced was difficult due to little vegetation and the tiny size of the corn crop plants. In contrast, in the fourth week, the conditions improve substantially, achieving the maximum detection of crop lines and the maximum percentage of weed Table 6.

This research uses image processing and analysis functions included in Matlab R2020b for the detection of corn crop lines and the detection of weeds present in images obtained from the DJI Mavic 2 Pro drone at 5, 10, and 15 m from height, during 4 weeks of plant growth (Tables 2 and 3). The results indicate that it is possible to detect up to 85% of crop lines and discriminate the weed from the corn crop by 34.61% (Table 6).

The images acquired employing a drone make it possible to detect weeds in corn crops with a coverage of up to 114 m^2 (Table 8), making it possible to reduce response times for large areas with little unmanned vehicle travel.

As future work, it is proposed to discriminate the weed, located between the crop plants, as well as to optimize the execution times with parallel processing using multicore and gpu architectures applying artificial intelligence techniques.

References

1. Ponnusamy, V., Natarajan, S.: Precision agriculture using advanced technology of IoT, unmanned aerial vehicle, augmented reality, and machine learning. In: Gupta, D., Hugo C. de Albuquerque, V., Khanna, A., Mehta, P.L. (eds.) Smart Sensors for Industrial Internet of Things. IT, pp. 207–229. Springer, Cham (2021). https://doi.org/10.1007/978-3-030-52624-5_14
2. Pusdá-Chulde, M., Salazar-Fierro, F., Sandoval-Pillajo, L., Herrera-Granda, E., García-Santillán, I., De Giusti, A.: Image analysis based on heterogeneous architectures for precision agriculture: a systematic literature review. In: Nummenmaa, J., Pérez-González, F., Domenech-Lega, B., Vaunat, J., Oscar Fernández-Peña, F. (eds.) CSEI 2019. AISC, vol. 1078, pp. 51–70. Springer, Cham (2020). https://doi.org/10.1007/978-3-030-33614-1_4
3. Puri, V., Nayyar, A., Raja, L.: Agriculture drones: a modern breakthrough in precision agriculture. J. Stat. Manag. Syst. **20**(4), 507–518 (2017). https://doi.org/10.1080/09720510.2017.1395171
4. Radoglou-Grammatikis, P., Sarigiannidis, P., Lagkas, T., Moscholios, I.: A compilation of UAV applications for precision agriculture. Comput. Networks **172**((February)), 107148 (2020). https://doi.org/10.1016/j.comnet.2020.107148
5. Costa, L., Nunes, L., Ampatzidis, Y.: A new visible band index (vNDVI) for estimating NDVI values on RGB images utilizing genetic algorithms. Comput. Electron. Agric. **172**(November 2019), 105334 (2020). https://doi.org/10.1016/j.compag.2020.105334
6. Wang, A., Zhang, W., Wei, X.: A review on weed detection using ground-based machine vision and image processing techniques. Comput. Electron. Agric. **158**(February), 226–240 (2019). https://doi.org/10.1016/j.compag.2019.02.005
7. García-Santillán, I., Peluffo-Ordoñez, D., Caranqui, V., Pusdá-Chulde, M., Garrido, F., Granda, P.: Computer vision-based method for automatic detection of crop rows in potato fields. In: Rocha, Á., Guarda, T. (eds.) Information Technology & Systems (ICITS 2018). Advances in Intelligent Systems and Computing, vol. 721, pp. 355–366. Springer, Heidelberg (2018). https://doi.org/10.1007/978-3-319-73450-7_34
8. FAO: Recomendaciones para el manejo de malezas. FAO (Organización las Nac. Unidas para la Aliment. y la Agric, vol. 1, pp. 1–61 (2018). ftp://ftp.fao.org/docrep/fao/010/a0884s/a0884s00.pdf
9. Pusdá-Chulde, M., De Giusti, A., Herrera-Granda, E., García-Santillán, I.: Parallel CPU-based processing for automatic crop row detection in corn fields. In: Artificial Intelligence, Computer and Software Engineering Advances, pp. 239–251 (2021)
10. García-Santillán, I., Guerrero, J., Montalvo, M., Pajares, G.: Curved and straight crop row detection by accumulation of green pixels from images in maize fields. Precis. Agric. **19**(1), 18–41 (2017). https://doi.org/10.1007/s11119-016-9494-1
11. García-Santillán, I., Montalvo, M., Guerrero, J., Pajares, G.: Automatic detection of curved and straight crop rows from images in maize fields. Biosyst. Eng. **156**, 61–79 (2017). https://doi.org/10.1016/j.biosystemseng.2017.01.013

12. Zhang, J., Li, M., Sun, Z., Liu, H., Sun, H., Yang, W.: Chlorophyll content detection of field maize using RGB-NIR camera. IFAC-PapersOnLine **51**(17), 700–705 (2018). https://doi.org/ 10.1016/j.ifacol.2018.08.114
13. Marques Ramos, A.P., et al.: A random forest ranking approach to predict yield in maize with UAV-based vegetation spectral indices. Comput. Electron. Agric. **178**(September), 105791 (2020). https://doi.org/10.1016/j.compag.2020.105791
14. García-Santillán, I., Pusdá, M., Caranqui, V., Landeta, P., Salazar, F., Granda, P.: "Crop/weed discrimination in potato fields using computer vision techniques I Discriminación de cultivo y malezas en campos de papa utilizando técnicas de visión por computador. IRISTI – Rev. Iber. Sist. Tecnol. Inf. **2019**(19), 95–107 (2019)
15. Zou, K., Chen, X., Zhang, F., Zhou, H., Zhang, C.: A field weed density evaluation method based on UAV imaging and modified U-net. Remote Sens. **13**(2), 1–19 (2021). https://doi. org/10.3390/rs13020310
16. García-Santillán, I., Pajares, G.: On-line crop/weed discrimination through the Mahalanobis distance from images in maize fields. Biosyst. Eng. **166**, 28–43 (2018). https://doi.org/10. 1016/j.biosystemseng.2017.11.003
17. Yan, G., et al.: Improving the estimation of fractional vegetation cover from UAV RGB imagery by colour unmixing. ISPRS J. Photogramm. Remote Sens. **158**(September), 23–34 (2019). https://doi.org/10.1016/j.isprsjprs.2019.09.017
18. Li, B., et al.: Above-ground biomass estimation and yield prediction in potato by using UAV-based RGB and hyperspectral imaging. ISPRS J. Photogramm. Remote Sens. **162**(December 2019), 161–172 (2020). https://doi.org/10.1016/j.isprsjprs.2020.02.013
19. DJI: Mavic 2 – DJI (2020). https://www.dji.com/mavic-2. Accessed 05 Apr 2021
20. MAthWorks: Image Processing Toolbox – MATLAB (2021). https://la.mathworks.com/pro ducts/image.html. Accessed 08 June 2021
21. Anthony Simon, N., Min, C.H.: Neural network based corn field furrow detection for autonomous navigation in agriculture vehicles. In: IEMTRONICS 2020 - International IOT, Electronics and Mechatronics Conference Proceedings (2020). https://doi.org/10.1109/IEM TRONICS51293.2020.9216347.
22. Zheng, H., et al.: Early season detection of rice plants using RGB, NIR-G-B and multispectral images from unmanned aerial vehicle (UAV). Comput. Electron. Agric. **169**(January), 105223 (2020). https://doi.org/10.1016/j.compag.2020.105223

Routing Security Using Blockchain Technology

Marcelo Gómez[1]($^{(\boxtimes)}$) (ID), Patricia Bazán[2](ID), Nicolás del Río[2](ID),
and Miguel Morandi[1](ID)

[1] IDECOM, UNSJ, San Juan, Argentina
{mgomez,morandi}@unsj.edu.ar
[2] LINTI, Facultad de Informática, UNLP, La Plata, Argentina
{pbaz,ndelrio}@info.unlp.edu.ar
https://www.linti.unlp.edu.ar/

Abstract. Route hijacking attacks exploit the mutual trust that BGP architecture is based on, rather than any vulnerabilities or protocol flaws. For this reason, these attacks are as old as the protocol itself, and today these failures continue to occur and research continues on what is the best strategy to provide security for routing on the Internet. New solutions, such as RPKI, are generating risks due to the centralization of the routing authority, they are not based on mutual trust, but depend on trust in the authority. This work seeks to implement a less centralized model, based on blockchain technology, where security is provided to the BGP protocol through the deployment of a specific application for the allocation of Internet resources in the Ethereum Ropsten network, and the subsequent use of this stored information.

Keywords: Inter-domain routing security · BGP · Blockchain

1 Goal and Contributions

The objective of this research is to analyze the properties of blockchain and its specific application in the allocation and delegation of resources of the Internet infrastructure, as well as in the security of external BGP routing against attacks from Route Hijacking or similar.

The arisen hypothesis we will discuss is that the deployment of a secure routing system between autonomous systems is facilitated by using blockchain to store the allocations and delegations of Internet resources. Additionally, it provides a flexible trust model, balances power among participating actors, simplifies administration, provides a highly auditable system, and solves distributed consensus by granting trust between its components without the use of digital certificates or centralized control.

As an additional contribution, we will seek to validate the architecture by implementing a functional prototype on Ethereum or similar network. This prototype includes the smart contracts that perform the needed operations for Internet resources management, and a client to interact with the implemented contracts.

M. Naiouf et al. (Eds.): JCC-BD&ET 2021, CCIS 1444, pp. 46–59, 2021.
https://doi.org/10.1007/978-3-030-84825-5_4

2   Use of Blockchain Technology to Validate Routing Information

The distributed nature of routing policies allows us to consider a blockchain-based model to deal with the routing security problem. In the thesis named "Digital Certificates: From a Hierarchical and Centralized Architecture to a Distributed and Decentralized One" [12] a reengineering and redesign of the Digital Certificate Architecture towards a decentralized and distributed model using blockchain[1] is proposed as a validation, synchronization and life cycle management mechanism for this architecture. The authors suggest that in order to achieve decentralization from a technical point of view, collaboration of different entities is required to jointly assume this role of a multifaceted central organism.

In its origin, blockchain applications were exclusive to financial systems with Bitcoin. Later, other fields of application were explored such as digital identity, authentication and security. By incorporating blockchain into routing security solutions, the hierarchical structure on which the RPKI infrastructure is based today could be discarded. Furthermore, the type of relationship that exist between the authorities (IANA, RIR) and the end users or ISPs would be established through smart contracts, achieving greater transparency and internet resources delegation reliability. Thus, the risks that exist with a central entity of management would be eliminated.

Blockchain technology and smart contracts facilitate the creation of an immutable and decentralized data source with the information necessary to speed up the mechanism by which routers perform validation of both, the origin and the AS-PATH[2]. In this way, they currently provide us with the means to exchange the necessary information that allows us to verify the validity of the messages sent between BGP neighbors in a reliable way.

Research on the use of blockchain technology to manage the allocation of resources and validate the routing information has been previously carried out with diverse approaches, including different types of blockchain and consensus algorithms to be used.

Some authors stand up for solutions with custom or permissioned blockchain, the most prominent are:

- Dmitri Tsumak, in the paper "Securing BGP using blockchain technology" [24], presents a solution that uses the Quorum blockchain platform.
- In "IPchain: Securing IP Prefix Allocation and Delegation with Blockchain" [19] the authors propose the development of a blockchain that makes use of the Proof of Stake consensus algorithm.

---

[1] Blockchain: It is a secure and globally shared data structure that maintains a single, consensual and immutable record of transactions.

[2] AS-PATH: BGP attribute that identifies autonomous systems (AS) through which the UPDATE message has passed. It lists the ASs traversed by a prefix in reverse order, with the last AS placed at the top of the list. The main purpose of AS-PATH is to prevent loops during inter-AS routing.

- In "Routechain: Towards blockchain-based secure and efficient bgp routing" [21], the authors propose a design with Clique, a modification of PoA[3] (Proof of Authority). The solution involves all ASs divided into subgroups, with each subgroup sharing a blockchain. Subgroups are built based on their geographic proximity in order to reduce propagation delays, improved scalability, and a faster achievement of consensus.

If we delve into customized solutions (own or based on private blockchain) we see that designing a distributed consensus protocol among ASs[4] is easier than designing one for a pseudonymous currency like Bitcoin, or a network like Ethereum, because the consenting entities are already well known. Despite this, some authors prefer a more generic infrastructure, such as Ethereum.

The following research propose solutions that are mounted on Ethereum:

- In "BGPcoin: Blockchain-Based Internet Number Resource Authority and BGP Security Solution" [25], Qianqian Xing proposes a working prototype deployed on the official Ethereum testnet.
- In "A Distributed Autonomous Organization for Internet Address Management" [4] the authors propose a DAO, a set of smart contracts on Ethereum.

The advantage of Ethereum-based solutions is the possibility of layered design, making the development of smart contract-based solutions independent from improvements in the blockchain used. This allows the evolution of the blockchain without affecting the smart contract deployed [4].

This last approach seems to us more pertinent than custom blockchains, since the goal of a scalable, secure and massively adopted network is increasingly closer with the development of Serenity (Ethereum 2.0). Some of the most outstanding investigations related to Ethereum Serenity are those related to migrating the network from Proof of Work to Proof of Stake [8,18] and the selection of a process to improve the scalability. This process called Sharding divides the network load into sub blockchains or shards (fragments), where the nodes only store the state and process the transactions of the shard to which they belong. To make this fragmentation possible, an update of several phases is carried out, and a chain (named Beacon Chain) containing all the logic to keep the shards safe and synchronized is implemented [1,22].

Actions to achieve consensus in a large number of participants require great efforts and investments in research and development, so it seems very reasonable

---

[3] Proof of Authority (PoA) is a family of consensus algorithms for permissioned blockchain whose relevance is the performance gains over typical BFT algorithms as a result of lighter message exchanges. PoA was originally proposed as part of the Ethereum ecosystem for private networks and was implemented in the clients Aura and Clique.

[4] ASs: An Autonomous System is a group of IP networks that have an own and independent routing policy. Only the routing information that the Autonomous System or organization wants to show can be seen from the Internet, but none of the complexity of internal routing. The Internet is nothing but a huge amount of inteconnected Autonomous Systems.

to mount the solution on an existing network (Ex: Ethereum). By delegating the responsibility for consensus to a network such as Ethereum 2.0 and decoupling the functions of the routing security solution from the blockchain's own design, the following advantages are obtained:

- Independence between the design, development, evolution of the blockchain and the consensus algorithm.
- Quick deployment and savings in maintenance costs.
- A greater logical decentralization than the one obtained with non-public blockchains.

3   Internet Resources

Although there is still a generalized perception about the decentralized nature of the Internet, the management of key Internet functions (IP Addressing Architecture, DNS and Routing) is partly hierarchical and centralized if we consider the control plane of the systems, since the data is usually decentralized.

Since the beginning of the Internet, every device needed an IP address to connect with each other, a unique number that identifies the device and allows it to be located by others. To ensure the uniqueness of addresses, they must be assigned and recorded in an organized manner.

The ways in which the allocation of addresses is recorded evolved over time, but always followed a centralized and hierarchical approach. From its beginnings when Jon Postel kept the record manually in his notebook, later formalized in the creation of the IANA, the Internet showed an exponential growth around the world, leading to the progressive creation of different Regional Internet Registries (RIRs) to supervise the adjustment of the allocation of resources to the needs of each region. To accomplish this, hierarchies were created and maintained from a central control body that guaranteed the required order [23].

The Internet-Draft "An analysis of the applicability of blockchain to secure IP addresses allocation, delegation and bindings" [11] highlights the applicability of blockchain technology while comparing some fundamental characteristics shared by IP prefixes and currencies or assets found in any blockchain. Both IP prefixes and cryptocurrencies can be unambiguously assigned to entities and cannot belong to two participants at the same time (prefixes are assigned to ASs and currencies to users or addresses). Prefixes can be delegated between ASs, just as cryptocurrencies can be transferred from one address to another. And finally, both can be divided up to a certain limit.

In "A Distributed Autonomous Organization for Internet Address Management" [4] the authors propose a decentralized management of IPv6 addresses through a set of smart contracts on the Ethereum blockchain, which implement all the necessary functions for management of a global set of addresses without any human intervention. They also suggest to limit human action only to the initial definition of some allocation rules before deploying the contract on the blockchain, mainly to define the size of the test block (e.g.: /20). Then, given that the IPv6 resource is practically unlimited, the conservation and equity in the distribution of resources could be achieved by a fee mechanism.

Although from a technological point of view BGP protocol is designed to work with mesh-type topologies and operate in a distributed manner, in practice, the decentralization of BGP is anchored to the centralized resource allocation function of the RIRs and to their implementation of the RPKI extension.

Even though technical community trust in RIRs, they view RPKI with some suspicious, since they do not want to transfer control of their routing to a centralized authority. There is no doubt that the implementation of RPKI will improve routing security, but the centralization and power concentration in the RIRs, could somehow lead to a technically shut down or disconnection of a AS from the Internet.

Power and control in the Internet topology are necessarily distributed among different control bodies, regionally organized technical communities and tier 1 networks. Given the Internet resources (ASN and IPs) distribution policies, "the technological choice to use (or not use) RPKI brings with it distinctive governance arrangements, with varying degrees and kinds of centralisation" [17]. Blockchain technology could help to find a balance between the parties involved.

4   BGP and Routing Security

The BGP protocol is what makes Internet routing possible, allowing communication between different ASs (autonomous systems) by exchange or publishing of routing information. BGP was initially designed with no inherent security considerations in mind. The design of BGP, as the successor to EGP, was carried out in the hierarchical or tree topology of the NSFNET, delegating responsibility for security to the administrators of the NSFNET Trunk network. However, some additional security mechanism is now vital for a normal network operation in the current Internet mesh topology.

Although RIRs do the allocation of network resources, the BGP protocol does not prevent a network administrator from intentionally or accidentally announcing a random prefix that does not correspond to them from their AS, regardless of their rights to advertise that route.

Along with network growth, trust between operators became weaker, increasing the number of attacks and route hijackings. Protection measures were fragile and insecure, like handwritten letters, email coordination and telephone calls between operators to agree on the IP blocks to be announced and on custom filters configuration.

IRR services are another way to verify entities right to internet resources, but although of great help, it does not provide signed information that guarantees the authentication of the right of use. This paved the way for the implementation of a security framework, called RPKI, to help network operators make informed and secure routing decisions.

RPKI is a community-driven system, in which the five Regional Internet Registries (RIRs), open source software developers and routing equipment providers participate. It combines the resource allocation model through RIRs, with the use of certificates based on the X.509 standard (with an extension to support IPs and ASNs - RFC 3779) [13]. Remarkably, it is an IETF standard, according to RFC 6480 - 6493.

It defines a public key infrastructure that creates a resource certificate chain following the same hierarchical structure than Internet number resource allocation. Except for IANA which does not operate a root certificate authority, the five RIRs run a root CA with a trust anchor that will derive on a chain of trust for the resources managed by each RIR [6].

Although most of the cases popularized by the press about route hijacking could be prevented by implementing RPKI, it does not validate the announcement path. Thus, it only prevents the attacks coming from the route origin.

As route origin validation is implemented in more places, foundation is being laid for path validation implementation. In fact, there are several efforts to offer out-of-band path validation. In particular, a proposed procedure currently being the most appealing within the IETF, uses a signed shared customer-provider relationships (C2P) database, which is built with a new RPKI object: Autonomous System Provider Authorization (ASPA). It is lightweight and fast to implement, detecting invalid AS-PATHs even during early and incremental adoption. ASPAs are digitally signed objects that allow verifying that an owner of a Customer AS (CAS) has authorized a particular Provider AS (PAS) to propagate IPv4 or IPv6 BGP route advertisements belonging to the customer to upstreams or AS Provider peers [15].

Although the implementation of RPKI + ASPA could represent a great progress in routing security and has several advantages (it is a lightweight implementation that does not require modifying the BGP UPDATE packages), some already mentioned concerns or risks have arisen mainly related to the centralization of the routing authority and the creation of single points of failure.

Several benefits can be obtained when applying blockchain rather than solutions based on a PKI, like routing security enrichment, better power balance between the participating entities, greater acceptance and lower implementation costs.

5   Blockchain Applied to Routing

Blockchain is the technology that could facilitate the construction of a shared database with cryptographical security, without relying on a hierarchical system since it can create a decentralized infrastructure that allows to validate routing information.

The main challenges that a blockchain-based solution should face are:

- Adoption motivation: Two examples to consider are the slow adoption of RPKI, and the null implementation of BGPsec despite being a standard. One of the reasons that could explain the slow deployment of RPKI is that the Certification Authorities (CA) have the final control of the resources, and this could be used to unilaterally remove the IP prefixes. Establishing a balance of power between RIRs and ISPs, and lowering implementation costs are also key to greater adoption.

– Balance of power between RIRs, ISPs and clients: A system that can get external routing security problems solved, without centralizing the power information governance, is the current challenge. In addition to providing less transparency, the risk that arises from centralized architectures is presented as a potential attack vector. In "On the Risk of Misbehaving RPKI Authorities" [10], the authors present the routing drawbacks that can arise when the threat model is changed. Rather than assuming PKI authorities trustworthiness and the route is under attack, it discusses the risks when authorities are not reliable (due to configuration errors, or to legal coercion by state-sponsored actors seeking censorship, information control or surveillance). Since IP addresses are a critical asset of ISPs, they would like to have a greater degree of control over them, but without losing the security of being certified by a CA, that is, balanced power between users and the CA [19].

– The implementation of the policies of the RIRs: Policies of the RIRs concerning resources distribution arise from forums and technical meetings open to the entire Internet community, carried out by the effort and participation of the RIRs after of internet development in each region. Regarding these guidelines or policies, options are very specific rules defined to allow human intervention to be eliminated from the allocation process (they can only be changed prior to the deployment of the contract), or more general and flexible rules defined maintaining a minimum human participation that interacts with the smart contract conducted by the allocation policies of each RIR.

Implementation cost: There are proposals, such as the BGPsec standard, that require modifying the structure of BGP messages (coexisting with the standard version), and the use of online cryptography, significantly increasing the necessary resources in routing equipment.

BGPsec was designed to solve the AS_PATH validation problem, but even leaving aside its complexity and high implementation costs, it allows to perform a downgrade attack to have compatibility with previous versions of BGP, making the work of the AS-PATH signature null, and turning path validation impossible.

It is important that the system designed using blockchain has low implementation costs, therefore the system should not replace BGP, but work in parallel, in order to validate its information, verifying the AS that originates the route and the full AS_PATH attribute.

6   Proposed Solution

After a meticulous review of the state of the art on the problem to be solved, the starting point for this investigation is the bgp_ethereum code from the Github repository [3].

The smart contract implemented must have functions that allow: ASs creation, prefixes assignment to a ASs, checking if a AS has been delegated a specific prefix, revocation or recovery of prefixes, etc. It must bear in mind that the parties involved will have addresses that will allow them to interact with the blockchain in different ways depending on whether or not they have the required permissions.

A deployment of the mentioned solution, the IANA.sol smart contract, was made on the Ropsten network[5]. After performing some testing and analysis, some improvements and variants to the original code were proposed. This contract has a dynamic arrangement of structure type data called "prefixes" , in which the assigned IP prefixes are stored, taking into account which SA they correspond to.

The requirements taken into account categorized according to the goal to be met are the following:

1. Requirements for the allocation and delegation of Internet resources through blockchain:
   - The management of resources (ASN, IPv4 and IPv6 addresses) must be simplified.
   - It should be more decentralized than the current model, but maintaining a certain level of control of the resources in the IANA and the RIRs.
   - It must provide up-to-date information about prefix assignments in order to verify ownership of the prefixes.
   - It must be fully auditable.
2. Requirements for blockchain implementation to provide BGP external routing security against Route Hijacking attacks:
   - The edge router that receives the BGP UPDATE announcements must be able to verify the origin of the route, that is, determine on the blockchain that the first AS in the received route is authorized to announce the prefix.
   - The edge router that receives the BGP UPDATE announcements must be able to validate the SAs path of the announcement, that is, the AS-PATH attribute.
   - In terms of startup, it should be able to be deployed incrementally without consumming large amounts of resources on the routers (memory, storage, and CPU).
   - BGP protocol must not be modified.

The chosen IPv4 network topology is the one used in the Mininet documentation [2] and is described in Fig. 1, where the relationships between the ASs and the IP prefixes used for the route hijacking attack emulation are shown [14].

The emulation employed Containernet as a testbed, a fork of the Mininet network emulator that allows Docker containers to be used as hosts in emulated

---

[5] The Ethereum blockchain has some test networks. The Ropsten testnet is the most similar to the Ethereum Mainnet, it allows blockchain developers to test their applications in a development environment, without the need to spend real ETH tokens.

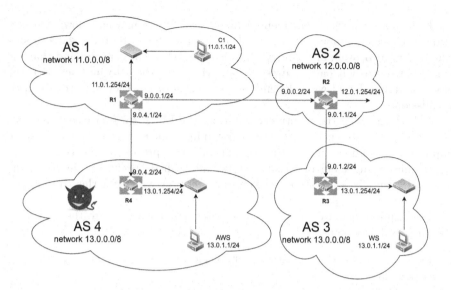

Fig. 1. IPv4 Network Topology - Route Hijacking Emulation.

network topologies [20]. This allows interesting functionalities to build network emulators and testbeds.

In the demo, two emulations were carried out, one of a successful Route Hijacking attack, and the other of an avoided Route Hijacking attack through blockchain technology.

The successful Route Hijacking attack demonstrated how the rogue AS (AS 4) falsely advertised a shorter path to reach a 13.0.0.0/8 prefix, causing other ASs to direct traffic destined for it through the shorter path. When the web server 13.0.1.1 was requested from the C1 client, the web page on the AWS attacker's server was loaded. Figure 2 shows the output of the "show ip bgp" command on R1.

In the simulation of the route hijacking attack avoided through the use of blockchain technology, the UPDATE messages were validated on the R1 router belonging to AS 1, invoking methods with blockchain reading operations implemented using client software developed in python language.

The objective of the python client is that the two requirements previously mentioned can be evaluated when receiving an UPDATE package:

1. To verify that the first AS in the received route is authorized to advertise the prefix.
2. To verify that the path of ASs of the announcement, the AS-PATH attribute, is valid.

Finally, taking into account the BGP route selection criteria (it evaluates which is the shortest as-path as long as "weight" or "local preference" has not been used), a higher local preference of 150 is configured for routes that were

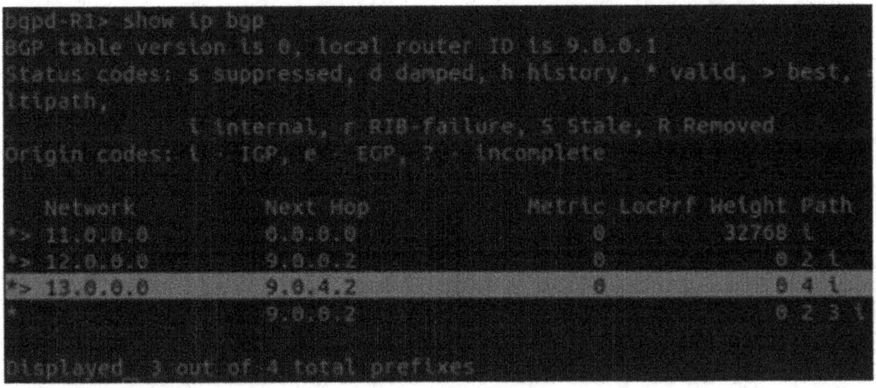

Fig. 2. Successful route hijacking attack.

fully validated, causing the correctly validated route to be preferred. When the web server 13.0.1.1 was requested from the client C1, the web page of the WS server belonging to AS 3 was loaded. Figure 3 shows the output of the "show ip bgp" command on R1.

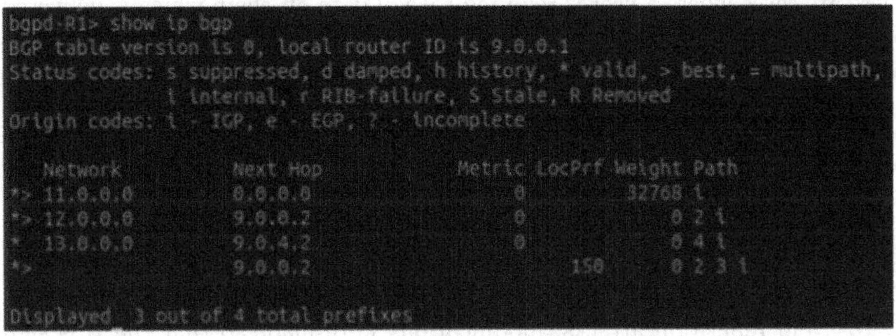

Fig. 3. Route hijacking attack bypassed by using blockchain.

For a blockchain-based implementation on commercial hardware, the RPKI-RTR protocol (RFC 8210) [7] could be modified. In the RPKI system there is a component called the Relying Party (RP), commonly called the RPKI validator. It collects ROA objects from distributed RPKI repositories, validates the signature of each entry to provide RPKI-compliant routers with validated route origins (VRP) through the RPKI-RTR protocol. Routers build a database with the information received from the cache and operators can use this attribute to define filters. In our case, the RPKI validator would be an interface between the information stored in the blockchain and the routers connected to the Internet, so the validator could be executed in a local transactional node of the blockchain.

Open network operating systems disengaged from hardware such as Cumulus Linux and Open Network Linux allow greater flexibility and innovation opportunities. They enable ISPs to implement new functionalities (such as a security model based on blockchain) while maintaining existing hardware. The impact of this business model relies on the independence of the agenda of big hardware manufacturers.

6.1   Contributions Made to the Smart Contract

Migration to Solidity V0.8.0

Major changes, new features and bug fixes are regularly introduced to Solidity, so its latest published version must be used when implementing contracts.

Using the ECDSA Library from Openzeppelin

The code was modified to use the OpenZeppelin ECDSA.sol library, which provides an audited and convenient signature verification library that is safe for production code. Also, sha256 hash functions were switched over the less consuming keccak256.

Signature Replay Attacks

There are cases where a user is required to sign data off-chain which is delivered to another authorized user who in turn will send it to the contract to invoke a function, with the endorsement of the user who made the signature. This process allows users to express their will to carry out a transaction outside the chain, and the confirmation is later updated within the blockchain through the authorized user [9]. In this case, the data signinig user is the AS or ISP, and IANA the authorized user.

The code initially used was prone to signature replay attack because the authorized entity (IANA), could resubmit the same signed data and perform unwanted operations that are expected to be performed only once.

To avoid repetition attacks, modifications were made so that the ASs sign the data together with a unique nonce value each time. The name of the function (or msg.sig) and the address of the smart contract in the signed data were also included, thus preventing the authorized entity from using the signed data in another function or even another smart contract.

Heartbeat Function

In a centralized RPKI-based model, RIRs have the ability to prevent the use of an IP prefix assigned to an AS by revoking the certificate. Although the proposed model maintains the IANA in the resource management role, it does not allow it to block the use of prefixes unless the AS does not perform the annual renewal and payment for the prefix use. Once the time-out expires, the smart contract allows the RIR to reclaim the resources. The reasons for which expiration may occur are:

- Oversight or decision of the head of the AS. If neglected, IANA/RIR should be contacted to avoid cancellation and carry out the renewal process as soon as possible.
- Loss of the private key due to carelessness, death, etc. In these cases the IANA can retrieve the prefixes after expiration. This is mandatory, otherwise address spaces and ASs would be lost permanently, without chance of recovering them or claiming payment for the use of the resource.

7   Conclusions and Future Work

It is not difficult to imagine a relatively near future when RPKI will be implemented in almost every AS, since RPKI and ASPA are the routing security solutions with more chances to prevail. Configuration errors or attacks that caused frequent route leaks will no longer cause any damage, and BGP attacks will become more advanced.

In this scenario, attacks that modify the AS-PATH with a valid origin will go unnoticed by RPKI, and the adoption of ASPA or some similar strategy shall be promoted to prevent attacks.

Nonetheless, this apparently inviolable system will have a single point of failure, its centralized authority, and the attackers will look for vulnerabilities in their computers, servers and in the people who have access to them.

For these reasons, it is extremely important to seek more decentralized, balanced, safe and democratic alternatives for the processes that govern us. In an increasingly interconnected future, excessive centralization doesn't seem like a good idea, leading us to investigate decentralized platforms that may be secure and scalable enough to meet that challenge.

In the Ethereum Mainnet network, the costs of fees to carry out transactions make the solution not economically viable at this time. For example, a transaction to assign a prefix to an AS consumes approximately 114,352 gas and the cost in Ethers of the transaction is 0.016695392 (with a gas price of 146 gwei), which is equivalent to USD 28.30 (0, 016695392 * 1.695). Therefore, it is necessary to look for alternative layer 2 solutions to make the project technically and economically viable prior to the implementation of Eth2.

The following improvements are planned in the near future:

Stack IPv6/IPv4 Dual Support
Most dual-stack implementations allow IPv6-only applications to interoperate with IPv4 and IPv6 nodes. IPv4 packets directed to IPv6 applications on a dual-stack node arrive at their destination because their addresses are mapped using IPv4-mapped IPv6 addresses (RFC 4038) [16].

The IPv4-mapped addresses, 0:0:0:0:0:FFFF: w.x.y.z or ::FFFF: w.x.y.z, are used to represent the addresses of an IPv4 node as an IPv6 type address (for example, the address ::FFFF:192.168.0.1 represents the IPv4 address 192.168.0.1. This notation is used for internal representation only, the address assigned to IPv4 is never used as a source or destination address within an IPv6 package, IPv6 does not support the use of IPv4-mapped addresses.

AS-PATH Verification

The following alternatives will be evaluated to verify the AS-PATH:

- The two side adjacencies method proposes that each AS registers its own peers in the blockchain, without differentiating the uplinks from the downlinks. The validity of the AS-PATH will depend on verifying the adjacency with the other end for each pair of ASs in the path. This method is used by the original repository but its disadvantage is that without a high adoption rate it does not provide a reliable way to automate route leak detection since the attacker could create a one-way adjacency. It can also cause problems with indirect adjacencies on some IXPs [5].
- The Autonomous System Provider Authorization (ASPA) method can be implemented by storing in the blokchain the different associations of the AS with its peers. This information allows to verify if that the owner of a Customer AS (CAS) has authorized a particular Provider AS (PAS) to propagate IPv4 or IPv6 BGP route announcements belonging to the customer, to the upstreams or peers of the Provider AS. Thus it would allow to detect invalid AS-PATHs even during early and incremental adoption [5].

References

1. Sharding on Ethereum - EthHub (Nov 2019). https://docs.ethhub.io/ethereum-roadmap/ethereum-2.0/sharding/
2. Mininet (June 2021). https://github.com/mininet/mininet
3. Abranches, M.: bgp_ethereum. library Catalog: github.com. https://github.com/mcabranches/bgp_ethereum. Accessed 15 Jul 2020
4. Angieri, S., García-Martínez, A., Liu, B., Yan, Z., Wang, C., Bagnulo, M.: A distributed autonomous organization for internet address management. IEEE Trans. Eng. Manag. **67**(4), 1459–1475 (2020). https://doi.org/10.1109/TEM.2019.2924737
5. Azimov, A., Bogomazov, E., Bush, R., Patel, K., Snijders, J.: Verification of AS_PATH using the resource certificate public key infrastructure and autonomous system provider authorization. Internet-Draft draft-ietf-sidrops-aspa-verification-07, Internet Engineering Task Force (Feb 2021). work in Progress. https://datatracker.ietf.org/doc/html/draft-ietf-sidrops-aspa-verification-07
6. Band, A.: The RPKI Documentation, p. 153. https://rpki.readthedocs.io/en/latest/. Accessed 27 Feb 2021
7. Bush, R., Austein, R.: The Resource Public Key Infrastructure (RPKI) to Router Protocol, Version 1. https://tools.ietf.org/html/rfc8210. Accessed 27 Feb 2021
8. Buterin, V., et al.: Combining GHOST and casper (May 2020). [cs] . arXiv: 2003.03052
9. Chittoda, J.: Mastering Blockchain Programming with Solidity: Write Production-Ready Smart Contracts for Ethereum Blockchain with Solidity. Packt Publishing Ltd., Birmingham (Aug 2019). google-Books-ID: wWOnDwAAQBAJ
10. Cooper, D., Heilman, E., Brogle, K., Reyzin, L., Goldberg, S.: On the risk of misbehaving rpki authorities. In: Proceedings of the 12th ACM Workshop on Hot Topics in Networks, HotNets 2013 (Nov 2013). https://doi.org/10.1145/2535771.2535787

11. Ermagan, V., Paillisse, J., Rodriguez-Natal, A., Cabellos-Aparicio, A., Vegoda, L., Maino, F.: An analysis of the applicability of blockchain to secure IP addresses allocation, delegation and bindings. library Catalog: tools.ietf.org. https://tools. ietf.org/html/draft-paillisse-sidrops-blockchain-02

12. Gallardo, I., Bazan, P., Venosa, P.: Arquitectura de certificados digitales: de una arquitectura jerárquica y centralizada a una distribuida y descentralizada. Revista Ibérica de Sistemas e Tecnologias de Informação **32**, 49–66 (2019)

13. Kent, S., Lynn, C., Seo, K.: X.509 Extensions for IP Addresses and AS Identifiers. https://tools.ietf.org/html/rfc3779. Accessed 5 Mar 2021

14. Kumar, V.: jvimal/bgp-Bitbucket. https://bitbucket.org/jvimal/bgp/src/master/. Accessed 25 Mar 2021

15. Labs, Q.: Eliminating opportunities for traffic hijacking (March 2019). https://qratorlabs.medium.com/eliminating-opportunities-for-traffic-hijacking-153a39395778

16. Shin, M.K., Hong, Y.G., Hagino, J., Savola, P., Castro, E.M.: Application Aspects of IPv6 Transition (2005). number: RFC 4038. https://www.rfc-editor.org/info/rfc4038

17. Mathew, A.J.: The myth of the decentralised internet. Internet Policy Rev. **5**(3), 1–16 (2016). https://doi.org/10.14763/2016.3.425, http://hdl.handle.net/10419/214020

18. Nakamura, R., Jimba, T., Harz, D.: Refinement and verification of CBC casper. In: 2019 Crypto Valley Conference on Blockchain Technology (CVCBT), pp. 26–38. IEEE, Rotkreuz, Switzerland (June 2019). https://doi.org/10.1109/CVCBT.2019.00008, https://ieeexplore.ieee.org/document/8787558/

19. Paillisse, J., et al.: Ipchain: securing ip prefix allocation and delegation with blockchain, pp. 1236–1243 (July 2018). https://doi.org/10.1109/Cybermatics_2018.2018.00218

20. Peuster, M., Karl, H., van Rossem, S.: Medicine: rapid prototyping of production-ready network services in multi-pop environments. In: 2016 IEEE Conference on Network Function Virtualization and Software Defined Networks (NFV-SDN), pp. 148–153 (Nov 2016). https://doi.org/10.1109/NFV-SDN.2016.7919490

21. Saad, M., Anwar, A., Ahmad, A., Alasmary, H., Yuksel, M., Mohaisen, D.: Routechain: towards blockchain-based secure and efficient bgp routing, pp. 210–218 (May 2019). https://doi.org/10.1109/BLOC.2019.8751229

22. Schwarz, C.: Ethereum 2.0: A Complete Guide. Scaling Ethereum — Part Two: Sharding. (July 2019). https://medium.com/chainsafe-systems/ethereum-2-0-a-complete-guide-scaling-ethereum-part-two-sharding-902370ac3be

23. Snyder, J.: The History of IANA (May 2016). https://www.internetsociety.org/ianatimeline/

24. Tsumak, D.: Securing BGP using blockchain technology. Master's thesis, Aalto University. School of Science (2018). http://urn.fi/URN:NBN:fi:aalto-201812146538

25. Xing, Q., Wang, B., Wang, X.: Bgpcoin: blockchain-based internet number resource authority and bgp security solution. Symmetry **10**(9), 408 (2018). https://doi.org/10.3390/sym10090408, https://www.mdpi.com/2073-8994/10/9/408

Comparison of Hardware and Software Implementations of AES on Shared-Memory Architectures

Victoria Sanz[1,2](✉), Adrián Pousa[1], Marcelo Naiouf[1],
and Armando De Giusti[1,3]

[1] School of Computer Sciences, III-LIDI, National University of La Plata,
La Plata, Argentina
{vsanz,apousa,mnaiouf,degiusti}@lidi.info.unlp.edu.ar
[2] CIC, Buenos Aires, Argentina
[3] CONICET, Buenos Aires, Argentina

Abstract. Nowadays, AES is one of the most widely used encryption algorithms. There are several implementations of AES, both in hardware and software. With the ever-increasing amount of sensitive data that need to be protected, it is natural to turn to parallel AES solutions that exploit the full computational power provided by emerging architectures in order to reduce encryption time. In this paper, we compare the performance of a hardware-based AES solution for multicore CPU (PAES-HW-CPU) with that of two other software-based AES solutions for multicore CPU (PAES-SW-CPU) and GPU (PAES-SW-GPU) respectively. The former is implemented using Intel AES New Instructions and the latter using the OpenSSL library. The results reveal that PAES-HW-CPU achieves higher performance. However, PAES-SW-GPU on 2 GPUs is competitive compared to CPUs with hardware support for AES and few cores and CPUs that do not support AES.

Keywords: Advanced encryption standard · Hardware encryption · Software encryption · Intel AES new instructions · OpenSSL

1 Introduction

Nowadays, the amount of sensitive data that is generated to be stored and/or transmitted over the network is constantly increasing. To protect sensitive data from potential threats encryption strategies are used. AES (Advanced Encryption Standard) [1] is one of the most widely used encryption algorithms and is considered secure enough to protect national information by the United States government [2].

There are several libraries that implement AES in software, being OpenSSL [3] one of the most used. At present, different processors (Intel, AMD, ARM) embed AES in hardware. In particular, Intel introduced the AES-NI [4] (AES

ⓒ Springer Nature Switzerland AG 2021
M. Naiouf et al. (Eds.): JCC-BD&ET 2021, CCIS 1444, pp. 60–70, 2021.
https://doi.org/10.1007/978-3-030-84825-5_5

New Instructions) instruction set to accelerate data encryption on Intel Xeon and Intel Core processor families.

Additionally, the time involved in data encryption is directly related to the amount of data to be encrypted and may be significant. Several works have focused on reducing this time, adapting AES to take advantage of the computing power of emerging parallel architectures.

On the one hand, several researchers have analyzed software-based AES solutions on different parallel architectures. In particular, different authors [5–8] parallelized AES on NVIDIA GPUs, achieving higher performance than the sequential version provided by OpenSSL. Other authors [9,10] compared the performance of AES on NVIDIA GPUs and multicore CPUs with 8 threads, and conclude that the GPU achieves better performance for input data less than 256 MB. In [11] we showed experimentally that multicore CPUs with a higher number of cores achieve better performance than GPUs, for input data that exceed 32 MB. However, in that work CUDA *streams* [12] (to overlap communication and computation) were not used since it is a newer technology.

On the other hand, several studies have assessed hardware-based AES solutions. Specifically, in [13] the authors implement a sequential AES solution using AES-NI and compare its performance against AES on an NVIDIA GPU. The results indicate that sequential AES implemented with AES-NI achieves better performance than AES on GPU and, also, they both improve the sequential software-based AES solution. Moreover, in [10] the authors run AES-NI on a multicore with up to 8 threads, for data less than 256 MB, and compare it against AES on a best-performing NVIDIA GPU. The results show that AES on this GPU outperforms sequential AES-NI. However, AES-NI with 4 threads is 1.4 times faster than AES on GPU.

From the previous works, it is concluded that hardware-based AES solutions are more efficient than software-based solutions, but require specific hardware support. Furthermore, there are other common encryption algorithms that are not supported by hardware. Thus, it is still of interest to study the performance of both types of encryption solutions and determine whether it is possible to achieve an acceptable performance with software-based solutions by adding more computing resources.

In this paper, we compare the performance of a hardware-based AES solution for multicore CPU (PAES-HW-CPU) with that of two other software-based AES solutions for multicore CPU (PAES-SW-CPU) and GPU (PAES-SW-GPU) respectively. The former is implemented using AES-NI instructions and the latter using the OpenSSL library. The results reveal that PAES-HW-CPU achieves higher performance. However, PAES-SW-GPU on 2 GPUs is competitive compared to CPUs with hardware support for AES and few cores and CPUs that do not support AES.

Our work differs from previous studies in two ways. First, we evaluate the scalability of the solutions presented here on architectures that include more computing resources. Specifically, we evaluate PAES-HW-CPU and PAES-SW-CPU on a CPU with 36 cores and PAES-SW-GPU on 1 and 2 GPUs. Second, the analysis was performed with larger input data.

The rest of the paper is organized as follows. Section 2 summarizes the AES algorithm, the architectural characteristics of NVIDIA GPUs and the AES-NI instruction set. Section 3 describes the different AES solutions used in this work. Section 4 shows our experimental results. Finally, Sect. 5 presents the main conclusions and future research.

2   Background

This section provides some background information on the AES algorithm, the GPU architecture and the AES-NI instruction set.

2.1   AES Algorithm

The AES (Advanced Encryption Standard) algorithm [1] divides the input data into fixed-size blocks (128 bits). Each block is represented as a 4 × 4 matrix of bytes, called *state* (Fig. 1). The algorithm described in the standard applies eleven *rounds* to each state, where each round is composed of a set of operations.

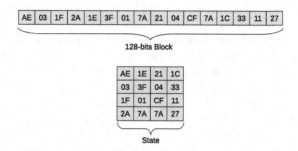

Fig. 1. AES state

Since AES is a symmetric algorithm, it uses the same key (*initial key*) to encrypt and decrypt the data. The key size is 128 bits, as indicated by the standard. From this key, ten more keys are generated through a mathematical procedure. The resulting keys (eleven in total) are called *sub-keys* and they are used one in each of the rounds.

The encryption process starts with the *initial round*. This round performs only the *AddRoundKey* operation, which combines each byte of the state with the corresponding byte of the *initial key* using bitwise XOR.

Each of the following nine rounds (*standard rounds*) applies 4 operations in this order:

- *SubBytes:* each state byte is replaced by another one. The new byte is taken from a 16 × 16 table (called Byte Substitution Table or S-box) that stores pre-computed values. This table is accessed taking the first 4 bits of the byte to be replaced as the row index and the last 4 bits as column index.
- *ShiftRows:* each row of the state is cyclically shifted to the left. Specifically, the ith row is shifted i times ($0 \le i \le 3$).
- *MixColumns:* a linear transformation is applied to each column of the state.
- *AddRoundKey:* this is the same as the initial round, but using the following subkey.

The *final round* performs 3 operations, *SubBytes*, *ShiftRows* and *AddRound-Key*, which work in the same way as in standard rounds. In this case, the *AddRoundKey* operation uses the last subkey.

Figure 2 shows the algorithm scheme.

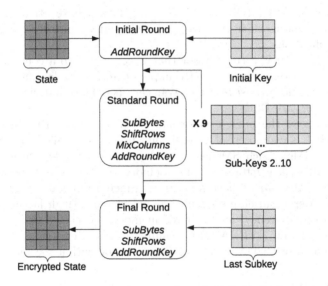

Fig. 2. Scheme of the AES algorithm

The decryption process applies the same procedure but in reverse order.

Other variants of the standard consider 192 or 256-bits keys and require increasing the number of rounds and consequently generating more sub-keys.

In this paper, we focus on evaluating the AES algorithm defined in the standard, which considers 128-bits keys, and only the encryption process, since decryption has similar performance.

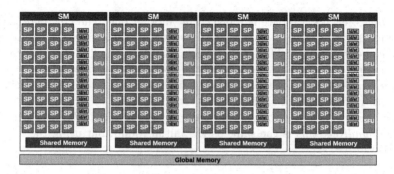

Fig. 3. NVIDIA GPU Architecture

2.2 GPU

In recent years, GPUs (Graphics Processing Units) have attracted attention of researchers due to their low cost and high performance for solving general purpose applications.

A GPU (*device*) is a coprocessor that is connected to a conventional CPU (*host*) via PCIe. Computing on a GPU implies transferring data from CPU memory to GPU memory (*host-to-device* transfer, aka H2D) and viceversa (*device-to-host* transfer, aka D2H).

Figure 3 shows the main components of an NVIDIA GPU. In general, an NVIDIA GPU is composed of several multiprocessors, called Streaming Multiprocessors (SMs). Each SM has multiple simple cores, known as Streaming Processors (SPs), load/store units for memory operations and special function units (SFUs). Also, GPUs have a multi-level memory hierarchy, whose components differ in size and access latency: global memory (high latency), constant memory (medium latency) and a shared memory in each SM (low latency).

Programming an NVIDIA GPU requires using extensions to C Language, such as OpenCL or CUDA, and compiling the code with a specific compiler.

2.3 Intel AES New Instructions

AES-NI [4] (AES New Instructions) is an instruction set designed to accelerate data encryption on Intel Xeon and Intel Core processor families.

Specifically, the instruction set consists of six instructions: four instructions for encryption/decryption and two for generating sub-keys.

Table 1 shows these six instructions and their functionality.

3   AES Implementations

This section describes the parallel implementations of AES developed in this work. Specifically, two software-based solutions for multicore CPU (PAES-SW-CPU) and GPU (PAES-SW-GPU) respectively, and a hardware-based solution for multicore CPU (PAES-HW-CPU).

Table 1. AES new instructions

Instruction	Description
AESENC	Performs one standard round of AES encryption
AESENCLAST	Performs the final round of AES encryption
AESDEC	Performs one standard round of AES decryption
AESDECLAST	Performs the final round of AES decryption
AESKEYGENASSIST	Generates the sub-keys used for encryption
AESIMC	Performs the Inverse MixColumns Transformation, in order to convert the encryption sub-keys to a form usable for decryption

It should be noted that the subkey generation process is done sequentially, because its execution time is negligible.

3.1 AES for Multicore CPU

Hardware-based and software-based solutions for multicore CPU, PAES-HW-CPU and PAES-SW-CPU respectively, use OpenMP to manage multiple threads. Both solutions consider the input data as consecutive states (16 bytes). Each thread takes a proportional set of successive states from the input and applies the encryption process to each state.

In PAES-SW-CPU each state is encrypted using the AES_encrypt function provided by the OpenSSL library, while in PAES-HW-CPU the encryption is carried out using the AES-NI instruction set described in Sect. 2.3.

3.2 AES for GPU

The software-based solution for GPU (PAES-SW-GPU) is developed using CUDA and performs the following steps. First, the host copies the subkeys and the Byte Substitution Table into the constant memory of the GPU, since they are read-only. Then, it copies the data to be encrypted into the global memory of the device (host-to-device transfer, aka H2D) and launches the kernel.

Similar to the solutions for CPU, PAES-SW-GPU considers the input data as consecutive states. The threads belonging to the same CUDA block work on successive states. For that purpose, they cooperate to efficiently load the states to be encrypted into shared memory. Then, each thread is responsible for encrypting one state, using the OpenSSL AES_encrypt function that we adapted for GPUs. After that, the threads cooperate to move the encrypted data from shared memory to global memory.

Finally, the host gets the encrypted data from the global memory of the GPU (device-to-host transfer, aka D2H).

Note that GPUs have limited memory capacity. Therefore, when the workload exceeds this capacity, it is divided into chunks that fit into global memory, and then they are transfered and encrypted one by one.

Also, it should be noted that H2D/D2H transfers are time-consuming, since they involve PCIe communication. It is possible to hide this latency with communication-computation overlapping, by using CUDA *streams* [12].

When the system has several identical GPUs, the workload (input data) is distributed equally among them. In this case, our solution creates as many threads as available GPUs (using OpenMP). Each thread runs on a dedicated CPU core and controls one GPU.

4   Experimental Results

Our experimental platform is a machine composed of two Intel Xeon E5-2695 v4 processors and 128 GB RAM. Each processor has eighteen 2.10 Ghz cores, thus the machine has thirty-six cores in total. Hyper-Threading and Turbo Boost were disabled. The machine is equipped with two Nvidia GeForce GTX 960; each one is composed of 1024 cores and 2 GB GDDR5 memory. Each CUDA core operates at 1127 Mhz.

Tests were performed using data of different sizes (2 GB, 4 GB, 8 GB, 16 GB and 32 GB) and focusing on the encryption process, since the decryption process has a similar performance.

Hardware-based and software-based solutions for multicore CPU, PAES-HW-CPU and PAES-SW-CPU respectively, were executed with the following system configurations: 6, 12, 18, 24, 30 and 36 threads/CPU cores. Also, both solutions were executed with 1 thread/CPU core (i.e. sequentially). All of these codes were compiled with ICC.

The software-based solution for GPU (PAES-SW-GPU) was executed on 1 and 2 GPUs, with 256 threads per block. This CUDA block size gives the best performance in practice. Our analysis considers the data transfer time (host-to-device and device-to-host, aka H2D and D2H), since it represents a significant portion of the total execution time (i.e. it is not negligible) [14]. Also, it evaluates two versions of this solution: without using and using CUDA streams. Both codes were compiled with NVCC.

For each test scenario (input and system configuration), we ran each solution 100 times and averaged the Gbps.

Figure 4 illustrates the average throughput (in Gbps) achieved by PAES-HW-CPU, for different data sizes and system configurations (number of threads/cores). In general, it is observed that the best performance is reached with 18 threads/cores, regardless of the data size. Adding more threads/cores does not bring significant performance gains. Also, it can be seen that the sequential solution (1 thread/core) reaches an average throughput of 26.04 Gbps, while the parallel solution with 18 threads/cores obtains an average throughput of 177.66 Gbps and a peak throughput of 190.13 Gbps with 8 GB data.

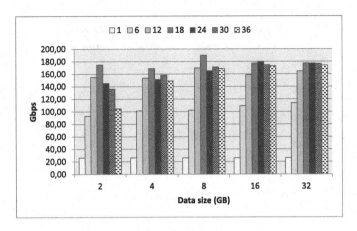

Fig. 4. Average throughput (in Gbps) of PAES-HW-CPU

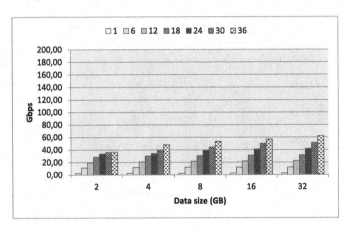

Fig. 5. Average throughput (in Gbps) of PAES-SW-CPU

Figure 5 shows the average throughput (in Gbps) achieved by PAES-SW-CPU, for different data sizes and system configurations (number of threads/cores). In this case, the best performance is reached with 36 threads/cores. Note that this software-based solution for CPU has a lower performance than the hardware-based solution for CPU. Specifically, the sequential solution (1 thread/core) achieves an average throughput of 2.32 Gbps, while the parallel solution with 36 threads/cores reaches an average throughput of 51.34 Gbps and a peak throughput of 61.88 Gbps with 32 GB data.

Figure 6 shows the average throughput (in Gbps) of PAES-SW-GPU for different data sizes, on 1 and 2 GPUs, without using and using CUDA *streams*. In the latter case, we experimentally determined that the best performance is achieved with 32 CUDA *streams*. As can be seen, when using CUDA *streams* the performance gain is more than 2x. A similar acceleration is also achieved

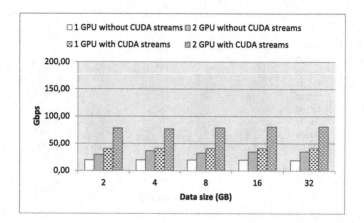

Fig. 6. Average throughput (in Gbps) of PAES-SW-GPU

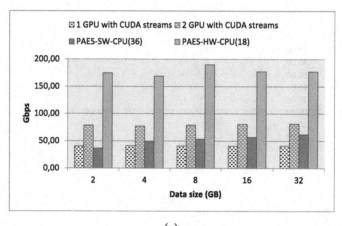

(a)

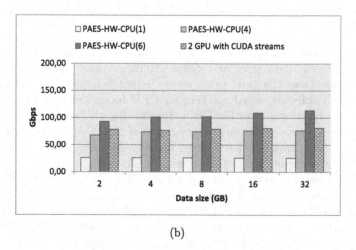

(b)

Fig. 7. Comparison of the different solutions

when using 2 GPUs. Specifically, the solution with 1 GPU and CUDA *streams* reaches an average throughput of 40.69 Gbps, while the solution with 2 GPUs and CUDA *streams* obtains an average throughput of 79.23 Gbps.

Figure 7a compares the average throughput (in Gbps) of the solutions that provide the best performance. From the results we conclude that the best alternative is the hardware-based solution for CPU, executed with 18 threads/cores. However, when the architecture does not provide hardware support for AES, the best option is to encrypt with the software-based solution on 2 GPUs. Moreover, from Fig. 7b we can deduce that this solution is competitive with the hardware-based solution for CPU: PAES-SW-GPU on 2 GPUs outperforms PAES-HW-CPU with 1 and 4 threads/cores and achieves an acceptable performance compared to PAES-HW-CPU with 6 threads/cores.

5   Conclusions and Future Work

In this paper, we compared the performance of a hardware-based AES solution for multicore CPU (PAES-HW-CPU) with that of two other software-based AES solutions for multicore CPU (PAES-SW-CPU) and GPU (PAES-SW-GPU) respectively.

From the experimental results we conclude that the best alternative is PAES-HW-CPU. On a platform equipped with 36 cores, this solution achieves the best performance (an average throughput of 177.66 Gbps) with 18 threads/cores. Also, the results show that PAES-SW-GPU on 2 GPUs reaches an average throughput of 79.23 Gbps. This solution is better compared to a CPU with hardware support for AES and few cores (4) or CPUs that do not support AES, and achieves an acceptable performance compared to a CPU with hardware support for AES and 6 cores.

As for future work, we plan to implement a solution of AES to fully exploit the resources of CPU-GPU heterogeneous systems (i.e., using both CPU cores and GPUs in a collaborative way) and compare its performance with the results presented here.

References

1. Federal Information Processing Standard Publication 197 (FIPS PUB 197): The Official AES Standard . http://csrc.nist.gov/publications/fips/fips197/fips-197. pdf
2. Lynn Hathaway: National Policy on the Use of the Advanced Encryption Standard (AES) to Protect National Security Systems and National Security Information (June 2003). http://csrc.nist.gov/groups/ST/toolkit/documents/aes/CNSS15FS. pdf
3. The OpenSSL Project: Cryptography and SSL/TLS Toolkit. https://www.openssl. org
4. Intel Corporation. Intel® Advanced Encryption Standard (AES) New Instructions Set. https://www.intel.com/content/dam/doc/white-paper/advanced-encryption-standard-new-instructions-set-paper.pdf

5. Manavski, S.A., et al.: CUDA compatible GPU as an efficient hardware accelerator for AES cryptography. In: Proceedings of the 2007 IEEE International Conference on Signal Processing and Communications (ICSPC 2007), pp. 65–68 (2007)
6. Di Biagio, A., et al.: Design of a parallel AES for graphics hardware using the CUDA framework. In: Proceedings of the 2009 IEEE International Symposium on Parallel & Distributed Processing, pp. 1–8 (2009)
7. Iwai, K., et al.: Acceleration of AES encryption on CUDA GPU. Int. J. Netw. Comput. **2**(1), 131–145 (2012)
8. Pousa, A., et al.: Performance analysis of a symmetric cryptographic algorithm on multicore architectures. In: Computer Science & Technology Series. XVII Argentine Congress of Computer Science Selected Papers, pp. 57–66. EDULP, Argentina (2012)
9. Ortega, J., et al.: Parallelizing AES on multicores and GPUs. In: Proceedings of the 2011 IEEE International Conference on Electro/Information Technology, pp. 1–5 (2011)
10. Nishikawa, N., et al.: High-performance symmetric block ciphers on multicore CPU and GPUs. Int. J. Netw. Comput. **2**(2), 251–268 (2012)
11. Pousa, A., et al.: Rendimiento del algoritmo AES sobre arquitecturas de memoria compartida. In: Proceedings of the XXIV Argentine Congress of Computer Science (CACIC), pp. 73–82 (2018)
12. Kirk, D., et al.: Programming Massively Parallel Processors (Third Edition), pp. 275–304. Morgan Kaufmann, Burlington (2017)
13. Guao, G. et al.: Different implementations of AES cryptographic algorithm. In: Proceedings of the 2015 IEEE 17th International Conference on High Performance Computing and Communications, 2015 IEEE 7th International Symposium on Cyberspace Safety and Security, and 2015 IEEE 12th International Conference on Embedded Software and Systems, pp. 1848–1853 (2015)
14. Sanz, V., et al.: Accelerating pattern matching with CPU-GPU collaborative computing. In: Vaidya J., Li J. (eds.) Algorithms and Architectures for Parallel Processing. ICA3PP 2018. Lecture Notes in Computer Science, vol. 11334, pp. 310–322. Springer, Cham (2018). https://doi.org/10.1007/978-3-030-05051-1_22

Machine and Deep Learning

Proposal for a Classifier for Public Tenders for Software Based on Standard IEEE830

Jorge Hochstetter[✉], Claudio Díaz, Mauricio Diéguez, and Jaime Díaz

Depto. Cs. de la Computación e Informática, Universidad de La Frontera, Temuco, Chile
jorge.hochstetter@ufrontera.cl

Abstract. Nowadays, governments and private sectors request industry software solutions through public tenders that use websites for mass distribution. Not only is demand organized, but a large number of software tenders is produced. This study focuses on the analysis of texts from these documents to characterize them efficiently in order to find a specific solution to the general problem of how to make a bid and how not to make a bid. An automatic classifier is proposed for the public tender process for software based on IEEE standard 830-1998, which categorizes text from a pragmatic point of view. Development phases and classification success rates are shown for each algorithm used in the different experiments. This system may be an alternative for the early analysis of public tenders for software with fuzzy requirements.

Keywords: Public tender · Software biddings · Automatic classifier · Requirements engineering

1 Introduction

For more than two decades there has been an economic trend toward outsourcing [1], with information technologies being one of the areas particularly affected by this process [2]. These changes obviously involve software development, where there is one market for software development services at the local level and another at the global level [3]. In this situation, it is frequently observed that when a public or private organization wishes to become involved in the selection process of a supplier to develop a specific software product, one of the go-to options, and particularly required if the purchaser is a government body, is to engage in the public tender process, which in this case here we will call PTSP (public tender for a software product).

This has meant that a significant number of software development projects is outsourced, attaching importance to the establishment of methodological conditions, budget, time and technology constraints, and a functionality framework, which are difficult to negotiate because they are established in the tender, leaving it to the offeror to decide to put forward a proposal or not.

Generally, procurement is not a topic in software engineering, i.e., the purchasing process is not part of any software development life cycle, or it works on the assumption that there is flexibility to address the requirements elicitation and specification phases

© Springer Nature Switzerland AG 2021
M. Naiouf et al. (Eds.): JCC-BD&ET 2021, CCIS 1444, pp. 73–88, 2021.
https://doi.org/10.1007/978-3-030-84825-5_6

as part of the life cycle. This can be interpreted as the project being formulated and addressed in its initial stage with nonexplicit limits for the requirements to be satisfied.

Neither of these last two options seems satisfactory with respect to how PTSP are dealt with and interpreted, and therefore we face a slightly more exhaustive search with respect to the phenomenon of procurement via PTSP. Showing that PTSP include requirements elicitation is paradoxical, because PTSP have reduced times and budgets.

Therefore, PTSP as they are undertaken today have a high level of risk for both the requestors and the offerors. For the requestors because it could mean not getting the product needed, and for the offerors, not having the minimum elements to adequately quantify the project. If the gap between stakeholders and developers is already wide for conventional projects [4], it may be assumed that it will not be better in projects where the requirements are not described by software development professionals as happens with a software tender. With the previous information, it can be said that the software industry generates its offers of software development projects in a scenario of uncertain and incomplete information. If we add to this the fact that the websites where the public calls are published can collect a considerable number of tenders in short periods, then we add complexity to the issue, since not only must it be decided which call can be applied to but also which subset of calls to study.

On the other hand, there are various automatic text analysis techniques that allow us to carry out complex tasks such as searches for grammar patterns, recognition of conceptual frameworks, concepts and relations between concepts [5] in addition to other simpler processes such as word frequency analysis or temporal modes of writing, but which, in a massive document set, have several uses for their analysis.

In particular, automated document classification is presented as a context-dependent process in which words are used, which complicates the task of deciding which category is best for a document by studying the words that comprise it. In addition, it must be considered that there are several classification algorithms with dissimilar performances for the same problem; thus, it is necessary to test and compare the performance of these algorithms when building the automatic classifier so as to use the one that best solves the classification of the formulations.

Then, from the scientific perspective, we can focus the problem on the techniques that are useful for distinguishing those bidding documents that contain more or fewer functional conditions of the product, more or fewer contain methodological conditions or more or fewer restrictions on the project. In this sense, IEEE Std. 830 [6] for software requirements specification in its version IEEE Std. 830-1998 [7] - frequently cited in software engineering studies- indicates that a good requirements document must include all the information presented in this standard and propose an organization for this information; in addition, it distinguishes the design, application, interface, performance and physical requirements [8].

Therefore, we used IEEE830-1998 [7] as the basis for the preparation of the categories in the creation of the prototype classifier, which will make it possible to contrast the quality of the requirements specifications in a PTSP, contrasting its composition with the criteria and regulations established by the standard.

On the one hand we endeavor to examine in depth how the requirements formulations are prepared in the PTSP, and on the other to contribute to establishing methodological parameters in relation to future studies related to classifier algorithms, indicating which of these offer the best response to a given tender.

In this regard, and insofar as we have been able to find, there is no generic solution to the problem of automatic classification based on IEEE Std. 830, which is why we intend to address the issue by limiting it in the domain of PTSP. The first approach we proposed was to use some analysis techniques suggested for requirements specifications. In particular our interest focused on requirements specification standard IEEE830-1998 and on some classification algorithms used [9, 10] for text analysis, with which the classification of early PTSP requirements was approached. In practical terms, the formulations of these documents, classified according to IEEE830, happen to be our classification objects: as a case study we have considered the PTSP in Chile.

Thus, our proposal is a complement to other proposals for requirements and PTSP analyses based on word frequency, increasing the type and number of metrics used to best characterize PTSP: as a case study we have considered the PTSP in Chile.

The Chilean government agencies that make purchases are bound by the Law of Public Purchases 19.886 passed in May, 2003 and which entered into force in October, 2004. This law forces the public sector to issue a call for public tenders via the well-known electronic platform Chilecompra (www.mercadopublico.cl) [14]. This way, software products are published and received via this platform, being available even after the bidding has closed.

2 Automatic Text Analysis

Computer science, as science, has channeled efforts into studying phenomena related to the computer processing of information [11]. Within this context, in the 1980s a computer science approach to linguistics appeared; this is how the first grammar formalisms emerged with a view to being processed computationally [12]. In that context, the terms of computational linguistics and natural language processing were coined; these refer to the same discipline that seeks to analyze and fully understand human languages [13]. The characteristics inherent in language make its correct processing difficult. In particular, automated document classification is presented as a context-dependent process in which words are used, which complicates the task of deciding the category to which a document belongs by studying the words that comprise it. Today automatic text analysis focuses on the recognition of concepts, relations between concepts and building ontologies [5]. This type of analysis can be useful for recognizing a specific domain, but not necessarily for distinguishing the conditions of a project or the number of requirements.

In our context we know there is a scenario of uncertain and incomplete information that encompasses PTSP, added to which in short periods a significant set of these tenders can be collected, which leads us to suggest that in order to solve the problem it is necessary to decide not only which call can be put forward, but which subgroup of calls we must study. As a result, and considering the complexity of the high volumes of data from physical and digitized PTSP documents, in addition to the high cost of processing them manually, the automation process associated with the handling of these documents becomes essential.

In this sense, we have drawn up a categorization in the creation of the prototype classifier, which will make it possible to contrast the quality of the requirements specifications in a PTSP, contrasting its composition with the criteria and regulations established by the standard.

A. *Automatic Classifiers*

Text categorization has been applied in such contexts as automatic document indexing, metadata generation, text filtering, semantic disambiguation, recognition of complex structures [14–16]. For example, Corso (2009) [17] sought to identify the level of confidence of some classification algorithms based on decision rules. In (Dapozo et al., 2007) [18], data pre-processing techniques were applied to improve the quality of the data corresponding to students admitted to a university. Some of these studies are oriented toward the selection of classification algorithms, the preparation of which consists of a series of steps as indicated next.

B. *Stages of Automatic Text Classification.*

The construction of a classifier in the approach of this study requires of several stages, which are illustrated in Fig. 1 and which we indicate next [16]:

- Selection of the documents that will be used to create the prototype classifier. In this stage the documents, texts or paragraphs are selected that will be used for the generation of the classifier.
- Selection of the labels used to classify the documents. The previously selected documents are labeled with the values we are going to include in the study. These are framed by IEEE Std. 830.
- Data pre-processing. So that the selected data can be processed by the classification algorithms, these data must pass through pre-processing to be able to retrieve only those values useful to the classifiers, attempting to discard the rest.
- Selection of the classification algorithm for use on the data. A classification algorithm is selected that will work on the data, adjusting the parameters where necessary.
- Execution of the classification. Once the classification algorithm has been selected, the classifier will be constructed.

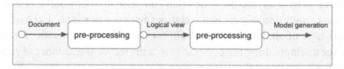

Fig. 1. Stages of automatic text classification [16].

For our objective, different classification algorithms were selected and experimented on. Finally, the results obtained are collected and, using these, some relevant conclusions are extracted for the classifiers seen.

C. *IEEE Standard 830 -1998*

The study developed points to the possibility of more efficiently characterizing PTSP documents from an automatic PTSP classifier based on IEEE830-1998 that includes the software requirements specification to obtain an approximation of the intention of the formulations of these documents, i.e., a more objective and accurate initial view of the software requirements specifications in documents [8].

IEEE830 basically defines and recommends certain parameters that should be included in every requirements specification. It seeks to assist both software customers and suppliers so they can understand exactly and accurately what it is the customer wants.

This standard characterizes what a good software requirements specification must possess, and defines a scheme so that a correct software requirements specification can be achieved. The characteristics and the scheme that establish the IEEE830 standard make it possible to define the categories needed to develop the automatic PTSP classifier.

In this case IEEE830-1998 was used to create a prototype of a PTSP classifier, where the classification algorithms with the best results evaluating a PTSP were examined in greater depth. The attributes included to develop the classifier for PTSP are based on IEEE830-1998, the classification algorithms with the best results evaluating a PTSP were examined in greater depth.

3 Automatic Classifier

The study was initially developed with a proposal for conceptual definitions of the IEEE830 standard for software requirements engineering, which reached a favorable assessment of the agreement and objectivity of classifying under this taxonomy.

The methodology used included the manual classification of PTSP compiled from the well-known electronic platform Chilecompra (www.mercadopublico.cl). In order to establish reliability in the measurement processes used, the Kappa index was applied, because it is the most used statistical index when dealing with categorical data [19]. Basically, this index is designed to measure the agreement between two observers who classify the same sample of n items in the same set of categories, or the tendency of the observer to assign values different from the value measured by the second observer [19].

It is important to note that the formulations are not necessarily classified by the literal, but also by the context, which represents the interpretation that it can suggest, since both the generic and specific categories are nominal and depend on the expert in the training phase.

D. *Text classification*

Two algorithmic proposals for classification were developed: the first to solve the classification related to generic requirements, i.e., to label the paragraphs with specific categories, which are presented in Fig. 2.

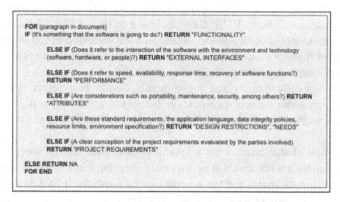

Fig. 2. Algorithmic proposal for the classification of generic categories.

The previous structure (Fig. 3) developed into a classification table as follows:

Table 1. Manual classification of generic categories.

Question	Type	Acronym
It is something the software is going to perform	Functionality	FN
Refers to the interaction of the software with technological medium	External interfaces	EL
Refers to the speed, availability, response time, recovery of the software functions	Performance	PE
Considerations such as portability, maintenance, security	Attributes	AT
Standard requirements, application language, data integrity policies, resource constraints, environment specification	Design constraints, needs	DC
Clear concessions of the project requirements evaluated by the parties involved	Project requirements	PR
None of the above	None of the above	NA

From Table 1, each paragraph in the documents was then classified with a label called "generic category", using abbreviations from the categories indicated in Table 1.

```
FOR (paragraph in document)
IF (A general introduction, general objectives, and goals) RETURN C1

ELSE IF (It's one of the following: objective, goals, benefits, what system will perform, integration with other systems) RETURN C1X

ELSE IF (It's a definition, an acronym, or an abbreviation) RETURN C13

ELSE IF (It's a list of referenced documents) RETURN C14

ELSE IF (It's a brief description of the contents and organization of the tender) RETURN C15

ELSE IF (It's a description of the factors affecting the product and its requirements; The context is described)
```

Fig. 3. Extract of algorithmic proposal for the classification of specific categories.

Continuing with this logic, a second algorithm was created to label the paragraphs with specific categories, of which an extract appears in Fig. 3.

This algorithm developed into another classification table, which appears next:

From Table 2, each paragraph in documents labeled "specific category" was classified using abbreviations in the categories indicated in Table 2. Next, we describe the construction of the prototype classifier, using the paragraphs classified in the generic and specific categories as test data.

B. *Construction of the classifier.*

According to [20], automatic document classification is the automatic allocation of a document set to various pre-existing categories. In this case, however, different sections of a document will be classified in relation to IEEE830 as described in the previous section. The steps to follow for the construction of the classifier are adapted from [20] and consist of (i) Construction of the test document, (ii) Preparation of the input data, (iii) Tests and (iv) Comparison of results.

(i) Construction of documents to classify: First, the test document was created, which contained a subgroup of PTSP document formulations, labeled and categorized, extracted from the Chilean public purchase portal. The process of labeling and categorizing was done manually and reviewed by two experts. This document has an arff format to be worked on in "Weka", a computer application for data analysis and mining [21], in the 64-bit version 3.7.9. In order to design and construct the classifier, 1,500 formulations corresponding to a set of 19 PTSP from municipalities were categorized, which are described by 5 attributes, i.e., each article in the set has 5 attributes that identify it. These attributes are described in Table 3.

(ii) Preparation of the input data: The next step was to pre-process the data that eliminated those words that did not yield relevant information for the classification; thus, the number of words to review was reduced, the classification times were reduced and the match rate of the classifier increased since the words or symbols that add confusion to the process were eliminated.

The formulations contained in the set were pre-processed. This consisted of the application of a filter on the words in the formulations. In this case in particular, an unsupervised filter was used on the attributes, called *StringToWordVector*, the main

Table 2. Manual classification of specific categories.

Question	Type	Acronym
Quite generic introduction about what the general objectives and goals will do	Introduction	C1
Includes some of the following: objective, goals, benefits it will provide, which the system will do	Purpose Scope of the system	C1X
A definition of an acronym or an abbreviation	Definitions	C13
It is a referenced document list	References	C14
It is a brief description of the contents and how the rest of the tender is organized	Document overview	C15
It is a description of the factors that affect the products and their requirements, the context is described	General description	C2
The main functions that the software must perform or are specifications of the actions or functions that the system to be developed will perform	Product functions Functions	C2X
It indicates the type of user for whom the application is designed	User characteristics	C23
It indicates any limitations and restrictions such as: company policies, hardware, security, communication protocols	Constraints	C3X
These are factors that if they change affect the requirements	Assumptions and dependencies	C25
These are possible improvements to the system in the future	Future requirements	C26
These are requirements at a level of detail sufficient to allow the designers to design a system that satisfies these requirements, and that make it possible to design the tests that confirm that the system fulfills the required needs	Specific requirements	C3
This is the definition of requirements that affect the user interface and the interface of other systems	External interfaces	C31
The requirements related to the load the system will have to support (number of simultaneous users, terminals	Performance requirements	C33

(*continued*)

Table 2. (*continued*)

Question	Type	Acronym
Attributes are detailed such as: reliability, maintainability, security, restricted access mechanisms, users authorized to carry out certain critical tasks	System attributes	C35
Represents an understanding between the customer and the supplier on contractual matters that pertain to the software production	Project requirements	C4
Representation of the amount allowed for the project	Cost	C41
The established terms are defined	Deadline	C42
Standardizes the forms and procedures in which information is handled among the actors	Reporting procedures	C43
Refers to a method or methods of development for the software to be used	Software development methods	C44
Systematic planning that protects the requirements given on quality	Quality assurance	C45
Validation and verification tests that protect each process	Validation and verification criteria	C46
Standardizes the acceptance procedures of a product	Acceptance procedures	C47
None of the above	None of the above	NA

Table 3. Formulation attributes.

Attribute	Description
id_doc	The identifier for each tender
id_parr	The identifier for each paragraph of a tender
texto	The body of the formulation
cat_gen	The generic category that corresponds to each formulation
cat_espec	The specific category that corresponds to each formulation

objective of which was to overturn the words in a vector of characters so as to organize the content of the articles for subsequent treatment by the classifier. In addition, depending on the configuration of the filter, some words or characters that did not contribute any value to the classification (for example, common words such as articles or pronouns, spaces, punctuation, etc.) were eliminated. These elements are known as *StopWords*.

With the configuration defined for the filter, 579 attributes were obtained on the 1500 instances, with which work began on the construction of the classifier.

(iii) Classification: This is the process that categorizes each formulation with respect to the categories defined in IEEE830. According to Venegas [22], the process to create an automatic text classification consists of discovering variables that are useful in the discrimination of the texts that belong to pre-existing classes. This definition indicates that these classifiers must be trained on a previously classified document set. This implies that within the work methodology, two document groups to work on must be considered: the training set and the test set, which do not have to contain the same formulations. These sets were obtained through the application of 2 types of options that Weka incorporates:

Cross Validation: This option consists of the separation of different sets with a certain number of attributes. These are called "Folds". The number of sets can vary, changing the number of Folds to be used. The default value that Weka uses is 10 Folds.

Percentage Split: This technique consists of separating the instances into two groups. The number of instances per group will be determined on the basis of a percentage of the total instances. The default value that Weka uses is 66%.

As part of the construction of the classifier, both methods were worked with, testing with different values for both *Cross Validation* and *Percentage Split*, so as to determine the effectiveness of the two methods. Considering this, next the different classification algorithms were evaluated. According to the characteristics of the document and the characteristics of the classification techniques described by Othman and Yau [23], Liu [24], Cunningham and Holmes [25], and Barnaghi [26], the decision was made to use the *BayesNet, NaiveBayes, J48, REPtree, DecisionTable* and *JRip* techniques. The same test options were used to separate the training and test sets. Several experiments were performed to find the best configuration in the different classification algorithms.

(iv) Comparison of results: In this stage the results obtained from the classification of the formulations with the different classification techniques were compared. This comparison was based mainly on two aspects: the number of formulations correctly classified and the confusion matrix resulting from each experiment.

The results obtained for the *Cross Validation* and *Percentage Split* options, in decision tree algorithms, the experiments were performed for the two categories: generic and specific.

- First with respect to the generic categories described in Table 4.

The previous table highlights that both the REPTree and JRip manage to classify the generic labels better, reaching higher classification percentages than BayesNet and generating the best models among the studied algorithms, obtaining a high goodness of fit. Next, we will compare the confusions matrices of the JRIP (above) and REPTree algorithms (below).

Figure 4 provides the distribution of the classified instances in the different categories, where without a doubt the diagonal concentrates the greatest amount of data of each

Table 4. Results from the generic categories

Algorithms	Cross Validation		Percentage Split	
	Folds	% Correct	%	% Correct
j48	5	89.46%	33	87.16%
j48	10	89.53%	66	88.43%
j48	15	90.06%	88	86.11%
REPTree	5	90.46%	33	88,35%
REPTree	10	91.33%	66	90,00%
REPTree	15	90.40%	88	88.88%
BayesNet	5	87.53%	33	85.97%
BayesNet	10	86.66%	66	87.05%
BayesNet	15	86.80%	88	90.00%
NaiveBayes	5	78.71%	33	72.63%
NaiveBayes	10	79.20%	66	77.84%
NaiveBayes	15	78.73%	88	78.33%
DecisionTable	5	89.33%	33	83.38%
DecisionTable	10	88.53%	66	87.05%
DecisionTable	15	88.73%	88	88.33%
JRip	5	90.93%	33	84.07%
JRip	10	91.06%	66	85.68%
JRip	15	90.86%	88	90.55%

```
=== Confusion Matrix ===              === Confusion Matrix ===

  a   b   c   d   e   f   g   <-- classified as      a   b   c   d   e   f   g   <-- classified as
449   0   0   8   9  12  11 |  a = fn        449   0   0  19   7   9  11 |  a = fn
  0   0   0   0   0   0   0 |  b = el          0   0   0   0   0   0   0 |  b = el
  0   0   5   0   0   0   0 |  c = pe          0   0   5   0   0   0   0 |  c = pe
 10   0   0 134  10   8   1 |  d = at         10   0   0 135   8   8   2 |  d = at
  1   0   0   0  48  10   0 |  e = dc          3   0   0   6  45   5   0 |  e = dc
 10   0   0   5   2 520  11 |  f = pr         13   0   0   5   1 520   9 |  f = pr
  5   0   0   1   1  13 210 |  g = na          5   0   0   2   0   7 216 |  g = na
```

Fig. 4. Distribution of generic categories.

corresponding row in both algorithms, which indicates that although there is confusion in some categories, this is minimal and is distributed homogenously among the other possibilities.

Both confusion matrices respond to similar patterns and their matrices are symmetrical. Only in some items can slight differences be seen; for example, the REPTree considered more classification errors in the category fn than at, whereas JRip considered the opposite.

- Second, the experiments were performed on the specific categories. The results obtained for both the *Cross Validation* and *Percentage Split* options in decision tree algorithms are described in Table 5.

Table 5. Results from the specific categories

Algorithms	Cross Validation		Percentage Split	
	Folds	% Correct	%	% Correct
j48	5	77.06%	33	71.44%
j48	10	78.00%	66	75.88%
j48	15	78.33%	88	78.33%
REPTree	5	79.86%	33	75.02%
REPTree	10	79.86%	66	78.82%
REPTree	15	79.33%	88	80.00%
BayesNet	5	77.20%	33	71.74%
BayesNet	10	77.46%	66	73.52%
BayesNet	15	77.06%	88	79.44%
NaiveBayes	5	66.33%	33	60.99%
NaiveBayes	10	66.93%	66	64.31%
NaiveBayes	15	67.66%	88	64.44%
DecisionTable	5	77.26%	33	70.14%
DecisionTable	10	77.40%	66	76.07%
DecisionTable	15	77.46%	88	77.22%
JRip	5	77.93%	33	74.62%
JRip	10	78.53%	66	76.86%
JRip	15	78.86%	88	82.77%

Table 5 contains the most outstanding by type. In the generic categories these were: REPTree (Decision trees), BayesNet (Bayesian) and JRip (Rules). It can be seen that REPTree is more consistent during the different training sessions, but that JRip reaches a higher percentage of cases classified correctly when trained with the *Percentage Split* (88%).

However, as can be observed through the experiments, the classifiers did not behave the same for all the categories, there being a type of hierarchy in the classification where for some their results were better, while for others they were poorer. Some specific categories were evaluated better, while others moderately well (Fig. 5).

It is observed in the confusion matrix that the greatest distribution of data is concentrated on the diagonal, which is good; however, some categories present more confusion

```
=== Confusion Matrix ===
```

a	b	c	d	e	f	g	h	i	j	k	l	m	n	o	p	q	r	s	t	u	v	w	x	<-- classified as
65	2	0	0	0	5	0	9	0	0	0	0	0	1	0	33	0	0	1	0	0	0	0	13	a = c1
6	20	0	0	0	2	0	5	0	0	0	0	0	0	0	4	0	0	1	0	0	0	0	0	b = c1x
0	0	0	0	0	0	0	0	0	0	0	0	0	0	0	0	0	0	0	0	0	0	0	1	c = c13
0	0	0	0	0	0	0	0	0	0	0	0	0	0	0	0	0	0	0	0	0	0	0	1	d = c14
0	0	0	0	0	0	0	0	0	0	0	0	0	0	0	0	0	0	0	0	0	0	0	1	e = c15
3	1	0	0	0	51	1	14	0	0	1	0	0	4	5	5	0	0	2	0	0	0	0	7	f = c2
0	0	0	0	0	0	15	0	0	0	1	0	0	0	3	0	0	0	0	0	0	0	1	1	g = c23
5	2	0	0	0	0	0	390	0	0	0	0	0	0	6	1	0	0	0	0	0	0	0	0	h = c2x
0	0	0	0	0	0	0	0	0	0	0	0	0	0	0	0	0	0	0	0	0	0	0	1	i = c25
0	0	0	0	0	0	0	0	0	0	0	0	0	0	0	0	0	0	0	0	0	0	0	1	j = c26
0	0	0	0	0	3	2	6	0	0	18	0	0	3	1	5	0	0	0	0	0	0	0	0	k = c3
0	0	0	0	0	0	0	0	0	0	0	0	0	0	0	0	0	0	0	0	0	0	0	1	l = c31
0	0	0	0	0	0	0	0	0	0	0	0	5	0	0	0	0	0	0	0	0	0	0	1	m = c33
0	0	0	0	0	6	3	10	0	0	3	0	0	46	2	2	0	0	0	0	0	0	0	1	n = c35
0	0	0	0	0	0	10	13	0	0	1	0	0	8	60	3	0	0	0	0	0	0	0	0	o = c3x
13	0	0	0	0	2	0	1	0	0	7	0	0	1	4	424	0	0	0	0	0	0	1	1	p = c4
0	0	0	0	0	0	0	0	0	0	0	0	0	0	0	4	10	0	0	0	0	0	0	1	q = c41
0	0	0	0	0	0	0	0	0	0	0	0	0	0	0	0	0	0	0	0	0	0	0	1	r = c42
0	0	0	0	0	0	0	0	0	0	0	0	0	0	0	0	0	0	13	0	0	0	0	3	s = c43
0	0	0	0	0	0	0	0	0	0	0	0	0	0	0	0	0	0	0	0	0	0	0	1	t = c44
0	0	0	0	0	0	0	0	0	0	0	0	0	0	0	0	0	0	0	0	0	0	0	1	u = c45
0	0	0	0	0	0	0	0	0	0	0	0	0	0	0	0	0	0	0	0	0	0	0	0	v = c46
0	0	0	0	0	0	0	0	0	0	0	0	0	0	0	0	0	0	0	0	0	0	0	0	w = c47
23	0	0	0	0	5	0	0	0	0	0	0	0	0	0	1	1	0	11	0	0	0	0	81	x = na

Fig. 5. Distribution of specific categories.

than others, which might be indicating that the classifier behaves well for some categories but not as much for others. For example, in the case of category c1, it tends to be confused with c4 and na.

4 Discussion

Our study focused on the characterization of PTSP documents based on results obtained by text classification algorithms. These in turn yield results that allow us to understand the composition of PTSP and in this particular case their relation to the requirements specifications of IEEE830-1998, which determines comprehensively how a software requirements specification should be composed. Labels were created from the standard mentioned; a division was made between generic and specific categories, where, in their evaluation, the generic categories showed a better connection than the specific categories. According to our interpretation, this is due to them being too specific; frequently, they are associated with a level of detail omitted in the tenders studied. In addition, as each set of specific categories comes from a more general category, most of the time the formulations that could be associated with a specific category are better defined within a similar generic category.

On the other hand, we understand that a PTSP is only one approach to a requirements specification phase. Proof of this is the existence of tenders that include the requirements phase as part of the tendered project itself. This could be due to the lack of a deep level of detail in the PTSP. Again, this phenomenon is associated with our results, where only some categories were used effectively, and among these, only some were considered by the classifiers. As an example, if we analyze the following text: *"The system must record each session from beginning to end"*, the classification algorithm of a specific category would have an 82.7% likelihood of classifying it correctly and in a generic category it would have a 91.3% likelihood. This is a particularly optimistic example, because it was chosen from among those categories that were classified with the highest rate of correct percentages.

5 Conclusions and Future Research

The work to obtain a good text classifier model requires many points and is susceptible to each of them. As they are elements that could influence decision making, each of these aspects demands from the precise detail that is needed.

The models generated by the classification algorithms that showed better results for the categories considered generic on the basis of the experiments and their evaluation make up a prototype classifier for PTSP, which could be used as an important starting point for the generation of an automatic classifier of PTSP. This could help discriminate or make decisions based on the components and requirements that can be retrieved from the study process of a given tender.

The models generated by the prototype classifier for the specific categories are a bit far removed from this, where future research will be needed to explain if it is possible to efficiently extract specific aspects of software requirements from PTSP.

Future studies that can be derived from the present study with regard to automatic text classifiers are:

- Clustering analysis, unsupervised classifiers: Using what is called "Clustering", it is possible to generate a number of "Labels" for the data studied. It is called unsupervised because the help of an expert is not necessary (only at first and for the data training set). Through certain characteristics of the data, they can be grouped into "clusters", where the content of the data generates the categories.
- Generation of a more specific model of categories for public tenders for software. These are not requirements in themselves, but at the same time they have aspects used by requirements engineering. IEEE Std. 830-1998 could be modified so that they fit into more categories with the form in which the public tenders for software are currently being developed.
- Generation of automated PTSP document preparation systems under some standard derived from IEEE830-1998 and fed with documents with no standards. This would simplify the preparation and analysis of PTSP tender documents, since it would separate the sections of greatest interest to the offerors. For example, the suppliers could be interested, in particular, in fulfilling certain restrictions related to technologies over those that have licenses, patents or other type of competitive advantage and thus increase their chances of success in their applications and reduce their operating costs. In this sense, the access to ordered documents would expedite the process.

References

1. McIvor, R.: Global services outsourcing. Cambrigde University Press, Cambrigde (2010).https://doi.org/10.1017/CBO9780511844911

2. Reyes, M., Llopis, J., Garcó, J.: El offshore outsourcing de sistemas de información. Univ. Bus. Rev. Econ. (38) (2006). http://ubr.universia.net/pdfs/UBR0042006080.pdf
3. Silva, C.: "La subcontratación en chile: aproximacion sectorial", *Polis*. Rev. la Univ. Boliv. **8**(24), 111–131 (2007)
4. Cleland, D.I.: Project Management Strategic Design and Implementation, fifth ed. McGraw Hill, New York, NY (2006)
5. Raigada, J.L.P.: Epistemología, metodología y técnicas del análisis de contenido. Socioling. Stud. **3**(1), 1–42 (2002)
6. IEEE, " Standard IEEE 830-1993: Recommended Practice for Software Requirements Specifications. Institute of Electronic and Electrical Engineers Press (1993)
7. IEEE, "IEEE Std 830-1998 IEEE Standard for Software Requirements Specification." IEEE Computer Society (1998)
8. Glinz, M.: On non-functional requirements. In: Proceedings of the 15th IEEE International Requirements Engineering Conference Delhi, India (2007). https://doi.org/10.1109/RE.200 7.45
9. Jureta, I.J., Mylopoulos, J., Faulkner, S.: Revisiting the core ontology and problem in requirements engineering. In: International Requirements Engineering, 2008. RE 2008. 16th IEEE, 2008, pp. 71–80 (2008)
10. Jureta, I.J., Mylopoulos, J., Faulkner, S.: A core ontology for requirements. Appl. Ontol. **4**(3), 169–244 (2009)
11. Barchini, G.E.: "Informática. Una disciplina bio-psico-socio-tecno-cultural," no. 12. p. 3 (2006)
12. Martín Antonínn, M.A.: "Panorama de la lingüística computacional en Europa," no. 1. pp. 11–24 (1999)
13. Graña Gil, J.: "Técnicas de análisis sintáctico robusto para la etiquetaciónn del lenguaje natural," no. 28. pp. 117–118 (2002)
14. Abelleira, M.A.P, Cardoso, C.A.: Minería de texto para la categorización automática de documentos. PhD in Computer Science por Carnegie Mellon University, Madrid, España (2010)
15. Sebastiani, F.: Machine learning in automated text categorization. ACM Comput. Surv. **34**(1), 1–47 (2002)
16. Granitzer, M.: Hierarchical text classification using methods from machine learning. Citeseer (2003)
17. Corso, C.L.: Aplicación de algoritmos de clasificación supervisada usando Weka. Córdoba Universidad Tecnológica Nacional, Facultad Regional Córdoba (2009)
18. Dapozo, G.N., Porcel, E., López, M.V., Bogado, V.S.: Técnicas de preprocesamiento para mejorar la calidad de los datos en un estudio de caracterización de ingresantes universitarios (2007)
19. de Ullibarri Galparsoro, L., Pita Fernández, S.: Medidas de concordancia: el índice de Kappa. Cad Aten Primaria **6**, 169–171 (1999)
20. Jiménez, R.S.: La documentación en el proceso de evaluación de sistemas de clasificación automática. Documentación de las Ciencias de la Información **30**, 25–44 (2007)
21. Hall, M., Frank, E., Holmes, G., Pfahringer, B., Reutemann, P., Witten, I.H.: The WEKA data mining software: an update. ACM SIGKDD Explor. Newsl. **11**(1), 10–18 (2009)
22. Venegas, R.: Clasificación de textos académicos en función de su contenido léxico-semántico. Rev. Signos **40**(63), 239–271 (2007)
23. bin Othman, M.F., Yau, T.M.S.: Comparison of different classification techniques using WEKA for breast cancer. In: Ibrahim F., Osman, N.A.A., Usman, J., Kadri, N.A. (eds.) 3rd Kuala Lumpur International Conference on Biomedical Engineering 2006. IFMBE Proceedings, vol. 15, pp. 520–523. Springer, Berlin, Heidelberg (2007). https://doi.org/10.1007/ 978-3-540-68017-8_131

24. Liu, H., Li, J., Wong, L.: A comparative study on feature selection and classification methods using gene expression profiles and proteomic patterns. Genome Inform. Ser. **13**, 51–60 (2002)
25. Cunningham, S.J., Holmes, G.: "Developing innovative applications in agriculture using data mining" (1999)
26. Barnaghi, P.M., Sahzabi, V.A., Bakar, A.A.: A comparative study for various methods of classification. In: International Conference on Information and Computer Networks (ICICN 2012). IPCSIT, 2012, vol. 27 (2012)

Optimizing a Gamified Design Through Reinforcement Learning - a Case Study in Stack Overflow

Jonathan Martin[1](✉)(iD), Diego Torres[1,2](✉)(iD), and Alejandro Fernandez[1](iD)

[1] LIFIA, CICPBA-Facultad de Informática, UNLP, La Plata, Argentina
{jonathan.martin,diego.torres,alejandro.fernandez}@lifia.info.unlp.edu.ar
[2] Depto. CyT, UNQ, Bernal, Argentina

Abstract. Gamification can be used to foster participation in knowledge sharing communities. While designing and assessing the potential impact of a gamification design in such a context, it is important to avoid work disruption and negative side effects. A gamification optimization approach implemented with deep reinforcement learning based on play-testing approaches helps prevent possible disruptive configuration and has the capability to adapt to different communities or gamification targets. In this research, a case of study for this approach is presented running over the Stack Overflow Q&A community. The approach detects the best configuration for a Contribution, Reinforcement, and Dissemination (CRD) gamification strategy using Stack Overflow historical data in a year. The results show that the approach funds proper gamification strategy configurations. Moreover, those configurations are robust enough to be applied along the time unseen periods.

Keywords: Deep reinforcement learning · Gamification · Knowledge building community · Optimization · Stack Overflow

1 Introduction

Stack Overflow is a well-known questions and answers (Q&A) community with a large number of users [2], more precisely with 12,615,110 registered users[1]. Stack Overflow covers the knowledge construction process from a question and answers perspective. Each user can vary between Question Author and Answer Author's roles to meet the community's requirements.

In order to lead the users to fulfill this role is important to encourage participation in the community. There are different approaches to encourage participation in a Q&A community. The use of Gamification [16] to encourage participation consists of applying elements taken from the realm of game and videogames to non-ludic environments without modifying its central structure [3,8,10].

---

[1] Information obtained on 25/06/20 at
https://data.stackexchange.com/stackoverflow/query/1255610.

© Springer Nature Switzerland AG 2021
M. Naiouf et al. (Eds.): JCC-BD&ET 2021, CCIS 1444, pp. 89–103, 2021.
https://doi.org/10.1007/978-3-030-84825-5_7

Stack Overflow already implements a gamification strategy that extends PBL (points, badges, and leader boards) with other gamification elements [7]. Those gamification strategies, as PBL, are an effective method to build and sustain a productive and active Q&A community directing the participation towards behaviors that improve the quality of content [6,8].

The result of applying a gamification approach to a community cannot be predicted entirely [9,14,18], and no guarantee that the desired effect will be achieved. It can generate disruptions to the community, create unproductive competition patterns between community members, or hinder participation [10,25]. An example of this is a design that promotes individual competition in a collaborative context due that collaboration should be the most relevant value [21].

If not done carefully, the gamification changes can disrupt the normal development of the activity aimed to improve. Play-testing is a process used as part of the iterative process for game design, development, evaluation, monitoring, and adaptation [23]. It could be applied to this context, but changes to the gamification can damage or fail to be adopted by the community. Another difficulty from play-testing is that it requires a functioning game, players, and time.

Other approaches consist of optimization strategies used to reduce the effort/cost of creating an effective gamification design where optimal pseudo-rewards guide the users in the activity [17]. However, this approach requires absolute knowledge of the decision environment.

This paper proposes as an alternative an approach to optimize the configuration of a gamified design, using a reinforcement learning agent to explore the space of configuration possibilities as in a play-testing approach. This approach would allow optimizing a configuration without disturbing the community and with fewer requirements of the traditional play-testing approach.

Consequently, a Contribution, Reinforcement, and Dissemination (CRD) strategy for gamified design optimization in knowledge-building communities is presented, using a reinforcement learning (RL) agent to explore the space of configuration possibilities. The agents look for configurations that reward desired user behaviors for the selected pair community/reward.

We evaluate the approach in a sub-community of Stack Overflow for one year. The evaluation was developed in 2 stages: a training stage in the first six months; and then a second evaluation stage in the following six months. Badges and ranks are the principal gamification components for both scenarios. The results show the stability of configurations obtained by this method during different time-lapses.

The rest of this article is organized as follows: Sect. 2 explore the related work; Sect. 3 presents a gamified design that serves as the basis for the rest of this work; Sect. 4 provides an overview of our approach; then, Sect. 5 introduces the evaluation over the dataset extracted from Stack Overflow. The results are described in Sect. 6, and they are discussed in Sect. 7. Finally, the Conclusions and further work are detailed in Sect. 8.

2   Related Work

Lieder et al. [17] explore ways to obtain an optimal gamification design by a mathematical framework. They introduce a gamification approach for problems that could be modeled as a Markov decision process; they compute optimal pseudo-rewards to guide the users in the activity for what is requested perfect knowledge of the decision environment or the possibility of approximate it. Our work achieves an "optimal gamification" but from an existing gamification design.

With an existing gamification design, the way to achieve an "optimal gamification" is to configure it to fit our purposes. This approach addresses the system configuration problem topic. The problem typically involves learning from analyzing actual executions or historical data, model specific aspects of the systems, and then adapt to actual conditions based on requirements [12]. A common way of tuning configurations is done manually by performance engineers, spending several hours of work [1]. There were proposed other methods less time-consuming and more precise to find configurations.

A rule-based approach like Multirelational Data Mining (MRDM) helps discover patterns. However, it requests gathering the metadata from the database of the system to configure, which describes the best approach of the analysis and transformation of the database into MRDM formats [4,22]. This approach favors quickly finding a suitable configuration at the expense of optimality.

A model-based approach is concerned with conducting experiments on a chosen set of configurations to observe their performance [11,15,24,26,30]. The restriction of using a limited number of configurations is a limitation that our approach overcomes because there are numerous configurations in practice with many dependencies between them and these can be used to get better optimization. Our approach instead evaluate all parameters and process them jointly over an RL process in order to exploit them.

Search-based approaches begin with an initial configuration to perform sequential experiments but require a statistical model to fit [4,19,30,31]. This kind of model is similar to the Lieder et al. model presented above and requires full knowledge of the decision environment.

Finally, as proposed in this work, learning-based approaches find the optimal configuration by reacting to feedback [5,32]. The RL approach used here fits better to our context where there are no correct input/output pairs required for other learning approaches that defined a correct configuration of gamification. However, a policy of satisfaction could be defined for our unknown environment by a reward function that measures the configuration found.

3   CRD Gamification Design

This work uses a Contribution - Reinforcement - Dissemination (CRD) gamification design based on Metagame [18], a knowledge-building CRD gamification design. CRD defines a PBL gamification strategy based on four main types of actions (inputs): Contribution, to represents the creation of content; Reinforcements, for content editing, data retrieval, status changes, or content groupings; Dissemination for actions linked to spreading the content, for example on social networks or within the community itself; and finally, Loggin actions.

The players (the users of the application) are awarded badges when they provide a certain number of inputs. There is one badge for each class of input, and there are multiple levels for each badge. To reach a higher level of a badge, more inputs of the corresponding class are required.

Players are also ranked according to the badges they obtain. For example, they start as "Visitors" (Rank 1), and they become "Explorers" (Rank 2) when they obtain the Login level 2 badge. After they obtained one "Contribution" badge, one "Reinforcement" badge, and one "Dissemination" badge, they become "Editors" (Rank 3)[2]. Then, after they obtain ten badges, they become "Prolific editors" (Rank 4). Finally, as long as they earn a new badge every month, they obtain and maintain the level of "Committed editors" (Rank 5).

The amount and type of badges a player requires to be promoted from one rank to another is part of the gamification configuration. How many inputs do users need to perform to get the 3rd level of Contribution badge? If the configuration sets a large number of inputs for promoting one badge, how does this impact the game's evolution? Will players be comfortable with this difficulty level?

In this article, the configuration space is reduced to five variables: the number of levels per badge; and, for each badge type, the number of inputs required to pass from one level to the next.

The simulation of the gamification design runs over a slice of historical data from the community. This selected slice becomes the simulation dataset.

The challenge is to find the correct values for the five variables of the configuration and then test those values in a "simulation of the game" with a historical dataset. The simulation is to avoid a harmful configuration that threatens the actual community.

The simulated game awards a badge to the users and computes the ranking. In an iterative process, users' distribution in the ranking could be analyzed to perform a fine-tune to the configuration. It could be repeated until a suitable configuration is reached (e.g., all ranks have users.).

There are two main issues in this approach. First, it is time-consuming; even with only five variables to set, the combined possibilities are many, and each change requests simulation with its analysis of the results. Secondly, it is based on the researchers' intuition regarding the effect that change in the configuration may have on the user's attitudes. The following section introduces an alternative approach that uses a reinforcement learning agent to explore the configuration space effectively.

---

[2] In the original work, they were called Citizen Scientists; we have changed the term for the sake of clarity.

4   Gamification Configuration with RL: Historical RL Framework

Reinforcement Learning (RL) is an approach to train machine learning models to make sequences of decisions. In RL, an agent takes actions in an attempt to maximize a cumulative reward [28]. Exploring the configuration space to find an acceptable configuration for the gamified design involves multiple iterations of updating the configuration, simulating the game on the defined dataset, and observing the effect. Having an agent instead of a person in charge of the exploration allows us to explore more alternatives in less time.

Figure 1 provides an overview of our approach to find an optimal game configuration using an RL agent. The game's configuration is modeled as an N-dimensional vector (1) of positive numbers. The game is simulated by providing a configuration and a slice of the community history (2) to the game engine (3). Once the simulation finishes, the list of badge assignments and users' ranking (4) is passed back to the agent. At each step (5), the RL agent (6) changes only one dimension of the configuration vector, by one, up or down. Then, the simulation runs. The agent uses a reward function (7) to update its model based on its last action outcomes. In one episode, the agent performs a maximum of 300 steps until it considers no further changes to the configuration are useful, then stops.

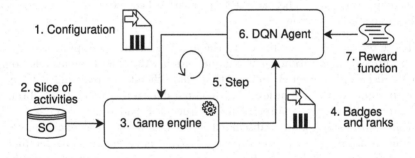

Fig. 1. Approach overview

This work uses a Deep Q-Network (DQN) [20], a reinforcement learning agent that uses a deep convolutional neural network to learn successful policies in high-dimensional state spaces like video games or robotics. Due to that, the DQN agent can handle complex, high-dimensional spaces. This means that it can deal with an even richer (and more complex) game configuration. DQN has become popular in the last few years due to the increasing availability of ready-to-use libraries (such as DeepMind's implementation for the Lua language) and services (such as OpenAI API). However, the type of agent could be configured according to the use case and analysis.

DQN is an implementation of Q-learning. Q-learning is a form of model-free reinforcement learning, which can be viewed as a method of asynchronous dynamic programming (DP). Learning proceeds in a similar way to Sutton's method of temporal differences (TD) [27]: an agent tries an action in a particular state and evaluates its consequences in terms of the immediate reward or penalty. By repeatedly trying all actions in all states, it learns by evaluating the long-term reward.

Although Q-learning is a very powerful algorithm, its main weakness is its lack of generality. If Q-learning is viewed as the updating of numbers in a two-dimensional array $(A * S)$, it is, in fact, similar to dynamic programming. This indicates that for states that the Q-learning agent has not seen before, it has no idea what action to take. In other words, the Q-learning agent does not have the ability to estimate the value of unseen states. To deal with this problem, DQN discards the two-dimensional matrix by replacing it with a Neural Network.

Two other techniques are also essential for DQN training:

Experience replay: Since the training samples in the typical RL setup are highly correlated, and less data-efficient, this will lead to higher convergence of the network. One way to solve the sample distribution problem is to adopt experience replay. Essentially, sample transitions are stored, which will then be randomly selected from the "transition pool" to update the agent's knowledge.

Separate target networks: The Target Network Q has the same structure as the one that estimates the value. Each C step, the target network is readjusted to the other. Therefore, the fluctuation becomes less severe, resulting in more stable training.

Those techniques were applied to the agent used in this approach to obtain an optimized configuration for the gamification. Also, the five-variable configuration discussed in Sect. 3, implies that the difficulty of reaching level $x + 1$ after obtaining the badge of level x, is comparable to the difficulty of obtaining the badge of level $x + 2$, after being awarded the badge of level $x + 1$. Such a linear relationship among subsequent challenges harms user engagement. To introduce variability, we define $inputs(x)$ as the number of inputs required to obtain a badge of level x (see Eq. 1). The larger the values of variables b and m, the greater the steps between levels. The values of $m_o c$ and $b_o c$ define the direction of those steps. Therefore, the configuration consists of 17 dimensions, the number of levels per badge (all 4 badges have the same number of levels), and values for the variables m, b, m_{oc} and b_{oc} for each of the four badges.

$$inputs(x) = \max \left(\sin \left(m_{oc} \times x + b_{oc} \right) \times (m \times x + b), 1 \right) \tag{1}$$

Following this approach, at the start of each reinforcement learning step, the agent produces a new configuration. The game is simulated using that configuration, on a predefined simulation dataset. Then, the reward function is applied to evaluate how well it did (i.e., is the resulting configuration better?) and notifies the agent about the performance. This process continues for a predefined number of episodes.

To enable the coupling of Stack Overflow to the simulator, we must detect the actions related to the gamification, obtain this history of actions, and finally integrate them into the simulation flow. Table 1 presents the mapping of Stack Overflow actions to CRD gamification actions.

Table 1. Stack Overflow events in the gamification context

Contribution	Reinforcement	Dissemination
Question creation	Question editing	Tag creation
Creating answers	Editing answers	Editing tags
Creation of comments	Rollback of questions	Rollback of tags
Post protection	Response rollback	Post migration
Locking posts	Changing post statuses	Creating links
	Merging of questions	Discussion of comments
	Making of suggestions for change	Tweeting of posts
	Application of suggestions for change	Question marked as a trend
		Question highlighted by the user community

5 Evaluation

The evaluation aims to evaluate the approach to obtain an optimal configuration for a gamification design in knowledge-building communities through reinforcement learning, introduced in this article. The evaluation is structured answering the following questions:

– **Q1:** How is the configuration obtained? The detail of variables and the final reward function.
– **Q2:** Is the difficulty of the gamification achievable and enjoyable by the player?. We followed the gamification flow aspects related to *challenge* and *player skill* [13,29]. In a minimalist way, the difficulty should change along the time and adapted to the skills the user incorporates.
– **Q3:** There are correlations among the number of badges the configuration assign?
– **Q4:** Could users reasonably achieve ranks?
– **Q5:** Is the detected configuration robust when it is applied with new community activities? How is the behavior in terms of the former questions? The goal here is to analyze the robustness of the configurations obtained by the agent's adjustments in the same community beyond the period known by the agent.

Therefore, the evaluation stages were divided into 2 stages: A training stage in the **first semester**; and a second evaluation stage in the **second semester** using the previous configuration.

5.1 Materials

The dataset for the evaluation was taken from the Python community from Stack Overflow (filtered by the *Tags* property with the value "python") of 2018. This translates to 242,822 questions, theirs answers, comments, and activity histories which result in 3,337,788 gamification actions. Among these actions, the Login actions were selected as the beginning of action's groups by the *RevisionGUID* tag. This dataset was divided into two parts of 6 months each: from January to June the first, and from July to December the second. This division was made with the goal of training the agent in the first half and evaluating its performance in the second part of the dataset in order to answer question Q5.

Finally, the Eq. 2 presents the reward function used to train the agent. The reward function drives the agent to look for configurations that value reinforcement inputs over contribution inputs, and dissemination inputs over both contribution and reinforcement inputs. The choice of this function was due to the fact that, as mentioned above, it rewards the behavior that we consider relevant in a knowledge building community. Also, this function will help in the evaluation of the result of applying the configuration obtained from the training in the test dataset.

$$reward = \sum_{u \in Users} rank(u) \times (ci(u) + ri(u) \times 5 + di(u) \times 10) \qquad (2)$$

where:

U = users that provided input to a featured article.
$rank(u)$ = the rank (1..5) of user u in the simulated gamified design.
$ci(u)$ = count of contribution inputs of user u
$ri(u)$ = count of reinforcement inputs of user u
$di(u)$ = count of dissemination inputs of user u

6 Results

6.1 First Semester

During the training process, the RL agent was trained using the first semester of the data set. The agent was trained for 100 episodes, obtaining a maximum score of 7,445,496 points awarded by the reward in combination with the dataset. Answering **Q1**, the agent returns a configuration with 10 badges per type with the parameters presented in Table 2. Dissemination receives the highest values in all of the variables representing high values for the oscillation ($m_o c$ and $b_o c$) and steps bigger than the other badges.

Table 2. Configuration for python community, first half of 2018.

Action type	#max_badges	m_{oc}	b_{oc}	m	b
Contribution	10	2	5	6	1
Reinforcement	10	3	9	7	7
Dissemination	10	14	19	14	13
Login	10	4	4	5	1

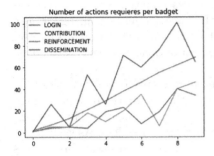

Fig. 2. Difficulty analysis: new actions required to obtain each badge.

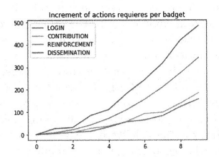

Fig. 3. Total actions required to earn each badge.

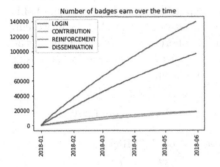

Fig. 4. First semester. Awarding of badges to users over time.

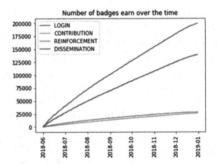

Fig. 5. Second semester - legacy configuration. Delivery of badges to users over time.

In order to answer **Q2**, Fig. 2 shows a difficulty analysis by comparing the number of new actions required to obtain each badge by action type. Badge levels are on the x axis, and the y axis indicates the number of inputs required to earn a badge. For example, a player has to perform 25 dissemination actions to achieve level 1 of the *Dissemination badge* (the line grows up from 0 to 1), then the same player needs only 7 new dissemination actions to be promoted to level 2 of *Dissemination badge* (the line decreases from 1 to 2). These oscillations in the lines in Fig. 2 means that the effort of the player to get a new badge is not always the same. The player had hard working periods with a lot of actions (challenges) and then a period of skills assimilation, in the line with having a balanced flow as we have mentioned in **Q2**. However, in the case of Reinforcement badges, the configuration proposed to have a lineal increment of difficulty along with the game.

The scaling of the difficulty could be seen in Fig. 3 that shows the accumulation of actions required to obtain each badge. As in the previous Figure, the x axis represents the badge levels and the y axis denotes the total of inputs required from the beginning to earn some badge. In this Figure, is possible to see a difference between the difficulty to earn a dissemination and reinforcement badges in comparison to the other badges; they become more challenging, at a faster pace than the others. It is because these actions are the main target of the reward and also the number of reinforcement actions are relevant elements in the activity of the community's users.

To answer **Q3**, Fig. 4 shows how the game would have assigned badges with this dataset and configuration. The x axis is the time along the first six months of data, and the y axis, the number of delivered badges. For example, in February 2018, the game delivered near than 20.000 Dissemination badges. As we can see, there is a correlation between reinforcement and contributions because both lines grow with similar values. As a complement of the former Figure, all players can achieve all the challenges to obtain the badges.

Finally, to answer **Q4**, Table 3 shows the distribution of players in each of the ranks with both the actual number and the percentage representation of this number over the total number of users in this dataset. From this data, we can observe the presence of users in all ranks and a coherent proportion of them: the distribution of the ranks is similar a pyramid with more presence in the easier ranks and a small group of players in the hardest rank.

Table 3. Rank of players in python community, first half of 2018.

	Rank 1	Rank 2	Rank 3	Rank 4	Rank 5
Real	61129	5084	3658	332	1446
Percentage	85.31%	7.09%	5.1%	0.46%	2.01%

6.2 Second Semester - Legacy Configuration

In order to answer **Q5**, the agent applies the configuration obtained to the second half of 2018 (Table 2). As an evaluation metric, the reward value given to this configuration over the simulation was considered; this value was 11,862,732 points. Although the value is significantly higher, this is due to the fact that the activity in the second half of the year is also significantly higher. So these reward values are also highly correlated to the simulation dataset.

As in the first half, information related to the difficulty, scaling is the same due to its relation with the configuration. Instead, the badge distribution increases significantly as it's shown in Fig. 5. This is related to the increment of user activity with respect to the previous dataset. However, the distribution of badges looks similar in both datasets and it means that the configuration has robustness for the same community along the time.

The Table 4 is presented showing the distribution of players in each of the ranks. These data show an expected proportion due to the continuation over time of the dataset. Along with this, we can observe that the increase in reward values is related to the number of players per rank, being almost double in the higher ranks, although in reality, the proportion between the two semesters is almost the same. It means that the configuration generated by the agents fits correctly beyond the period known by the agent.

Table 4. Range of players in python community, second half of 2018 with legacy configuration.

	Rank 1	Rank 2	Rank 3	Rank 4	Rank 5
Real	86090	7365	5483	658	2125
Percentage	84.63%	7.24%	5.39%	0.64%	2.08%

7   Discussion

This section presents an analysis of the results obtained in the application of the deep reinforcement learning approach to obtain an optimal configuration for a gamification design in the Python sub-community of Stack Overflow.

From the configuration obtained by the agent answering the **Q1**, we can observe a more pronounced separation into two groups of badges, dissemination, and reinforcement versus contribution and login. While among all the training a priority ordering of badges dictated by the reward function is preserved as much as possible, in these particular cases the impact of the reward function is further accentuated. Also, we can observe from the **Q2** and **Q3** answers, how the agent manages the difficulty curve of badges such as dissemination to allow an easy initial acquisition, thus providing access to the first ranks. While with badges such as the reinforcement badge, the difficulty curve is flattened at higher levels to aid in the preservation of the last rank with its temporary feature. These results show that the configuration found by the agent presents characteristics to be achievable and enjoyable by the player.

The first relevant difference found when working with the data divided into the first and second semesters for the **Q5** was based on the fact that the magnitudes of activity in both sets were different. The second-semester data set was larger than the first semester data set, and this could condition the performance of the agent trained in the first semester.

However, we were able to observe that the configuration obtained in the first semester turned out to be effective, although probably not optimal due it wasn't optimized for this period, in the simulation of the second semester. This is due to the fact that, although the magnitudes are different and this will disturb the agent's configuration process, the activity proportions and the form of user activity did not vary from one semester to another, so the configuration remained within acceptable margins.

These magnitude differences exist also in the distribution of users by ranks. But this difference didn't generate a negative impact on the proportional distribution of users. The answer to the **Q4** shows that all the ranks were covered in a pyramid shape, except by the last rank. It is a temporal dependant rank and as it was a simulation, it is conditioned by the ending date of the simulation. In both rank distribution, there is a big part of the users that stay in the first rank. It's common in communities where new users only participate one time to make a question and after never more. Table 5 shows a comparison of the ranks obtained with the strategy presented in this paper in contrast with a manual configuration of badges distribution from a previous paper [18]. In this table, an increment of players in higher ranks can be observed buy it still maintains its pyramidal shape, which means that the players are able to achieve high ranks.

Table 5. Ranks comparative.

	Rank 1	Rank 2	Rank 3	Rank 4	Rank 5
Previous approach [18]	96.2%	2.28%	1.52%	0.0%	-
First half of 2018	85.31%	7.09%	5.1%	0.46%	2.01%
Second half of 2018	84.63%	7.24%	5.39%	0.64%	2.08%

Although the article is based on using a specific gamification design, other types of gamification design are an exciting aspect of research. In this case, we base the search for the optimal configuration for a badge-based configuration (5 variables detailed above). What does it imply to use a different gamification strategy with or without badges? What does happen if it requires a higher number of variables? As a first approach to use a different gamification strategy, we have to identify and map the user's activities of the community with the actions of the gamification strategy. This mapping is required in order to have a simulation to optimize. Moreover, a new reward function based on the values of the new simulator has to be created. Also, it is necessary to identify the configuration variables and create methods that allow the RL agent to changes them. If a high number of variables is requested, the agent will have to learn the relevance of more actions and the changes that those made in the configuration, but the process presented in this approach will not change.

Another important aspect is to extend the approach to contemplate a gamification strategy in a tailored way. The overall logic and purpose of gamification are maintained, e.g., promoting collaborative work, quality content production, and dissemination. Furthermore, it optimizes the way players are motivated by adapting the gamification alternatives. Each player can give their best based on their behavioral profile in conjunction with the overall purpose.

8   Conclusions

This work introduced an approach to optimize a gamified design to reward desired user behaviors without disturbing the functionality of an existing community. This approach is base on play-testing using a deep reinforcement learning strategy.

The optimization was performed over a simulation of gamification by a deep reinforcement learning agent. It allows us to adapt the distribution of badges by a change in the parameters of the badges distribution function. Those parameters are defined by the reinforcement learning agent while it tries to optimize a reward function.

As an evaluation of the approach, the integration of the knowledge-building community, Stack Overflow, is presented. For this purpose, notions of the community's data structure were also introduced, as well as the data extraction and mapping process. Also, a reward function to encourages communication and dissemination in the community is developed to train the agent and as a metric of performance for the configuration obtained.

The configurations obtained by the agent during the training show an improvement over a previous manual configuration approach. This new approach helps to configure gamification that allows the players to flow over the ranks; without them having to change their main behavior in the community. The agent also detects and values correctly different types of actions by the importance of the reward function and its occurrence in the dataset. It helps to fit the difficulty of the gamification to the community and the target goal reducing the possibility of harming the community. It was proved that the configurations of a previous period can be successfully maintained along the time for the same community archiving similar badges and users in rank distributions.

As future work, given the sensitivity of the agent to the input data, it would be relevant to evaluate ways of overcoming this limitation or explore regularization strategies with respect to the input values. Then, try to optimize the configuration for the second dataset with the pretrained agent is the next logical step.

In order to facilitate this future work, it is necessary to consider the creation of a framework to evaluate and optimize the integration of gamification and communities. It will allow us to get a better abstraction between the agent and the environment for training. Finally, this abstraction will allow us to change or optimize the agent implementing novel deep reinforcement learning algorithms to obtain more accurate configuration in gamification with more complex configurations or action space. The capability of change easily the agent will allow comparing different RL agents for this specific task.

References

1. Allen, S.T., Jankowski, M., Pathirana, P.: Storm Applied: Strategies for Real-Time Event Processing. Manning Publications Co. (2015)
2. Anderson, A., Huttenlocher, D., Kleinberg, J., Leskovec, J.: Discovering value from community activity on focused question answering sites: a case study of stack overflow. In: Proceedings of the 18th ACM SIGKDD International Conference on Knowledge Discovery and Data Mining, pp. 850–858 (2012)
3. Beza, E., et al.: What are the prospects for citizen science in agriculture? Evidence from three continents on motivation and mobile telephone use of resource-poor farmers. PloS One 12(5), e0175700 (2017). https://doi.org/10.1371/journal.pone. 0175700
4. Bilal, M., Canini, M.: Towards automatic parameter tuning of stream processing systems. In: Proceedings of the 2017 Symposium on Cloud Computing, pp. 189–200 (2017)
5. Bu, X., Rao, J., Xu, C.Z.: A reinforcement learning approach to online web systems auto-configuration. In: 2009 29th IEEE International Conference on Distributed Computing Systems, pp. 2–11. IEEE (2009)
6. Burke, B.: Gamification 2020: what is the future of gamification. Gartner Inc, 5 Nov (2012)
7. Cavusoglu, H., Li, Z., Huang, K.W.: Can gamification motivate voluntary contributions? the case of stackoverflow Q&A community. In: Proceedings of the 18th ACM Conference Companion on Computer Supported Cooperative Work & Social Computing, pp. 171–174 (2015)
8. Deterding, S., Dixon, D., Khaled, R., Nacke, L.: From game design elements to gamefulness: defining "gamification". In: Proceedings of the 15th International Academic MindTrek Conference: Envisioning Future Media Environments, pp. 9–15. MindTrek 2011, ACM, New York, NY, USA (2011). https://doi.org/10.1145/2181037.2181040
9. Devers, C.J., Gurung, R.A.R.: Critical perspective on gamification in education. In: Reiners, T., Wood, L.C. (eds.) Gamification in Education and Business, pp. 417–430. Springer, Cham (2015). https://doi.org/10.1007/978-3-319-10208-5_21
10. Domínguez, A., Saenz-De-Navarrete, J., De-Marcos, L., Fernández-Sanz, L., Pagés, C., Martínez-Herráiz, J.J.: Gamifying learning experiences: practical implications and outcomes. Comput. Educ. 63, 380–392 (2013). https://doi.org/10.1016/j.compedu.2012.12.020
11. Fischer, L., Gao, S., Bernstein, A.: Machines tuning machines: configuring distributed stream processors with Bayesian optimization. In: 2015 IEEE International Conference on Cluster Computing, pp. 22–31. IEEE (2015)
12. Geldenhuys, M.K., Thamsen, L., Gontarskay, K.K., Lorenz, F., Kao, O.: Effectively testing system configurations of critical iot analytics pipelines. In: 2019 IEEE International Conference on Big Data (Big Data), pp. 4157–4162 (2019). https://doi.org/10.1109/BigData47090.2019.9005504
13. Göbel, S., Wendel, V.: Personalization and adaptation. In: Dörner, R., Göbel, S., Effelsberg, W., Wiemeyer, J. (eds.) Serious Games, pp. 161–210. Springer, Cham (2016). https://doi.org/10.1007/978-3-319-40612-1_7
14. Hamari, J., Koivisto, J., Sarsa, H.: Does gamification work? - A literature review of empirical studies on gamification. In: 2014 47th Hawaii International Conference on System Sciences, pp. 3025–3034 (2014). https://doi.org/10.1109/HICSS.2014. 377

15. Jamshidi, P., Casale, G.: An uncertainty-aware approach to optimal configuration of stream processing systems. In: 2016 IEEE 24th International Symposium on Modeling, Analysis and Simulation of Computer and Telecommunication Systems (MASCOTS), pp. 39–48. IEEE (2016)
16. Kasurinen, J., Knutas, A.: Publication trends in gamification: a systematic mapping study. Comput. Sci. Rev. **27**, 33–44 (2018)
17. Lieder, F., Griffiths, T.L.: Helping people make better decisions using optimal gamification. In: Proceedings of the 38th Annual Conference of the Cognitive Science Society, pp. 2075–2080 (2016)
18. Martin, J., Torres, D., Fernandez, A., Pravisani, S., Briend, G.: Using citizen science gamification in agriculture collaborative knowledge production. In: Proceedings of the XIX International Conference on Human Computer Interaction, p. 8 (2018)
19. McKay, M.D., Beckman, R.J., Conover, W.J.: Comparison of three methods for selecting values of input variables in the analysis of output from a computer code. Technometrics **21**(2), 239–245 (1979)
20. Mnih, V., et al.: Human-level control through deep reinforcement learning. Nature **518**(7540), 529–533 (2015). https://doi.org/10.1038/nature14236
21. Ozdener, N.: Gamification for enhancing web 2.0 based educational activities: the case of pre-service grade school teachers using educational wiki pages. Telematics Inform. **35**(3), 564–578 (2018)
22. Padhy, N., Panigrahi, R.: Multi relational data mining approaches: a data mining technique. arXiv preprint arXiv:1211.3871 (2012)
23. Radoff, J.: Game on: Energize your Business with Social Media Games. Wiley, Hoboken (2011)
24. Rasmussen, C.E., Nickisch, H.: Gaussian processes for machine learning (gpml) toolbox. J. Mach. Learn. Res. **11**, 3011–3015 (2010)
25. Seaborn, K., Fels, D.I.: Gamification in theory and action: a survey. Int. J. Hum. Comput. Stud. **74**, 14–31 (2015)
26. Shahriari, B., Swersky, K., Wang, Z., Adams, R.P., De Freitas, N.: Taking the human out of the loop: a review of Bayesian optimization. Proc. IEEE **104**(1), 148–175 (2015)
27. Sutton, R.S.: Learning to predict by the methods of temporal differences. Mach. Learn. **3**(1), 9–44 (1988)
28. Sutton, R.S., Barto, A.G.: Reinforcement learning : an introduction. MIT Press (1998). https://dl.acm.org/citation.cfm?id=551283
29. Sweetser, P., Wyeth, P.: GameFlow: a model for evaluating player enjoyment in games. Comput. Entertain. **3**(3) (2005). https://doi.org/10.1145/1077246.1077253
30. Trotter, M., Liu, G., Wood, T.: Into the storm: descrying optimal configurations using genetic algorithms and bayesian optimization. In: 2017 IEEE 2nd International Workshops on Foundations and Applications of Self* Systems (FAS* W), pp. 175–180. IEEE (2017)
31. Trotter, M., Wood, T., Hwang, J.: Forecasting a storm: divining optimal configurations using genetic algorithms and supervised learning. In: 2019 IEEE International Conference on Autonomic Computing (ICAC), pp. 136–146. IEEE (2019)
32. Vaquero, L.M., Cuadrado, F.: Auto-tuning distributed stream processing systems using reinforcement learning. arXiv preprint arXiv:1809.05495 (2018)

A Comparison of Neural Networks for Sign Language Recognition with LSA64

Iván Mindlin[1] ⓘ, Facundo Quiroga[1](✉) ⓘ, Franco Ronchetti[1,2] ⓘ,
Pedro Dal Bianco[1] ⓘ, Gastón Ríos[1] ⓘ, Laura Lanzarini[1] ⓘ,
and Waldo Hasperué[1,2] ⓘ

[1] Instituto de Investigación en Informática LIDI (Centro CICPBA),
Facultad de Informática, Universidad Nacional de La Plata, La Plata, Argentina
{fquiroga,fronchetti}@lidi.info.unlp.edu.ar
[2] Comisión de Investigaciones Científicas de la Pcia. De Bs. As. (CIC-PBA),
La Plata, Argentina

Abstract. Sign Language Recognition models have been steadily increasing in performance in the last years, fueled by Neural Network models. Furthermore, generic Neural Network models have taken precedence over specialized models designed specifically for Sign Language. Despite this, the completeness and complexity of datasets has not scaled accordingly. This deficiency presents a significant challenge for deploying Sign Language Recognition models, specially given that Sign Languages are specific to countries or even regions. Following this trend, we experiment with three models built on standard recurrent and convolutional neural network layers. We evaluate the models on LSA64, the only Argentinian Sign Language dataset available. Coupled with simple but carefully chosen hyperparameters and preprocessing techniques, these models are all able to achieve near perfect accuracy on LSA64, surpassing all previous models, many specifically designed for this task. Furthermore, we perform ablation studies that indicate that temporal data augmentation can provide a significant boost to accuracy, unlike traditional spatial data augmentation techniques. Finally, we analyze the activation values of the three models to understand the types of features learned, and find they develop on hand-specific filters to classify signs.

Keywords: Sign Language Recognition · Neural Networks · LSA64 ·
Convolutional Neural Networks · Recurrent Neural Networks ·
Computer vision

1 Introduction

Automatic Sign Language Recognition (SLR) aims to convert signs, typically captured in video, to text in a given written language. SLR is therefore an important field that can make a significant contribution to bridge the gap between deaf and non-deaf communities [1].

© Springer Nature Switzerland AG 2021
M. Naiouf et al. (Eds.): JCC-BD&ET 2021, CCIS 1444, pp. 104–117, 2021.
https://doi.org/10.1007/978-3-030-84825-5_8

SLR systems typically consist of a pipeline of tasks which start with the recognition of the shape of the hands of the signer, their movement and position, the shape of lips and face expressions, plus the objects in the scene, in every frame of the video. Afterwards, the signs in the video must be identified, using both information about how signs are made and the syntax and semantics of the sign language. Afterwards, the sentences in sign language must be translated to some target written/spoken language, such as English or Spanish [1,16]. Von Agris et al. [16], Cooper et al. [2] and Koller [7] present excellent general reviews of the standard techniques of the field.

In this work we focus on sign-level recognition, where videos have been previously segmented and contain a single sign. Also, we focus only on manual features, since the dataset employed non-expert interpreters which did not perform the corresponding facial expressions for signs.

1.1 Sign Language and Datasets

Sign language is a natural language conveyed through hand gestures, face expressions, and other non verbal information. According to the World Federation of the Deaf, there are over 300 sign languages (SLs) used around the world, and 70 million deaf people are also signers. Many of these communicate exclusively in sign language. Furthermore, aside from the deaf community, very few people are fluent in use sign language. The availability of interpreters is low and their cost high. Additionally, many deaf people have difficulties with reading and writing, and are therefore excluded from many important tools of the written world such as internet and email communication.

There are, nonetheless, many challenges to developing an effective SLR system. Besides the lack of a standard sign language, each language may also have dialects that evolve naturally within each country and region. While SLs from different countries share several grammatical rules, these are not universal either. Therefore, to create a recognition system for a specific language, a corresponding dataset is needed.

The creation of SL datasets is more difficult than for other similar problems such as speech recognition, since signers are few, there are no universally employed annotation tools and video is costly to store and process [1]. Since SL is very context dependent as well, a truly realistic dataset should include not only several samples of each sign, but also a variation of environments and contexts.

Consequently, current sign language datasets are neither extensive enough or of a sufficient quality to train models that provide a level of performance that can allow effective usage for daily tasks such as web-browsing. However, they can be used to evaluate current models, and pave the way for future systems when the data available increases.

1.2   Sign Language and Neural Networks

Sign Language Recognition has transitioned in recent years (2015–2021) from using specialized models to standard neural network-based ones [1,7], similarly to other related fields such as Speech Recognition. This transition is fueled mostly by advances in the area of Neural Networks, with the rise of Convolutional Neural Networks (CNNs) and Recurrent Neural Networks (RNNs) as state of the art spatial and temporal models, respectively. Additionally, there has been a slight increase in the amount of data available for training SLR models, which in turn allows for Neural Networks and other data-driven models to be more effective for this problem [7].

While previous models relied on domain knowledge to extract relevant image features for hand movements and shapes, CNNs can model spatial features with little or no annotation or preprocessing steps [7], which allows using lower quality annotations. Therefore, the shift towards neural network models for SLR has implied a shift towards global features as well [7].

Unlike Hidden Markov Model (HMM) approaches, CNNs + RNNs models can also be trained end-to-end, allowing the network to learn both spatial and temporal characteristics of the problem without explicit temporal feature engineering [7].

1.3   Contributions

In this work, we review the state of the art on the LSA64 dataset, and identify common trends and working strategies. In this way, we show how to train standard recurrent and convolutional neural networks models to surpass the state of the art in terms of accuracy for LSA64. Furthermore, we perform detailed ablation studies to assess which strategies and models help in obtaining state of the art recognition. Finally, we analyze model activation to understand how the networks represent signs and their most important features.

2   LSA64 Dataset

2.1   Description

The LSA64 dataset consists of 64 signs from the LSA (*Lengua de Señas Argentina* or Argentinian Sign Language) recorded with RGB cameras [13]. It includes 3200 videos of 10 non-expert subjects who perform 5 repetitions of each sign. (Fig. 1).

Subjects were recorded using colored gloves, with a different color for each hand. Only 22 out of the 64 classes use both hands to perform the sign (Fig. 2). Additionally, the dataset was recorded in two sessions; in the first one, only right handed signs were recorded, with no glove for the left hand; in the second, left hands did had gloves. Therefore, models need to learn to ignore left-hand shapes and movements for the other 42 classes.

Fig. 1. Sample frames taken from LSA64 videos. The background is uniform, there are no other objects in the scene and subjects were captured clearly with no blur or other undesired noise.

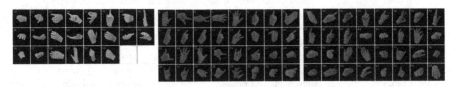

Fig. 2. Sample handshapes from LSA64, for the left hand with green gloves (left) and right hand with red gloves (center and right). (Color figure online)

2.2 Previous Results

The LSA64 dataset has been previously employed by various authors to evaluate SLR models (Table 1). In all cases, these evaluations correspond to subject-dependent experiments. Most experiments use LSTMs as classifiers to model the temporal information of the signs and 2D or 3D CNNs for the spatial aspect. Only very few cases use HMMs [13] or SVMs with a bag of words approach [5,11]. Some researchers use hand-engineered features [5,9,11–13], but this practice is increasingly less common as indicated in Sect. 1. Instead, some researchers are adding new types of features such as skeletal pose data and/or optical flow, and using neural networks and model fusion to improve performance [5,8,9].

As Table 1 indicates, models obtain more than 95 accuracy in most cases. The general trend in Table 1 indicates that the subject-dependent, word-level recognition problem posed by LSA64 can be considered a mostly solved problem. Therefore, the dataset can be used primarily to validate the performance of new models and not as a measure for state of the art results, in the same way that the MNIST or CIFAR10 datasets are used in general in computer vision research.

Furthermore, Table 1 shows an advance of our experimental results presented in Sect. 3. These results suggest that a combination of well trained RNN+CNN models with adequate preprocessing and data augmentation can achieve performance on par with many of the aforementioned specialized models, without incurring in overly complicated neural network designs.

3 Experiments

In this section we describe the experiments conducted to assess the optimal combination of model, preprocessing and data augmentation methods to reach a high performance classifier.

Table 1. Accuracy of several models and features on the LSA64 dataset. Accuracies where obtained by using a single a random split of 80 of the data for training and the rest for testing, stratified to preserve class distributions. Accuracies marked with † averaged 5 repetitions of the previous procedure; those with ‡ averaged 30 repetitions. The entry marked with only ↓ used a subset of 40 classes of LSA64. In all cases, the accuracies were subject dependent.

Classifier	Feature	Accuracy	Year
HMM+GMM	Radon Transform + Hand segmentation	95.95 ‡	2016 [13]
Custom Bayesian	Radon Transform + Hand segmentation	97.00 ‡	2016 [12]
SVM	Cumulative Shape Difference	85.00	2018 [11]
LSTM	Skeletal + LDS Histograms	98.09 †	2018 [9]
LSTM	Skeletal + RGB + Optical Flow	97.94 †	2018 [8]
LSTM + DSC	Skeletal + RGB + Optical Flow	**99.84** †	2018 [8]
LSTM	RGB + Optical Flow	99.37 †	2018 [8]
LSTM	Inception CNN + Hand segmentation	95.20	2018 [10]
Bi-directional LSTM	Inception CNN	96.00	2018 [14]
LSTM + MEMP	3D CNN	99.06	2019 [17]
Kernel Extreme Learning Machines	MobileNet CNN + Skeletal + Motion Template Fusion	97.81	2020 [5]
LSTM	3D CNN	98.50 ↓	2021 [3]

In Sect. 3.2 and Sect. 3.3 we describe spatial and temporal preprocessing techniques, including a type of data augmentation. Section 3.4 shows the effect of training with different temporal resolutions. Section 3.5 presents an analysis of the activations of the convolutional layers. Finally, Sect. 3.6 shows the effect of using hand segmentation as a preprocessing step.

3.1 Setup

We experimented with three different models we name ConvLSTM, MobileNet and Conv3D, chosen for diversity of approaches[1]. All of them use convolutional layers to process spatial information in the videos but differ mainly in their temporal encoding.

Our first model, named ConvLSTM (Fig. 3), uses ConvLSTM layers. These are a variation of Long Short Term Memory (LSTM) that use convolutional instead of fully connected layers [15] to encode their internal state. An architecture based on ConvLSTM layers is able to simultaneously learn spatial and temporal features.

The small total number of frames in LSA64 may make it difficult for this type of network to learn spatial features. To test this hypothesis, we also evaluate a network similar in architecture that uses a pre-trained image model. In this way, the network only has to learn temporal relationships between frames, relegating the spatial encoding to the pre-trained model.

---

[1] Experiment code, including model details and other supplementary materials can be found at https://github.com/midusi/lsa64_nn.

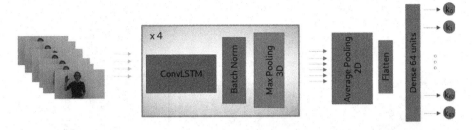

Fig. 3. ConvLSTM: four ConvLSTM layers model both spatial and temporal information. They have 16, 32, 64 and 64 filters respectively with 3×3 kernels.

For this architecture we named MobileNet (Fig. 4) we used a pretrained version of the model of the same name to extract image features. MobileNet is a lightweight and efficient convolutional based model that was trained using the ImageNet dataset [4]. For the recurrent layers, we found Gated Recurrent Units (GRUs) had significantly better results and therefore used them to replace the corresponding LSTM layers of ConvLSTM.

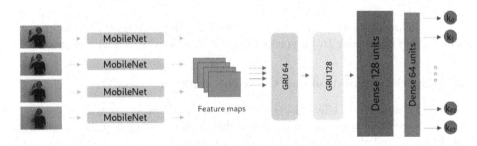

Fig. 4. MobileNet: two GRU layers fed with features extracted with a MobileNet pretrained model. GRU layers only model temporal information.

Finally, 3D convolution layers (Conv3D) are a variant of classical 2D convolutions that add a temporal dimension and can learn spatio-temporal features by capturing the motion information encoded in multiple adjacent frames [6]. Unlike recurrent layers, they observe all frames at the same time to generate features, and therefore can use less complex representations. To test this alternative representation, we use a network based named Conv3D (Fig. 5) that is also similar to the ConvLSTM model, but replaces those layers with 3D convolutions.

We trained all models for 48 epochs, using a batch size of 32, Adam optimizer with learning rate 0.001, and categorical cross entropy as loss function. Given the small sample size of LSA64, we used 5-fold cross validation in all experiments.

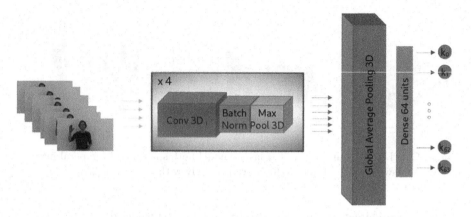

Fig. 5. Conv3D: four Conv3D layers which model both sequence and spatial information. They have 16, 32, 32 and 64 filters respectively with 3×3 kernels. The temporal and spatial structure is then removed by a 3D global average layer, and classified by fully connected layers.

We selected models hyperparameters empirically, constrained to our hardware limitations[2].

The following subsections present detailed ablation experiments to determine which types of features and preprocessing techniques work well with each model.

3.2   Spatial Resolution and Color Information

Spatial resolution can affect the scale of objects that can be recognized, such as handshapes. Color information is another factor that can weigh in the complexity of the data, and therefore affect overall performance.

To test the effect of these parameters on the models, we train and test models using spatial resolutions of 64×64 and 128×128, and grayscale or RGB color spaces. For the ConvLSTM and MobileNet models, memory limitations only allowed experimenting with 64×64 pixels. Additionally, since MobileNet was trained with RGB images, we did not test grayscale images with that model.

Figure 6 suggests only a slight increase in accuracy when increasing the complexity of the image. It is possible that colored gloves do not contribute to discerning information if layers are capturing other parts of the image. Nonetheless, since the increase in parameters is very slight, we used RGB in all further experiments.

Surprisingly, 64×64 images that fully contain the subject perform very well. Although 128×128 images performed slightly better for Conv3D, we also used 64×64 in further experiments due to memory constraints.

---

[2] We executed all experiments using an Intel(R) Xeon(R) CPU @ 2.30 GHz CPU, a single 12 GB NVIDIA Tesla K80 GPU, and 13 GB of RAM.

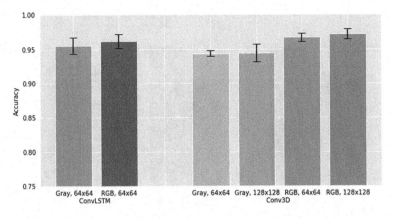

Fig. 6. Effect of image resolution and color information on Conv3D and ConvLSTM accuracy.

3.3 Temporal Data Augmentation via Resampling

Since each sign has a different duration, the corresponding videos have different lengths. In order to train the models efficiently with batches of samples, we resampled the videos to a fixed number of frames. To this end, we used a resampling technique where we eliminate frames in a uniform fashion and repeat the first and last frames in order to obtain the same number of frames for all videos. Resampling in this fashion is therefore also a source of data augmentation, where the model is biased to learn to ignore specific cues in starting/ending frames and also non-linear speed variations. It also simplifies training by standardizing the number of frames in a batch.

We generate 4 resampled videos for each original sample. Given this increase in effective number of samples, correspondingly we reduce the number of epochs from 48 to 12 when training models with this technique. Figure 7 shows an improvement throughout all models when using this technique, increasing the mean accuracy and also decreasing classification variance. Due to its simplicity and positive effect we decided to use it in all further experiments.

3.4 Sensitivity to Temporal Resolution

Using fewer frames per video allows for faster training and inference, so we experimented with various temporal resolutions to assess how many frames are actually necessary to correctly classify a sign. Figure 8 shows the accuracy of the models when trained/tested with videos resampled to different number of frames (i.e., resampling size). In all cases, the best results are obtained when training and testing with the same resampling size.

ConvLSTM and Conv3D cannot accurately classify videos that differ too much from the training videos' length. This is more noticeable when testing models trained with 8 frames. This could be attributed to the fact that these

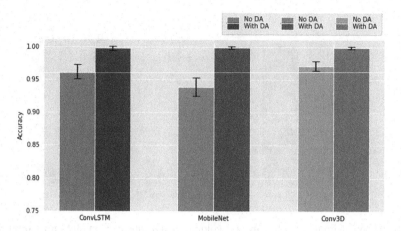

Fig. 7. Effect of data augmentation on model accuracy. Error changes from 4% and 6% respectively to less than 1% in all cases.

models need to learn the visual representations alongside learning the sequence of each video, and using less frames effective reduces total the number of images processed by the convolutional layers. In the case of Conv3D, which performs even worse than ConvLSTM, there is an additional aspect to consider. 3D convolutions do not process each frame individually, but instead operate over a block of frames. Because of this the sequence information it encodes is highly dependent on observing all frames at the same time, instead of just one as with recurrent models, making it more susceptible to different temporal lengths.

On the other hand, since MobileNet only learns the temporal structure of the videos it is less sensible to this effect. MobileNet models trained with 8 frames perform worse when tested with other resampling sizes, but generalize very well when trained with 16 o 32 frames.

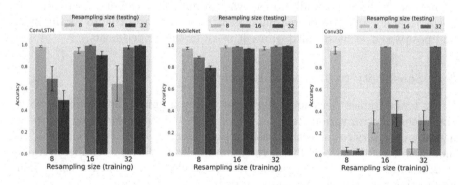

Fig. 8. Effect of resampling testing videos to 8, 16 and 32 frames. Each group of bars shows the accuracy of the model when trained with a fixed sample length, but evaluated with different sample lengths.

3.5   Activation and Hand Features

Activation values are the result of applying an input to a given layer. If a particular activation has a relatively high or low value, it generally indicates it encodes information that can significantly affect the output of the network. For the case of Convolutional layers, feature maps can be considered as entire activations that learn to capture different aspects of an image.

Figures 9 and 10 show feature maps of the first layers of the three models for two different signs. We manually selected feature maps that had a high response to the hands, of which there were several in each model[3]. The first corresponds to a video of class 17 where only the right hand is used and the second to a video of class 60 where both hands are used. In both cases, all three models have features with high activation values for hand pixels. This would indicate that all models understand that both hands are part of the sign if they are present and have developed specific filters for them.

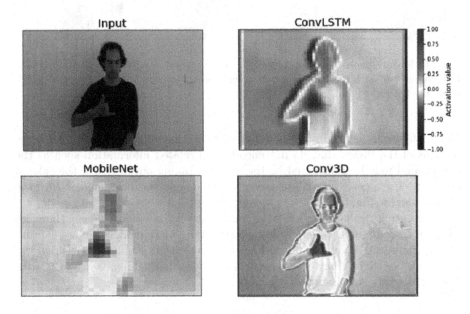

Fig. 9. Feature maps corresponding to the input image, selected from the first convolutional layer of each model. The input image corresponds to a video of sign 17 which uses only both hands.

3.6   Hand Segmentation

In the previous section, we analyzed all model activations in three of their layers and observed that in all cases the hand of the signer produced high activations,

---

[3] See the supplementary material in the code repository for more examples.

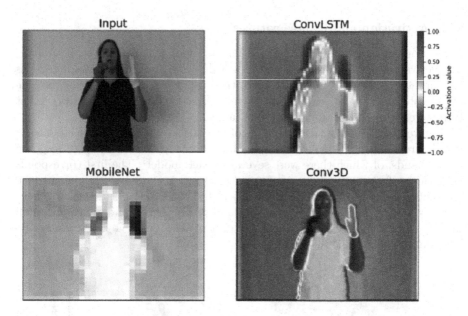

Fig. 10. Feature maps corresponding to the input image, selected from the first convolutional layer of each model. The input image corresponds to a video of sign 60 which uses only the right hand.

but the following layers of the model may ignore this information. Furthermore, sections of the image that do not encode sign related information such as the background may be considered by the models. Taking advantage of the colored gloves, we use a color filter to segment the hands and train the models with the filtered videos (Fig. 11).

Segmenting the hands reduces the complexity of the frames and can therefore ease the difficulty of learning visual representations since models need to capture mainly shape and sequence information. We can see that in effect models perform just as well or slightly better by visualizing only segmented hands (Fig. 12), with Conv3D slightly surpassing all previous results.

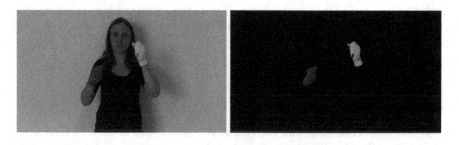

Fig. 11. Left: raw LSA64 frame. Right: hands segmented with a color filter.

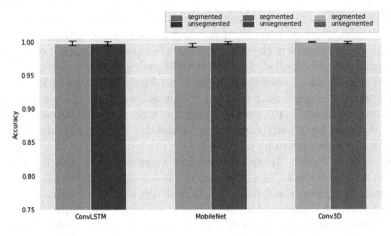

Fig. 12. Comparison of the accuracies of models trained with segmented hand images vs unsegmented (original). In all three cases, the differences in accuracy are not significant.

3.7 Summary of Results

Table 2 shows a summary of results. All models were able to reach very high accuracies using different features and architectures, surpassing the state of the art which uses a much complex model [17]. Conv3D with color filtering achieved the highest accuracy, but other models perform very similarly. Moreover, all surpass or are very close to the previous state of the art [8].

Table 2. Comparison of results on LSA64 for different models and preprocessing. The Conv3D model surpasses the previous state of the art.

Model	Features	Accuracy (%)	σ
ConvLSTM	16 frames	99.49	0.0033
ConvLSTM	32 frames	99.73	0.0031
ConvLSTM	32 frames + segmented hands	99.79	0.0034
MobileNet	16 frames	99.38	0.0043
MobileNet	32 frames	99.89	0.0017
MobileNet	32 frames + segmented hands	99.49	0.0020
Conv3D	16 frames	99.60	0.0015
Conv3D	32 frames	99.84	0.0018
Conv3D	32 frames + segmented hands	**99.96**	0.0006
LSTM + DSC [8]	Skeletal + RGB + Optical Flow	99.84	-

4   Conclusions and Future Work

We evaluated three standard video recognition models based on RNNs (LSTM/GRU) and CNNs (2D and 3D) on the LSA64 dataset. We also performed ablation studies to understand the effects of several hyperparameters. The accuracies obtained surpass all previous results on the dataset.

Besides this advance in the state of the art for LSA64, our main conclusion is that simple but well-applied standard models are sufficient to solve the LSA64 recognition problem. Therefore, LSA64 is no longer challenging for standard models, and we suggest using it only for validation of new models or methodologies. Since LSA64 is the only Argentinian sign language dataset, this also implies the need for a more complex and extensive dataset for this language if recognition systems are to be improved.

Our ablation studies also spanned several dimensions and identified key areas for effective recognition. First, we tested various spatial resolution and color information parameters and found that these did not significantly affect accuracy. Video length (number of frames), did show a significant impact in accuracy. Models tested and trained with 16 and 32 frames presented better accuracies. Using less frames (8 in our experiments) significantly decreased this accuracy. The use of data augmentation via temporal resampling, on the other hand, had a noteworthy impact, reducing error by 4–6% and decreasing model variance.

MobileNet models, when evaluated with different video lengths than those used for training, showed great invariance to this transformation. ConvLSTM and Conv3D based models, however, were susceptible this modification of the temporal encoding and therefore performed significantly worse.

Our analysis of model activations showed that hand specific features were considered for the classification. Additionally, by experimenting with hand segmentation on the videos, we asserted that the models indeed can use only this information to correctly classify signs

In future work, we plan on expanding this analysis and methodology to other well known sign language datasets, such as RWTH-Phoenix. We also plan on using more recent pretrained CNN models such as EfficientNet, and evaluating the impact of its different versions on accuracy.

Our ablation studies also lacked other typical spatial data augmentation techniques such as rotation or cropping, which we plan on performing. Another aspect that was missing from our analysis was the computational budget required to run each model, since SLR systems typically need to run in real time or portable devices.

In terms of model interpretability, we also intend to compare the activations of models trained with full frames vs those trained with segmented hands to assess the impact of the background on the model.

References

1. Bragg, D., et al.: Sign language recognition, generation, and translation: an interdisciplinary perspective. In: The 21st International ACM SIGACCESS Conference on Computers and Accessibility, p. 16–31. ASSETS 2019, Association for Computing Machinery, New York, NY, USA (2019). https://doi.org/10.1145/3308561.3353774

2. Cooper, H., Holt, B., Bowden, R.: Sign language recognition. In: Moeslund, T.B., Hilton, A., Krüger, V., Sigal, L. (eds.) Visual Analysis of Humans: Looking at People, chap. 27, pp. 539–562. Springer, London (2011)

3. Elsayed, E.K., Fathy, D.R.: Semantic deep learning to translate dynamic sign language. Int. J. Intell. Eng. Syst. 14 (2021). https://doi.org/10.22266/ijies2021.0228. 3

4. Howard, A.G., et al.: Mobilenets: efficient convolutional neural networks for mobile vision applications. arXiv preprint arXiv:1704.04861 (2017)

5. Imran, J., Raman, B.: Deep motion templates and extreme learning machine for sign language recognition. Vis. Comput. 36(6), 1233–1246 (2020)

6. Ji, S., Xu, W., Yang, M., Yu, K.: 3D Convolutional Neural Networks for Human Action Recognition. IEEE Trans. Pattern Anal. Mach. Intell. 35(1), 221–231 (2013). https://doi.org/10.1109/TPAMI.2012.59

7. Koller, O.: Quantitative survey of the state of the art in sign language recognition. CoRR abs/2008.09918 https://arxiv.org/abs/2008.09918 (2020)

8. Konstantinidis, D., Dimitropoulos, K., Daras, P.: A deep learning approach for analyzing video and skeletal features in sign language recognition. In: 2018 IEEE International Conference on Imaging Systems and Techniques (IST), pp. 1–6. IEEE (2018)

9. Konstantinidis, D., Dimitropoulos, K., Daras, P.: Sign language recognition based on hand and body skeletal data. In: 2018–3DTV-Conference: The True Vision-Capture, Transmission and Display of 3D Video (3DTV-CON), pp. 1–4. IEEE (2018)

10. Masood, S., Srivastava, A., Thuwal, H.C., Ahmad, M.: Real-time sign language gesture (word) recognition from video sequences using CNN and RNN. In: Bhateja, V., Coello Coello, C.A., Satapathy, S.C., Pattnaik, P.K. (eds.) Intelligent Engineering Informatics, pp. 623–632. Springer Singapore, Singapore (2018)

11. Rodríguez, J., Martínez, F.: Towards on-line sign language recognition using cumulative SD-VLAD descriptors. In: Serrano C., J.E., Martínez-Santos, J.C. (eds.) CCC 2018. CCIS, vol. 885, pp. 371–385. Springer, Cham (2018). https://doi.org/10.1007/978-3-319-98998-3_29

12. Ronchetti, F., Quiroga, F., Estrebou, C., Lanzarini, L., Rosete, A.: sign languague recognition without frame-sequencing constraints: a proof of concept on the argentinian sign language. In: Montes-y-Gómez, M., Escalante, H.J., Segura, A., de Dios Murillo, J. (eds.) IBERAMIA 2016. LNCS (LNAI), vol. 10022, pp. 338–349. Springer, Cham (2016). https://doi.org/10.1007/978-3-319-47955-2_28

13. Ronchetti, F., Quiroga, F., Estrebou, C.A., Lanzarini, L.C., Rosete, A.: Lsa64: an argentinian sign language dataset. In: XXII Congreso Argentino de Ciencias de la Computación (CACIC 2016) (2016)

14. Shah, J.A., et al.: Deepsign: a deep-learning architecture for sign language. Master's thesis, University of Texas at Arlington (2018)

15. Shi, X., Chen, Z., Wang, H., Yeung, D.Y., Wong, W.K., Woo, W.C.: Convolutional LSTM network: A machine learning approach for precipitation nowcasting. arXiv preprint arXiv:1506.04214 (2015)

16. Von Agris, U., Zieren, J., Canzler, U., Bauer, B., Kraiss, K.F.: Recent developments in visual sign language recognition. Univ. Access Inf. Soc. 6(4), 323–362 (2008)

17. Zhang, X., Li, X.: Dynamic gesture recognition based on MEMP network. Future Internet 11, 91 (2019). https://doi.org/10.3390/fi11040091

Big Data

Optimizing Sparse Matrix Storage for the Big Data Era

Raúl Marichal, Ernesto Dufrechou$^{(\boxtimes)}$, and Pablo Ezzatti

HCL, Instituto de Computación (INCO), Facultad de Ingeniería,
Universidad de la República, 11300 Montevideo, Uruguay
{rmarichal,edufrechou,pezzatti}@fing.edu.uy

Abstract. The efficient handling of sparse matrices is essential in many applications. In particular, they are critical in Big Data applications that involve large graphs, as these are often represented as sparse matrices. In this context, it is necessary to provide matrix storage formats that save memory, avoid pointless computations, and enable convenient memory accesses. Reordering techniques, which permute the rows and columns of the matrix to achieve better nonzero patterns, have long been applied in the sparse numerical linear algebra field. However, their use has focused on reducing the matrix bandwidth or the fill-in during the LU factorization. In this work, we study the application of reordering techniques to enhance sparse hybrid storage formats. Concretely, we develop an evolutionary algorithm (EA) to provide the matrix reordering, following different optimization goals. The results show that the nonzero patterns obtained after applying the EA's reorderings are superior to those obtained through standard reorderings, regarding the use of hybrid sparse matrix formats.

Keywords: Big data · Graph theory · Sparse matrices · Hybrid formats

1 Introduction

The use of sparse matrices has a long history in scientific computing. Since the 1950s, when sparse matrices to improve linear programming methods were first proposed, the research related to this type of structure has not stopped its development. In the 1970s and 1980s, this evolution focused on the solution of partial differential equations (PDEs), where sparse matrices arise due to the application of the finite element method (FEM). Later, in the 1990s and 2000s, the sparse matrices spread across all the numerical linear algebra (NLA) fields. In the last decade, with the irruption of several new scientific computing problems, especially concerned with social networks and artificial intelligence, sparse matrices are revisited to address problems from graph theory. A clear example of the several important efforts that connect sparse matrices with the Big Data field is J. Kepner and J. Gilbert's book [13], which offers a detailed mapping between graph problems and matrix operations.

© Springer Nature Switzerland AG 2021
M. Naiouf et al. (Eds.): JCC-BD&ET 2021, CCIS 1444, pp. 121–135, 2021.
https://doi.org/10.1007/978-3-030-84825-5_9

When a matrix is composed mostly by coefficients of certain fixed value (usually zero), saving storage space and optimizing the computations requires a sparse storage format. This implies storing only the nonzero coefficients, adding indexing data to compute the nonzero values' location in the original matrix. These strategies, in conjunction with specialized algorithms, allows saving memory volume and avoiding pointless computations. However, as sparse matrices typically involve indirection and poor locality in data access, there are also some drawbacks. These characteristics imply that sparse matrix algorithms belong to the *memory-bound* class. Therefore a large share of the research on sparse matrices is devoted to the design of storage formats that make the most efficient use possible of the memory hierarchy, at least for the most common computations.

In this work, we advance in developing strategies that use reordering techniques to find better sparse storage formats. We are interested in improving the nonzero pattern of the matrix to leverage a hybrid format that stores part of the matrix in diagonal format (DIA) storing the rest in standard formats such as CRS or COO. Although the application of reorderings, such as the Reverse Cuthill-McKee (RCM) or Approximate Minimum Degree (AMD) methods, is not new in NLA, it generally points to other purposes, i.e., reducing the matrix bandwidth or the fill-in during the LU factorization. Concretely, we develop an evolutionary algorithm to provide the matrix reordering and modify the fitness function to optimize different matrix properties. Then, we reorder the matrices and explore the resulting nonzero pattern's effect. The obtained results show that the evolutionary algorithm's reorderings produce more convenient nonzero patterns, from the point of view of hybrid storage formats.

The rest of the paper is structured as follows. In Sect. 2 we include a brief review of the main topics related to our work, among others, sparse matrix storage formats, reordering techniques, and the connection between Big Data and sparse matrices. A description of our proposal follows in Sect. 4. Section 5, presents the study and the experimental results. Finally, Sect. 6, summarizes the main conclusions arrived at and proposes several lines of future work.

2   Large Sparse Matrices

In the last years, an essential part of the high-performance computing (HPC) community's challenges were related to the Big Data field, addressing problems derived from social network applications, graph databases, and artificial intelligence. Several of those challenges require the efficient processing of large graphs. A significant paradigm in this line is that of mapping graph problems to algebra ones. In [13], J. Kepner and J. Gilbert explain this paradigm in detail, describing the close relationship between graph and matrix operations. The application of these ideas, in turn, has already spread into different fields, as it can be observed in [12].

In the rest of this section, we describe some essential concepts of sparse matrices and provide a brief review of related work.

2.1   Sparse Matrices

According to Tim Davis [8]:

> "The large matrices that arise in real-world problems in science, engineering, and mathematics tend to be mostly zero, or sparse. Sparse matrix algorithms lie in the intersection of graph theory and numerical linear algebra. A graph represents the connections between variables in the mathematical model, such as the voltage across a circuit component, a link from one web page to another, the physical forces between two points in a mechanical structure, and so on, depending on the problem at hand. The numerical linear algebra arises because these matrices represent systems of equations whose solution tells us something about how the real-world problem behaves. Google's page rank algorithm, for example, requires the computation of an eigenvector for a matrix with as many rows and columns as there are pages on the web"

This definition evidences the close link between graphs and linear algebra.

It is most evident that storing the large number of zeros presented by this sort of matrices is highly inefficient. As an example, a dense matrix of $10^4 \times 10^5$ elements using double precision floating point (64 bits) for the coefficients implies $10^4 \times 10^5 \times 8$ Bytes $= 8 \times 10^9$ Bytes $= 8$ GBytes. In contrast, a sparse matrix with the same dimensions but only 10^7 nonzero coefficients (1%) would occupy only 0.08 GBytes if only the nonzero elements are stored. However, it is generally necessary to store indexing information that allows the computation of the nonzero elements' positions in the original matrix. Different ways to represent this indexing information give place to a myriad of sparse matrix representations or formats. Each of these formats has its strengths and weaknesses. For example, formats can be designed to occupy more or less storage space, perform better in particular matrix operations, take advantage of some specific hardware platform, or store matrices with a specific characteristic exceptionally well [4].

Sparse Matrix Formats. Some of the essential sparse matrix storage strategies are COOrdinate format, Compressed Row Storage - CRS, Compressed Column Storage - CCS, Compressed Diagonal Storage - CDS (or DIA), and the Ellpack-Itpack format (ELL). We include a brief description of each format using the matrix A in Fig. 1 as an example.

- COO (COOrdinate format): This format is maybe the most straightforward strategy to represent a sparse matrix. It employs three vectors of dimension nnz elements. One vector d of floating-point values stores the nonzero coefficients, while two vectors (r and c) store each nonzero's row and column index. Figure 1 shows a depiction of this format.
- CRS (Compressed Row Storage): As COO, this format also employs three vectors. If the matrix's nonzeros are placed in the vectors row-wise, vectors d and c are identical to those of COO. Vector r, however, is "compressed". It stores the index of the first element of each row in the other two vectors. To

$$A = \begin{pmatrix} 1 & 2 & 0 & 0 & 3 & 4 & 0 \\ 0 & 5 & 0 & 6 & 0 & 0 & 0 \\ 0 & 7 & 8 & 9 & 0 & 0 & 0 \\ 1 & 0 & 0 & 2 & 0 & 0 & 0 \\ 0 & 3 & 0 & 0 & 4 & 5 & 0 \\ 0 & 0 & 6 & 0 & 7 & 8 & 0 \\ 0 & 0 & 0 & 0 & 0 & 0 & 9 \end{pmatrix}$$

$$d = \begin{pmatrix} 1 & 2 & 3 & 4 & 5 & 6 & 7 & 8 & 9 & 1 & 2 & 3 & 4 & 5 & 6 & 7 & 8 & 9 \end{pmatrix}$$
$$f = \begin{pmatrix} 1 & 1 & 1 & 1 & 2 & 2 & 3 & 3 & 3 & 4 & 4 & 5 & 5 & 5 & 6 & 6 & 6 & 7 \end{pmatrix}$$
$$c = \begin{pmatrix} 1 & 2 & 5 & 6 & 2 & 4 & 2 & 3 & 4 & 1 & 4 & 2 & 5 & 6 & 3 & 5 & 6 & 7 \end{pmatrix}$$

Fig. 1. Example matrix and its representation in COO format.

access a nonzero entry placed on $A(i, j)$, it is necessary to fetch the indices $p_1 = r(i)$ and $p_2 = r(i + 1)$, and look for the index p that $p_1 \leq p < p_2$ and $c(p) = j$. Finally, the value is in $d(p)$.

- CCS (Compressed Column Storage): This format is analogous to CRS but enforcing a column-wise order on r and d while compressing vector c.
- DIA (DIAgonal format): If the sparse matrix's nonzero pattern is close to a band matrix, or the nonzeros are placed forming diagonals, this format is an exciting option. DIA stores the nonzeros in a rectangular $n \times d$ matrix where n is the sparse matrix dimension and d the number of diagonals. A separate vector of size d stores the offset of each diagonal with respect to the main diagonal (Fig. 2).
- ELL (Ellpack-itpack): This format stores the nonzero coefficients in a dense structure of $n \times k$, where n is the number of rows of the sparse matrix and $k = max_i(nnz\,(A_i))$, with A_i the row i. The column index of each nonzero is stored in the corresponding position of another dense matrix with the same dimensions. For rows with less than k nonzero elements, the arrays are padded with zeros. Figure 3 presents an example of this format.

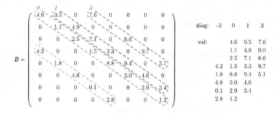

Fig. 2. Matrix B stored in DIA.

2.2   Reordering Techniques

A reordering consists of finding a permutation p applied to rows and columns to achieve a more convenient nonzero pattern for the matrix. Practitioners have

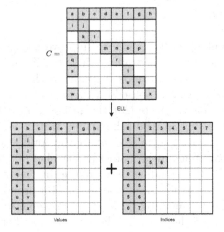

Fig. 3. Matrix C stored ELL.

widely used reordering techniques with sparse matrices since the 1970s when the methods that seek to reduce the matrix bandwidth were among the most used in NLA. These ideas are helpful for two reasons. On the one hand, they can allow the use of simpler data structures. For instance, a sparse matrix that allocates all its nonzeros in a small band around the diagonal could be stored using a simple dense structure. On the other hand, reorderings can improve the data locality in the computations even if standard sparse matrix formats are used.

Considering that matrices can be seen as the representation of a graph, a reordering is equivalent to renumber the nodes of the graph. This concept is mainly present in the solution of PDEs by the finite element method, where the sparse matrix represents the relationship between the nodes of the grid in which the equation is discretized. Because we are interested in leveraging dense diagonals of the matrix by applying a hybrid matrix storage format, the minimization of bandwidth is especially interesting in our case. Finding a reordering that minimizes the bandwidth of a matrix is an $\mathcal{NP}$-complete problem [18]. This situation motivates the development of heuristics to address it.

The Cuthill-McKee [7] is based on a Breadth-First-Search. The algorithm traverses the sparse matrix's associated graph starting from an initial node and its neighbors. Each time a node is visited, its unvisited neighbors are appended to a list of nodes to visit. Once all nodes have been visited, they are numbered in the order they were added to the list. If the initial node is level 1, its neighbors can be considered level 2, their unvisited in level 3, proceeding similarly for the rest. The most important variant of CM is the Reverse CM (RCM), which reverses the numbering of nodes inside each level. In both previously described methods, the selection of the initial vertex is critical. Another algorithm for bandwidth minimization is the Sloan algorithm [24], but it is not as widely applied as RCM, and libraries containing efficient implementations are difficult to find.

3 Related Work

The search for efficient data structures to improve the performance of sparse matrix operations is not new. For example, in 1999, Pinar and Heath proposed packing blocks of contiguous nonzeros to mitigate the indexing overhead and formulated a reordering heuristic based on the Travelling Salesperson Problem (TSP) to enlarge such blocks [21]. In [25], the authors study the effect of reducing the matrix bandwidth using RCM on the Sparse Matrix-Vector product (*spmv*) with the ELLPACK format. They also evaluate the application of delta encoding to compress the column index matrix of ELL. Pichel et al. [20] perform a similar but more complete study, including other reordering methods, such as AMD, Metis, and their heuristic [19]. Mironowicz et al. [16] propose a task-scheduling for the *spmv* based on a sparse hybrid format that separates blocks with many nonzeros from the rest of the matrix. The authors also benefit from the RCM reordering to boost the performance of their approach.

To reduce the memory footprint of the ELL, SELL-based formats [2,15,17] cut the matrices in slices that are padded to a different row length. This implies reordering the matrix's rows such that rows with a similar number of nonzeros are grouped. Guo et al. [11] propose a SELL-based hybrid format (EVC-HYB) that sorts the rows by number of nonzeros, representing the shorter rows in ELL and the longer rows in CSR-vectorized format. Choi et al. [6] added the idea of blocking to ELL, creating the format BELLPACK. They also provide mechanisms to adjust the parameters of their implementations of BELLPACK and BCSR outperforming state-of-the-art versions for the latter.

Regarding the improvement of the reordering heuristics, we focus on bandwidth reduction, which we found to be the most applied in sparse matrix format optimization. In this sense, Gonzaga de Oliveira and collaborators have implemented and evaluated numerous techniques for bandwidth and profile reduction, mainly applied to symmetric matrices. In [5] the authors give a systematic review of 29 heuristics for bandwidth reduction. A similar study, this time reviewing 74 heuristics for profile reduction, is performed in [3]. An evaluation of reordering techniques for bandwidth and profile reduction to reduce the computational cost of Incomplete Cholesky Conjugate Gradients (ICCG) can be found on [10]. More recently, the authors proposed an ant-colony-based hyperheuristic approach for matrix bandwidth reduction, seeking to accelerate the convergence of the ICCG method [9]. The proposed ACHH, in contrast to the most common heuristics, generates or selects heuristics for specific application problems with relatively low cost (if training time is not considered). In [23], the authors propose a biased random-key genetic algorithm (BRKGA) for bandwidth reduction. The novel technique achieves good bandwidth reduction results, but the authors did not compare the computational cost with state-of-the-art metaheuristics.

Other works that apply genetic or evolutionary techniques to bandwidth reduction obtain good bandwidth results at a considerably high computational cost compared to state-of-the-art [14,22].

4   Proposal

As we stated previously, the data locality, the reduction of indirect accesses and the volume of data storage are substantial aspects of sparse linear algebra. In this work, we leverage new heuristics for matrix reordering to obtain nonzero patterns that are better suited to specific sparse storage formats. Specifically, we try to move from classic storage, like COO or CRS, to dense storage strategies or hybrid ones. To advance the objective mentioned above, we design an evolutionary algorithm that looks for permutations according to different optimization criteria, such as reducing the number of non-empty diagonals (making them denser), which can be helpful for hybrid formats that store a part of the matrix in DIA. In this section, we present the essential characteristics of our evolutionary algorithm, and in the next, we experimentally evaluate the proposal.

4.1   Evolutionary Algorithm

Evolutionary algorithms search for solutions to different problems via the emulation of the biologic evolution of living beings. Specifically, these algorithms work with a population of potential solutions to the problem, called individuals, applying operations such as recombinations and mutations, and evaluating a *fitness* function to tell which individuals are closer to the optimal solution of the problem. The following generation of individuals is assembled according to the individuals' fitness value and some selection criteria.

Our EA works on individuals (or chromosomes) that are permutation vectors. We address different criteria for the fitness function. Although the recombination operation is usually essential, after some preliminary evaluation with the *Order Crossover* [1] operator, we decided to omit its application. The reason is that we are employing a permutation vector representation, and thus the computational cost of this operator becomes prohibitive. To compensate for this weakness, we empower the exploration capabilities by including two different mutation operators, `fliplr` y `swap`. The former reverses the positions of the elements of one individual (i.e., individual [1–4] becomes [1–4]). This operator is applied to half of the population. The latter interchanges two elements of one individual (`swap`). This operator is applied with a *Mutation rate* probability.

We employ the following general configuration for all the experiments. This parameters are aligned with the specialized literature:

- *Population*: 240 individuals.
- *Initialization*: 3 groups of 80 individuals. First group is a matrix identity (i.e. a vector with values of 1 to n). Second group is the permutation obtained with the RCM strategy. The last group, are random permutations.
- *Generations*: 2500.
- *Mutation rate*: 0.2.

4.2   Experimental Setup

The hardware platform employed in our experimental evaluation presents an Intel i7-4770 processor (4 cores at 3.40 GHz) and 16 GB of DDR3 RAM (approximately 26 GB/s of bandwidth). For the test cases, we selected a group of matrices from the SuiteSparse Matrix Collection. Specifically, for each study, we start with the bfwb62 matrix (an electromagnetism problem) and, later, we extend the study to other 16 matrices with different characteristics but similar dimensions, considering the computational restrictions. In Table 1 we summarize the main characteristics of these matrices.

Table 1. Characteristics of the matrices employed in the experimental evaluation.

Matriz	Dim(n)	nnz
bfwb62	62	342
662_bus	662	2474
S10PI_n1	528	1317
Si2	769	17801
Spectro_10NN	531	7422
Trefethen_700	700	12654
bfwb782	782	5982
dendrimer	730	63024
dwt_503	503	6027
goddardRocket	831	8498
lowThrust_1	584	6133
lshp_577	577	3889
lshp_778	778	5272
nos6	675	3255
orsirr_2	886	5970
steam2s	600	5660
young4c	841	4089

5   Experimental Study

This section describes the different studies carried out in our work. Concretely, we start this section with the optimization of the matrix bandwidth, comparing the results of our EA with traditional strategies (such as RCM). Next, we adjust our EA's fitness function to minimize the number of non-empty diagonals of the reordered matrix. Finally, we adjust the optimization criteria once again, this time with a specific hybrid storage strategy in mind.

5.1 Bandwidth Reduction, EA$_{bw}$

The first of the proposed studies evaluates the EA's ability to reduce the matrix bandwidth (EA$_{bw}$). To assess the solution's quality, we compare it with the reordering yield by the RCM method, which is the classic approach for this objective. In this case, we set the fitness function to be the (minimization of the) matrix bandwidth. As we stated previously, the first experiments are performed on the bfwb62 matrix. Figure 4 displays the original ordering and the result of applying the reordering delivered by RCM and EA$_{bw}$. Although the images are very similar, the EA manages to slightly improve the matrix profile, with a bandwidth reduction of 1.

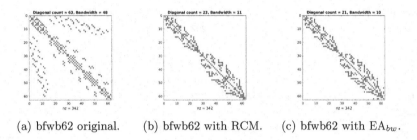

(a) bfwb62 original.   (b) bfwb62 with RCM.   (c) bfwb62 with EA$_{bw}$.

Fig. 4. Three reordering of bfwb62 matrix.

The experimental evaluation is summarized in Table 2 with a row for each matrix. For each test case we include the *bandwidth* (*BW*) and the number of diagonals (or *diagonal count DC*). The table includes the percentage of reduction of each quantity relative to the original matrix, achieved by the application of the RCM method (RCM-Orig) and our evolutionary algorithm (EA$_{bw}$). The final column shows the direct comparison between RCM and EA$_{bw}$ (EA$_{bw}$-RCM). The experimental results show that, in general, the bandwidth results obtained by our heuristic are similar to those of the reordering offered by the RCM method. In a few cases, our method outperforms the RCM, but these improvements are limited to 1%. This confirms that RCM is a remarkable tool for this objective since it offers good results with a bound computational cost.

5.2 Reducing the Number of Diagonals (EA$_{dc}$)

The second study aims to obtain a matrix permutation that minimizes the number of non-empty diagonals. Although this criterion seems closely related to reducing the matrix bandwidth, it is important to remark that the two are different. The reduction in the matrix bandwidth usually implies a reduction in the number of diagonals, but the opposite is not valid.

In this case, we set the fitness function as (the minimization of) the number of diagonals.

Table 2. Results of reordering strategies for *bandwidth* reduction.

Matriz	Original		RCM		EA_{bw}		BW reduction (%)		
	DC	BW	DC	BW	DC	BW	RCM-Orig.	EA_{bw}-Orig.	EA_{bw}-RCM
662_bus	463	335	237	118	237	118	64.78%	64.78%	0.00%
S10PI_n1	97	509	29	14	27	13	97.25%	97.45%	7.14%
Si2	1013	552	649	324	649	324	41.30%	41.30%	0.00%
Spectro_10NN	994	518	192	96	190	95	81.47%	81.66%	1.04%
Trefethen_700	21	512	655	327	655	327	36.13%	36.13%	0.00%
bfwb782	593	593	71	35	71	35	94.10%	94.10%	0.00%
dendrimer	1355	708	853	426	835	417	39.83%	41.10%	2.11%
dwt_503	477	452	129	64	129	64	85.84%	85.84%	0.00%
goddardRocket	723	777	575	287	573	286	63.06%	63.19%	0.35%
lowThrust_1	509	487	607	303	595	297	37.78%	39.01%	1.98%
lshp_577	325	563	53	26	53	26	95.38%	95.38%	0.00%
lshp_778	411	762	61	30	61	30	96.06%	96.06%	0.00%
nos6	7	30	33	16	33	16	46.67%	46.67%	0.00%
orsirr_2	437	554	245	122	245	122	77.98%	77.98%	0.00%
steam2	123	330	152	76	152	76	76.97%	76.97%	0.00%
young4c	5	29	59	29	59	29	0.00%	0.00%	0.00%

Following the methodology described in Sect. 5.1 we start with a proof of concept with the `bfwb62` matrix. As before, Fig. 5 displays the profile of this matrix with the different reorderings. These images show that the EA_{dc} achieves a substantial reduction in the number of diagonals compared with the original nonzero pattern and the RCM method. More in detail, the reduction in the number of diagonals relative to the RCM reordering is 21%. Additionally, an 18% reduction in the matrix bandwidth is also achieved (which outperforms the previously commented strategy).

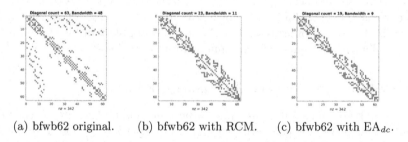

(a) bfwb62 original.   (b) bfwb62 with RCM.   (c) bfwb62 with EA_{dc}.

Fig. 5. Three reordering of `bfwb62` matrix.

Table 3 presents the results for the set of matrices described in Table 1. Considering that our set of test cases includes matrices of different characteristics,

Table 3. Results of reordering strategies with the aim of the diagonals number reduction.

Matriz	Original		RCM		EA_{dc}		DC reduction (%)		
	DC	BW	DC	BW	DC	BW	RCM-Orig.	EA_{dc}-Orig.	EA_{dc}-RCM
662_bus	463	335	237	118	205	118	48.81%	55.72%	13.50%
S10PI_n1	97	509	29	14	27	13	70.10%	72.16%	6.90%
Si2	1013	552	649	324	649	324	35.93%	35.93%	0.00%
Spectro_10NN	994	518	192	96	190	95	80.68%	80.89%	1.04%
Trefethen_700	21	512	655	327	21	512	−3019.05%	0.00%	96.79%
bfwb782	593	593	71	35	71	35	88.03%	88.03%	0.00%
dendrimer	1355	708	853	426	773	386	37.05%	42.95%	9.38%
dwt_503	477	452	129	64	129	64	72.96%	72.96%	0.00%
goddardRocket	723	777	575	287	465	324	20.47%	35.68%	19.13%
lowThrust_1	509	487	607	303	427	468	−19.25%	16.11%	29.65%
lshp_577	325	563	53	26	53	26	83.69%	83.69%	0.00%
lshp_778	411	762	61	30	61	30	85.16%	85.16%	0.00%
nos6	7	30	33	16	7	30	−371.43%	0.00%	78.79%
orsirr_2	437	554	245	122	245	122	43.94%	43.94%	0.00%
steam2	123	330	152	76	123	330	−23.58%	0.00%	19.08%
young4c	5	29	59	29	5	29	−1080.00%	0.00%	91.53%

we separate the obtained results into three groups. The first group is composed of the matrices for which the original pattern is better than that obtained after reordering with RCM. In this group, composed by matrices Trefethen_700 y nos6, which are structured matrices, the original variant is possibly the best option, and the EA_{dc} reaches the same results. The second group includes the matrices for which RCM offers reductions in the number of diagonals, as it is the case of lshp_577, lshp_778 and dwt503. In these cases, the EA_{dc} reaches similar results than the RCM. Finally, in the last set of matrices, where both the original and RCM reordering patterns are not good options, our proposal can achieve remarkable differences. Specifically, for four of these six matrices, the EA_{dc} reordering outperformed the RCM by more than 10%. The best result is obtained by the lowThrust1 matrix, where the benefits over the RCM are around 29%. As a summary of this study, we can highlight that the RCM is not a robust method for minimizing the number of diagonals.

5.3   Increasing the *nnz* in Few Diagonals (EA_{hyb})

After evaluating the reordering techniques to minimize the bandwidth and the number of diagonals of a sparse matrix, in this section, we study the maximization of the number of nonzero coefficients lying in a limited number of diagonals. This objective is primarily related to the efficient use of sparse hybrid formats. In these sorts of formats, the matrix is decomposed into two different parts, one with a reasonably regular pattern to be stored in a dense structure, and the other with an irregular pattern to be stored in a standard format such as COO or CSR. For example, in the HYB format, the regular part has the same (or similar) number of nonzeros in every row and is stored in ELL, while the rest of the coefficients are stored in a COO structure.

A hybrid strategy alternative to HYB, is to store the most populated diagonals of the matrix in DIA format, while the rest is stored on COO or CSR. For this strategy to be effective, most nonzeros should be located in a reduced number of diagonals. To assess if a reordering strategy can help achieve such nonzero patterns, we modify our original evolutionary algorithm to contemplate these criteria (EA_{hyb}).

With this aim, we change the fitness function to be the (maximization of) number of nonzero coefficients in a certain number of diagonals (which was set to 2% of n for the following experiments).

Table 4. Results of reordering strategies with the aim of maximizing the nnz in a limited number of diagonals.

Matriz	2% diag	Original				RCM				EA_{hyb}			
		DC	BW	nnz in 2%	%nnz in 2% diag	DC	BW	nnz in 2%	%nnz in 2% diag	DC	BW	nnz in 2% diag	%nnz in 2% diag
662_bus	14	463	335	951	38.44%	237	118	966	39.05%	529	651	1701	68.76%
S10Pl_n1	10	97	509	1223	92.86%	29	14	1058	80.33%	65	513	1256	95.37%
Si2	16	1013	552	7029	39.49%	649	324	4256	23.91%	1099	768	7200	40.45%
Spectro_10NN	10	994	518	208	2.80%	192	96	2182	29.40%	340	530	3130	42.17%
Trefethen_700	14	21	512	9610	75.94%	655	327	2818	22.27%	21	512	9610	75.94%
bfwb62	2	63	48	94	27.49%	23	11	86	25.15%	83	60	108	31.58%
bfwb782	16	593	593	3733	62.40%	71	35	2926	48.91%	609	597	3785	63.27%
dendrimer	14	1355	708	8000	12.69%	853	426	4551	7.22%	1425	729	9168	14.55%
dwt_503	10	477	452	2190	36.34%	129	64	1919	31.84%	537	493	2813	46.67%
goddardRocket	16	723	777	2937	34.56%	575	287	1472	17.32%	727	789	4291	50.49%
lowThrust_1	12	509	487	2377	38.76%	607	303	836	13.63%	721	547	2554	41.64%
lshp_577	12	325	563	2487	63.95%	53	26	2680	68.91%	277	571	3072	78.99%
lshp_778	16	411	762	3583	67.96%	61	30	3920	74.36%	355	766	4310	81.75%
ncs6	14	7	30	3255	100.00%	33	16	2893	88.88%	7	30	3255	100.00%
orsirr_2	18	437	554	5170	86.60%	245	122	2491	41.73%	437	554	5170	86.60%
steam2	12	123	330	2413	42.63%	152	76	2116	37.39%	230	595	2518	44.49%
young4c	16	5	29	4089	100.00%	59	29	2295	56.13%	5	29	4089	100.00%

The first observation from this study is that the new heuristic (EA_{hyb}) does not offer any benefits for reducing bandwidth or the number of diagonals. Thus, in all cases, the original or RCM offers a better solution than the EA. However, this behavior is completely expected since the fitness function of EA_{hyb} is not directly related to these two criteria.

Considering the focus of this study, maximizing the number of nonzero coefficients in the limited number of diagonals, the most important conclusion derived from the results of Table 4 is that the reordering obtained with EA_{hyb} outperforms, or at least matches the original nonzero pattern and the reordering yield by RCM for all the evaluated cases. Two remarkable cases are the 662_bus and goddardRocket matrices, where the EA achieves 68.8% and 50.5% of nonzero coefficients in 2% of the diagonals, respectively. In the same cases, the original ordering presents 38.4% and 34.6%, and the RCM presents 39.1% and 17.3% for the same values. These results motivate further studies in this line of work.

Another aspect to mention is the behavior of RCM for this criterion, where the heuristic offers benefits for some cases but gets worse results for others. It can be concluded that the RCM is not a good option to improve this variant of a hybrid format.

6 Concluding Remarks and Future Work

We have revisited the state of the art of sparse matrices' storage formats and advanced in applying reordering techniques to improve hybrid formats. Specifically, we developed evolutionary algorithms that follow different optimization criteria. The first effort, using the minimization of the bandwidth as the optimization criteria, reaffirms that RCM is a high-quality heuristic for this purpose, although on some occasions, our algorithm offers slightly better results. In the second study, where the fitness function was adjusted to minimize the number of non-empty diagonals, our proposal outperforms both the original pattern and the RCM heuristic. Finally, the idea of maximizing the number of nonzero coefficients in a restricted number of diagonals (in our work 2% of the matrix dimension) allows reducing the storage demands of the studied hybrid sparse format notoriously.

As future lines of work, we identify several interesting ideas:

- Extend the evaluated data set. This is important to arrive at more accurate conclusions.
- Include other criteria for the optimization. In particular, exploring other thresholds and manage criteria adaptively.
- Develop a high-performance library to handle different hybrid sparse storage formats.

References

1. Umbarkar, A.J., Sheth, P.D.: Crossover operators in genetic algorithms: a review. ICTACT J. Soft Comput. **06**(01), 1083–1092 (2015)
2. Anzt, H., Tomov, S., Dongarra, J.: Implementing a sparse matrix vector product for the SELL-C/SELL-C-σ formats on Nvidia GPUs (2014)
3. Barreto, J.A., de Oliveira, S.L.G.: A systematic review of heuristics for profile reduction of symmetric matrices. In: Proceedings of the International Conference on Computational Science, ICCS 2015, Reykjavík, Iceland. Procedia Computer Science, vol. 51, pp. 221–230. Elsevier (2015)
4. Belgin, M., Back, G., Ribbens, C.J.: Applicability of pattern-based sparse matrix representation for real applications. Procedia Comput. Sci. **1**(1), 203–211 (2010)
5. Chagas, G.O., de Oliveira, S.L.G.: Metaheuristic-based heuristics for symmetric-matrix bandwidth reduction: a systematic review. In: Proceedings of the International Conference on Computational Science, ICCS 2015, Reykjavík, Iceland, vol. 51, pp. 211–220. Elsevier (2015)
6. Choi, J.W., Singh, A., Vuduc, R.: Model-driven autotuning of sparse matrix-vector multiply on GPUs. ACM SIGPLAN Not. **45**(5), 115–126 (2010)

7. Cuthill, E., McKee, J.: Reducing the bandwidth of sparse symmetric matrices. In: Proceedings of 1969 24 National Conference, pp. 157–172. ACM Press (1969)
8. Davis, T.: Suitesparse matrix collection web page. https://people.engr.tamu.edu/davis/research.html. Accessed 14 Feb 2020
9. de Oliveira, S.L.G., Silva, L.M.: An ant colony hyperheuristic approach for matrix bandwidth reduction. Appl. Soft Comput. **94**, 106434 (2020)
10. de Oliveira, S.L.G., Bernardes, J.A.B., Chagas, G.O.: An evaluation of reordering algorithms to reduce the computational cost of the incomplete Cholesky-conjugate gradient method. Comput. Appl. Math. **37**(3), 7 (2018)
11. Guo, D., Gropp, W., Olson, L.N.: A hybrid format for better performance of sparse matrix-vector multiplication on a GPU. Int. J. High Perform. Comput. Appl. **30**, 103–120 (2016)
12. Jamour, F.T., Abdelaziz, I., Kalnis, P.: A demonstration of magiq: matrix algebra approach for solving RDF graph queries. Proc. VLDB Endow. **11**(12), 1978–1981 (2018)
13. Kepner, J., Gilbert, J.: Graph Algorithms in the Language of Linear Algebra. Society for Industrial and Applied Mathematics, USA (2011)
14. Koohestani, B., Poli, R.: A genetic programming approach to the matrix bandwidth-minimization problem. In: Schaefer, R., Cotta, C., Kołodziej, J., Rudolph, G. (eds.) PPSN 2010. LNCS, vol. 6239, pp. 482–491. Springer, Heidelberg (2010). https://doi.org/10.1007/978-3-642-15871-1_49
15. Kreutzer, M., Hager, G., Wellein, G., Fehske, H., Bishop, A.R.: A unified sparse matrix data format for modern processors with wide SIMD units. arXiv, abs/1307.6209 (2013)
16. Mironowicz, P., Dziekonski, A., Mrozowski, M.: A task-scheduling approach for efficient sparse symmetric matrix-vector multiplication on a GPU. SIAM J. Sci. Comput. **37**(6), C643–C666 (2015)
17. Monakov, A., Lokhmotov, A., Avetisyan, A.: Automatically tuning sparse matrix-vector multiplication for GPU architectures. In: Patt, Y.N., Foglia, P., Duesterwald, E., Faraboschi, P., Martorell, X. (eds.) HiPEAC 2010. LNCS, vol. 5952, pp. 111–125. Springer, Heidelberg (2010). https://doi.org/10.1007/978-3-642-11515-8_10
18. Papadimitriou, C.H.: The $\mathcal{NP}$-completeness of the bandwidth minimization problem. Computing **16**(3), 263–270 (1976)
19. Pichel, J.C., Singh, D.E., Carretero, J.: Reordering algorithms for increasing locality on multicore processors. In: 2008 10th IEEE International Conference on High Performance Computing and Communications, pp. 123–130 (2008)
20. Pichel, J.C., Rivera, F.F., Fernndez, M., Rodrguez, A.: Optimization of sparse matrixvector multiplication using reordering techniques on GPUs. Microprocess. Microsyst. **36**(2), 65–77 (2012)
21. Pinar, A., Heath, M.T.: Improving performance of sparse matrix-vector multiplication. In: Proceedings of the 1999 ACM/IEEE Conference on Supercomputing, SC 1999, p. 30es. ACM, New York (1999)
22. Pop, P., Matei, O., Calin-Adrian, C.: Reducing the bandwidth of a sparse matrix with a genetic algorithm. Optimization **63**, 12 (2014)
23. Silva, P.H.G., Brandão, D.N., Morais, I.S., de Oliveira, S.L.G.: A biased random-key genetic algorithm for bandwidth reduction. In: Gervasi, O., et al. (eds.) ICCSA 2020. LNCS, vol. 12249, pp. 312–321. Springer, Cham (2020). https://doi.org/10.1007/978-3-030-58799-4_23

24. Sloan, S.W.: An algorithm for profile and wavefront reduction of sparse matrices. Int. J. Numer. Meth. Eng. **23**(2), 239–251 (1986)
25. Xu, S., Lin, H.X., Xue, W.: Sparse matrix-vector multiplication optimizations based on matrix bandwidth reduction using Nvidia CUDA. In: 2010 Ninth International Symposium on Distributed Computing and Applications to Business, Engineering and Science, pp. 609–614 (2010)

Modelling Network Throughput of Large-Scale Scientific Data Transfers

Joaquin Bogado[1]([✉]), Mario Lassnig[2], Fernando Monticelli[3], and Javier Díaz[1]

[1] LINTI, Facultad de Informática, UNLP, IFLP, UNLP, CONICET,
La Plata, Argentina
jbogado@linti.unlp.edu.ar
[2] European Organization for Nuclear Research (CERN), Geneva, Switzerland
Mario.Lassnig@cern.ch
[3] IFLP, UNLP, CONICET, La Plata, Argentina
Fernando.Monticelli@cern.ch

Abstract. Rucio is an open-source software framework that provides scientific collaborations with the functionality to organize, manage, and access their data at scale. The data can be distributed across heterogeneous data centers at widely distributed locations [1]. Since its commissioning in 2014, Rucio has become the de-facto standard for scientific data management, even outside CERN community [6]. The rich amount of data gathered about the transfers by Rucio presents a unique opportunity to better understand the complex mechanisms involved in file transfers across the Worldwide LHC Computing Grid (WLCG). This work focuses on the study of a recently published dataset [4] to reconstruct the lifetime of transfers and reveals important information that can be used to predict the Time To Complete (TTC) of transfers across the WLCG.

Keywords: Data transfer simulation · Distributed computing modelling · Performance metrics

1 Introduction

Rucio is the scientific data management system of the ATLAS Experiment, one of several experiments installed around the Large Hadron Collider (LHC) at CERN. Rucio works as a file catalog that tracks data placement and movement across the Worldwide LHC Computing Grid (WLCG). The size of the files, number of accesses are stored in the system, creation, submission, starting, and ending timestamps of the requests are stored in Rucio Database, both to comply with data retention policy and with monitoring purposes. The ATLAS Rucio instance processed file transfer requests in the order of 25 per second during July 2019, totalling more than 67 million transfer requests. This number does not include the deletion requests, which are also processed by Rucio.

Supported by CONICET - IFLP - CERN - LINTI.

There are ongoing efforts in order to model data transfers since the commissioning of Rucio in 2014. The work cited in [7] focuses on Transfers Time To Complete (TTC) predictions. The work cited in [3] focuses on the prediction of the length of the queues of the system, with emphasis on the importance of network throughput. The most relevant related work is [2]. There, the authors focuses on the prediction of the network throughput. However, in order to get a prediction, the authors use data that is not available in Rucio at real time, and thus, the methods explained are not applicable in the scenario described in this work.

The ability to predict the ending time of a transfer after its creation allows to make scheduling decisions early in the lifetime of the transfer or group of transfers, called rules. We call this to times *Transfers TTC* and *Rules TTC*. Better scheduling techniques will likely lead to network and storage optimization.

Rucio stores 4 time stamps related to transfer requests states. Creation time, submission to transfer tool time, network starting time, and ending time. These data allow us to reconstruct the lifetime of each transfer processed by the system in a detailed way, at a time resolution of seconds. Rucio also stores the rule id of the transfer, associated to groups of transfers that belongs to the same dataset. This should allow us to group the transfers associated to a rule, and to reconstruct the rule life time.

Rucio handles transfers between sites, but also handles the deletion requests in order to comply with the data retention policy. Both transfers and deletions requests are stored in the REQUESTS and REQUESTS_HISTORY tables: the REQUESTS table stores the current requests with no final state while the REQUESTS_HISTORY table is the archive of finished requests that will not be updated anymore, i.e., the requests in final state. Deletions requests do not directly affect Rucio Storage Elements (RSEs) [1] transfer performance and can be ignored. Only transfers requests were took into account for this work.

Rucio doesn't do file transfers. Instead, it delegates the actual transfer of files between WLCG endpoints to the several instances of the File Transfers System FTS [5] transfer tool. The instance selected to do the transfers of the files depends on the destination of the file transfer request. These instances operate at the WLCG level and serve transfers from several Virtual Organizations (VOs) and not only ATLAS specific transfers. The Rucio database does not contain information about the transfer tool other than which FTS instance that is used for each transfer request. Information about FTS queues state, scheduling and retries, number of nodes, and configuration are hidden from Rucio. Transfers in an FTS server from other Virtual Organizations (VOs) are also hidden from Rucio.

The main hypothesis is that the load in FTS queues has a noticeable impact on the difference of the submission time and starting time of a transfer. The more transfers are queued at FTS the more time will elapse between the submission time and starting time of a transfer. Ergo, a model that can predict the Network Time of a transfer with 100% of accuracy will not necessarily predict accurately the Transfer TTC, as the Network Time represents a small fraction of the total time.

The studied dataset has been made publicly available in [4].

We present a novel model that can predict the rate of a transfer based on the transfer size. We use the Fraction of Good Predictions (FoGP) metric to evaluate this model as a predictor of the Transfers TTC and Rules TTC.

2 A Metric to Compare Accuracy Among Models

The metric selected to compare models in this work is described in [8] (p. 16) as percentage of predictions with less than X percent Relative Error. We call this metric Fraction of Good Predictions ($FoGP$), expressed as a number between 0 and 1, in which X is the threshold of relative error below of which a prediction is considered good.

Formally, with the trivial function g defined in Eq. 1, $FoGP$ is defined as in Eq. 2.

$$g(y_i, \hat{y}_i, \tau) = \begin{cases} 1 & \text{if } RE(y_i, \hat{y}_i) \leq \tau; \\ 0 & \text{else.} \end{cases} \tag{1}$$

$$FoGP(y, \hat{y}, \tau) = \frac{1}{n} \sum_{i=0}^{n-1} g(y_i, \hat{y}_i, \tau) \tag{2}$$

As an example, assume that certain models made a prediction for y. We calculate the $FoGP$ with threshold 0.05 and we obtain the 0.5 as results. Formally, that can be expressed as $FoGP(y, \hat{y}, 0.05) = 0.5$. This means that 50% of the predictions in $\hat{y}$ are less than 5% in distance from it their real values.

This metric presents several important properties. First is easy to understand and interpret. Second, it is robust to outliers both in y as in $\hat{y}$. Third, is robust to the scale of both y and $\hat{y}$. And fourth, unlike other metrics like Mean Absolute Error or Mean Squared Error, allows to compare very different models and predictions over a wide range of values with respect to the scale in absolute terms.

3 A Model for the Network

The transfers dataset cited in [4] includes data at the individual file transfer request level. Four timestamps are important to reconstruct the lifetime of a request, namely created, submitted, started, and ended. From these timestamps, three states in the transfer lifetime can be distinguished. From the point where the transfer request is created until it is submitted to the FTS transfer tool, the request is under Rucio's responsibility. That means one of Rucio's daemons is responsible to submit transfer requests to FTS, continuously observe their status, and update the Rucio database upon state changes. These submissions can be delayed at Rucio's discretion, i.e., when a certain number of transfers have been already submitted to a particular FTS server, to avoid over-loading it. Thus, the difference between submitted and created timestamps is known as Rucio Time or *RTIME*.

After the request is submitted to FTS, but before the actual transfer starts, the transfer request is under FTS' responsibility. FTS queues the requests, sorts them, and processes them per link. A request transfer could be delayed in FTS queues only at FTS Optimizer discretion. The FTS Optimizer is an algorithm that aims to increase network usage between links, by managing the number of concurrent transfers a link can handle based on transfer failures on that link. If a link presents a failure, the Optimizer reduces the number of concurrent transfers and vice versa. The difference between the started timestamp and submitted timestamp is known as FTS Queue Time, or *QTIME*.

Once FTS starts processing the transfer request, the actual transfer of the file begins. The difference between ended and started timestamps is known as Network Time or *NTIME*. During this period the transfer will be using the network resources. The larger the file the longer the Network Time will be, and the wider the link the faster transfers for files of the same size will be. Rucio knows the created and submitted timestamps almost instantly after the events have happen. The started and ended timestamps are known to Rucio after FTS report it, that is, some seconds after the completion of the transfer.

Among with the four timestamps already mentioned, the transfers dataset contains the sizes of the files requested to be transferred, and the links affected by the transfers.

Network information like topology and link bandwidth are hidden to Rucio, and thus, not included in the analyzed dataset [4]. The links are known to be heterogeneous. While the links between some of the tier-1 sites are dedicated 10 Gbps, this is not the situation for tier-2 sites and even for some small tier-1 sites.

The *rate* of a transfer is the amount of bytes completed or transferred in a given amount of time. This rate can be approximated using Eq. 3. The size in bytes of a transfer is divided by the Network Time, which gives the mean rate of the transfer in bytes per second. First, this rate cannot be calculated before the transfer in question ends, and second, this in an approximation of the mean rate of the transfer.

No information about the instantaneous rate of a transfer is stored in the Rucio database. Thus it is not possible to know the real rate of a transfer at a given time. Moreover, from Rucio's database point of view, this rate can only be computed after the transfer ends, because the starting and ending timestamps are only know once the transfer request has finished.

$$xfer_{rate} = \frac{xfer_{size}}{xfer_{ended} - xfer_{started}} \tag{3}$$

The mean rate of the transfers should remain constant for a given link, as the rate a transfer progresses depends on the link throughput and link throughput is constant. If all the transfers for a link during a period of time are considered and the for each transfer, the rate is calculated as in 3, the histogram should have a normal distribution with a clear mean value. Figure 1 shows this is not the case. This could happen due to several reasons. First, a particular transfer usually is sharing the link with other transfers. Moreover, this number is not constant during the Network Time, as other transfer can be submitted or end during this period. Second, if a file is big enough, the rate will be I/O bound, as network bandwidth is usually higher than the read/write bandwidth of the storage. Third, if these files are read/written from different storage pools it is easy to saturate even wide links, e.g., if each pool averages 80–100 MiB/s, then between 9 and 11 transfers can saturate a 10 Gbps link. If that is the case, again the mean rate should converge to a constant. As this does not happen accordingly to Fig. 1, another possible explanation is that the link bandwidth is not being fully utilized.

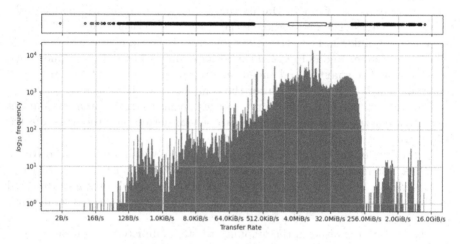

Fig. 1. Rate of the transfers according to Eq. 3 for the transfers of the link BNL-ATLAS_AGLT2, for all the transfers in the dataset [4]. The mean transfer rate is 30.26 MiB/s. The rate distribution is not normally distributed.

A relation between the size of the transfers and the rate was discovered during the research and is shown in Fig. 2. The Figure shows the rate of a transfer as a function of its size, with log_2log_2 scale, for the transfer requests in the link AGLT2_BNL-ATLAS, which represents the network between two large data centres in the US. Two characteristics can be distinguished here. For transfers with size less than 256 MiB the rate is directly proportional to the size of the transfer. For transfers bigger than 256 MiB the rate does not increase proportionally to the size of the transfer. Similar behaviour has been seen on most of the links with enough statistics.

If the rate is a function of the transfer size then it is not linear for all the sizes. For some file sizes the transfers are bound by the storage throughput. Also, the transfers suffer a delay product of the time it took to establish the connection

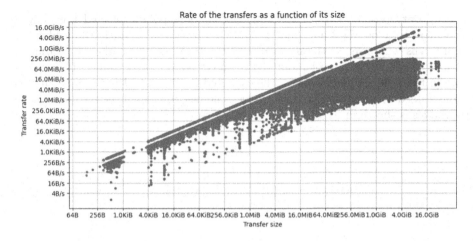

Fig. 2. The rate of the transfers as a function of its size for the same set of transfers in Fig. 1.

between the source and destination site. This should be less than few seconds but could be not negligible, especially for short transfers.

If this is the case, it is possible to express the rate of a transfer as a function of its size as in Eq. 4. The mean rate of a transfer $rate_{xfer}$ can be approximated as the size of the transfer $size_{xfer}$ divided by the time the transfer needs to finish. This time can be expressed in seconds, as the size of the transfer divided by the $rate$ that depend on the size, plus an *overhead*. All this should be bound or be less than some limit at which the file can be read from or be written to the storage. Therefore, the $rate$, the *overhead*, and the $diskrw\_limit$ are unknowns. This equation has infinite solutions for a single transfer. However, for a set of transfer of a given link it is possible to approximate a solution using ordinary least squares method. Moreover, some of the algorithms used to find the solution can diverge and find no solutions at all or find several solutions for the same set of data if initial conditions are randomized.

$$rate_{xfer} = \frac{size_{xfer}}{\left(\frac{size_{xfer}}{rate}\right) + overhead)} < diskrw\_limit \tag{4}$$

The least squares fit needs to be done for transfers of the same link.

For all the transfers from BNL-ATLAS to AGLT2, i.e. link `955b9f5678222e4` in dataset [4], transfers were separated in training and testing datasets. The training dataset contains all the transfers created between June, 8th 2019 and July, 4th 2019. The testing dataset contains all the transfers created between July, 11th 2019 and July 29th 2019. The training dataset contains 121680 transfers and the testing dataset 76093 transfers. The results for 300 different solutions of $rate$, *overhead*, and $disk\_limit$ were found. Each solution was found by choosing at random 500 points in the size/rate plane from the training set, and by solving the least squares for Eq. 4 using `least_squares` function from the `scipy.optimize` package. The number of random points selected was proven sufficient to allow the least squares algorithm to converge. Initial values for the unknowns where set to the mean rate of the training set for the *rate* variable, 1 for the *overhead* variable, and 100 to the *diskrw_limit* variable. This values are in the order of magnitude of the expected results. The least squares fit was constrained to allow only positive values. The distribution of the results for each variables is shown in Fig. 3.

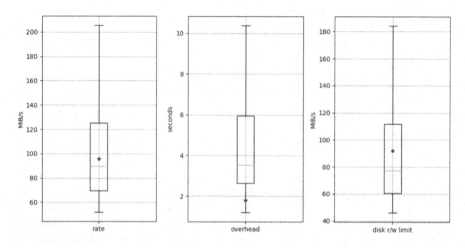

Fig. 3. Distribution of the results for multiple fits of each variable. Ranges of the solutions are (51.79 MiB/s, 1670.88 MiB/s) for the rate, (1.19 s, 17.00 s) for the overhead, and (46.02 MiB/s, 299.14 MiB/s) for the storage read/write limit. The results for the unknowns which predict best the training set are 95.72 MiB/s for the rate, 1.81 s for the overhead, and 92.04 MiB/s for the storage bandwidth limit

In order to determine which set of results is able to make the best predictions of the Network Time based on the size of the transfer, the $FoGP(y, \hat{y}, \tau = 0.1)$ was calculated for each set of results. In this case, y is the observed Network Time for the transfers in the training set, and $\hat{y}$ is the predicted Network Time, obtained after computing $\frac{size_{xfer}}{rate_{xfer}}$, where the $rate_{xfer}$ is approximated using Eq. 4, replacing the variables for a particular set of results. Blue asterisks in Fig. 3 show the set of results that obtains the best FoGP, 95.72 MiB/s for *rate*, 1.81 s for *overhead*, and 92.04 MiB/s for *diskrw_limit*. Using these values, the $FoGP(y, \hat{y}, \tau = 0.1) = 0.3024$ means that 30.24% of the Network Time predictions have less than 10% relative error. If the same analysis is done using the observed rate instead of the Network Time, then the same set of results is returned as best but the FoGP metric is around 1% lower. This set of results were used to predict the Network Time for the transfers in the testing dataset, obtaining a $FoGP(y, \hat{y}, \tau = 0.1) = 0.2838$.

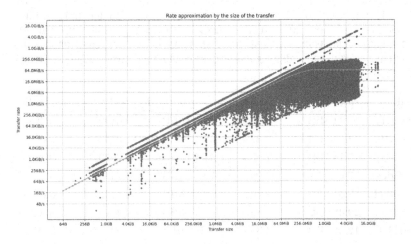

Fig. 4. Rate approximation using the size of the transfer as input. In blue dots, the sizes and rates of the transfers in the test dataset. In orange, the approximation of the rate for a given size, replacing *rate, overhead*, and *diskrw_limit* in Eq. 4 for the best set of results according to the FoGP criteria ($rate = 95.72$ MiB/s, $overhead = 1.81$ s, $diskrw\_limit = 92.04$ MiB/s) (Color figure online)

Figure 4 shows the observed size and rate of each transfer in the test dataset. The orange dots are the approximated rate for a given size using the best set of results following the FoGP criteria to replace the values in Eq. 4.

4 Network Time as Transfer TTC and Rule TTC Estimator

As the ultimate goal is to predict the Transfer TTC and Rule TTC, this section studies the possibility to use the Network Time of the transfer as a predictor. First, the observed Network Time was used to predict the Transfer TTC in order to study the properties of the estimator. For each transfer request for the 10 most popular links, the $FoGP(y, t_{NT}, \tau = 0.1)$ was computed, being y the Transfer TTC, the total time of the transfer request need to finished since its creation until it finishes, and t_{NT} the observed Network Time. The Transfer TTC can be obtained by subtracting the ending timestamp from the creation timestamp, but also can be obtained trough the sum of Rucio Time, FTS Queue Time, and Network Time. Thus, if the Network Time is an important fraction of the Transfer TTC, the $FoGP(y, t_{NT}, \tau = 0.1)$ should be high. However the numbers obtained for the 10 more popular links and summarized in Table 2 show that the Network Time contribution to the Transfer TTC seems small. Figure 6 shows the distribution of these times against each other for the 9 more popular

Table 1. Summary of the results for the 10 most popular links. Link hashes correspond to `CERN-PROD-->TRIUMF-LCG2`, `IFIC-LCG2-->SMU_HPC`, `BNL-ATLAS-->TRIUMF-LCG2`, `CERN-PROD-->IN2P3-CC`, `CERN-PROD-->INFN-T1`, `CERN-PROD-->NDGF-T1`, `BNL-ATLAS-->CERN-PROD`, `CERN-PROD-->CERN-PROD`, `UNI-BONN-->wuppertalprod`, and `CERN-PROD-->BNL-ATLAS`.

Link	rate	overhead	diskrw_limit	FoGP (train)	FoGP (test)
55ada41..	16.11 MiB/s	8.25 s	12.92 MiB/s	0.6479	0.4986
69fda49..	4486.83 MiB/s	2.27 s	1281.95 MiB/s	0.0760	0.0064
ab50c34..	15.74 MiB/s	7.60 s	11.89 MiB/s	0.6970	0.3853
5d0adae..	579.06 MiB/s	1.09 s	21.40 MiB/s	0.3408	0.3278
7b65b5d..	59.91 MiB/s	2.83 s	83.78 MiB/s	0.1342	0.0472
9b06f74..	29.48 MiB/s	1.83 s	15.78 MiB/s	0.2515	0.0552
38043af..	12.55 MiB/s	4.35 s	7.70 MiB/s	0.2050	0.0989
0a88060..	196.29 MiB/s	4.00 s	71.39 MiB/s	0.1445	0.0241
c64d4d3..	53598.56 MiB/s	1.01 s	4042.04 MiB/s	0.8519	0.0000
6343052..	25.42 MiB/s	2.78 s	24.05 MiB/s	0.3767	0.3463

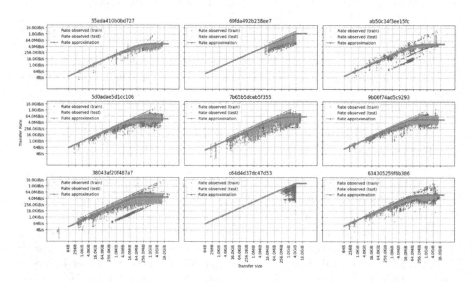

Fig. 5. Rate/Size of the transfers for the most popular links. `CERN-PROD→CERN-PROD` (0a880607b497131) link was excluded. `UNI-BONN→wuppertalprod` (c64d4d37dc47d53) link lacks statistics in test dataset which explains 0.0 FoGP on Table 1.

links. Here it is possible to see how the Network Time is small with respect to the Rucio time or the FTS queue time, and with respect to the Transfer TTC in general. The FTS Queue Times have a distribution with the median indicated with the orange line, and are generally far from the mean value indicated with a green triangle, meaning the distributions are heavy tailed.

Table 2. Summary of the $FoGP(y, t_{NT}, \tau = 0.1)$, which is the percentage of predictions with less than 10% relative error, using the observed Network Time as predictor of y. The variables correspond to y the Transfer TTC, $y\prime$ the Rucio time plus the Network Time (RTIME + NTIME), and $y\prime\prime$ the FTS queue time plus the Network Time (QTIME + NTIME). Link hashes correspond to CERN-PROD→TRIUMF-LCG2, IFIC-LCG2→SMU_HPC, BNL-ATLAS→TRIUMF-LCG2, CERN-PROD→IN2P3-CC, CERN-PROD→INFN-T1, CERN-PROD→NDGF-T1, BNL-ATLAS→CERN-PROD, CERN-PROD→CERN-PROD, UNI-BONN→wuppertalprod, and CERN-PROD→BNL-ATLAS

Link	y	$y\prime$	$y\prime\prime$
55ada410b0bd727	0.0151	0.0257	0.2751
69fda492b238ee7	0.0000	0.0000	0.0037
ab50c34f3ee15fc	0.0230	0.0393	0.1651
5d0adae5d1cc106	0.0078	0.0283	0.1401
7b65b5dceb5f355	0.0088	0.0199	0.0940
9b06f74ad5c9293	0.0074	0.0242	0.0806
38043af20f487a7	0.0468	0.0768	0.1497
0a880607b497131	0.0025	0.0135	0.0389
c64d4d37dc47d53	0.0000	0.0000	0.0003
634305259f6b386	0.0072	0.0131	0.2322

In the case of Rules TTC the same analysis was made. The Network Time approximation using polynomial fitting of Eq. 4 cannot be applied directly as not always all the transfers in a rule use the network of the same link. However, the observed Network Time can be computed for historical rules and this observed time can be used to predict the same rules in order to check if this is a good predictor for the Rule TTC. The Rule Network Time r_{NT} is defined as the difference between the maximum ending timestamp and the minimum starting timestamp of all those transfers with the same rule_id, that is all the transfer of the rule.

This definition of rule Network Time could not represent the actual time that the transfers of a rule are using the network. Imagine the case of a rule with two transfer requests. Both transfers are submitted to FTS at the same time but for some reason, the first starts but the second does not. If the first transfer ends before the second transfer starts, then the Network Time defined this way will overestimate the real Network Time. There will be gaps in time when the rule is not using the network, because transfers are queued in FTS, that will be computed as Network Time.

Figure 7 shows the FoGP measured for different τ thresholds, in which the observed Network Time of the rule is used to predict the Rule TTC for all the rules in the dataset. The results for $\tau = 0.1$ is 0.2128, meaning the 21.28% of the predictions have less than 10% relative error.

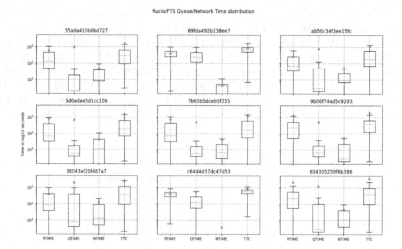

Fig. 6. Rucio/FTS Queue/Network Time/Transfer TTC distribution for 9 more popular links. `CERN-PROD→CERN-PROD` link was excluded. `UNI-BONN→wuppertalprod` (c64d4d37dc47d53) link presents an abnormal population of transfers with Network Time of 1 s for 69% of all the transfers sampled. Reasons for this behaviour is unknown.

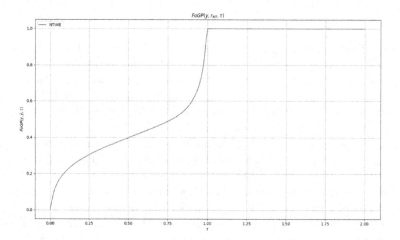

Fig. 7. FoGP for several τ thresholds, when the r_{NT} estimator is used to predict the Rule TTC y, for all the rules in the dataset [4].

5   Conclusions and Future Work

The results for the best *rate, overhead* and *diskrw_limit* vary for every link. For some, the amount of overhead seems to be excessive. This could be due to lack of statistics in some size ranges or for other unknown reasons. If the network throughput is effectively constant, then the transfer rate will be dependent on the history of the active transfers during the Network Time. That is, the transfer will share the link, and thus the throughput, with several transfers that will be done in parallel. Moreover, the number of active transfers will not be constant, as during the Network Time of one transfer, some other transfers can start and finish. From the Rucio database it is possible to reconstruct the history of active transfers for finished transfers. Through the study of Rucio data it is possible to check if the link network throughput converges to a value. But in order to apply any method to real time, FTS or other transfer tool needs to provide the timestamp the transfers request is submitted to the network at the moment of the submission, instead of at the ending transfer time in order to know the real number of active transfers in the network per link in real time.

On the other hand, the usage of the Network Time as predictor of Transfer TTC or Rule TTC is limited, as demonstrated in Sect. 4. Even if a model to predict the Network Time with 100% of accuracy exist, then using this value will allow to predict the Rule TTC only around 21% of the time within 10% or less relative error.

Future models should include other information available like queue lengths in Rucio or FTS, aggregated per link. The dataset used for this work allows for the reconstruction of the state of the system in great detail and further study of the data will help us to better comprehends its predictive power.

References

1. Barisits, M., et al.: Rucio - scientific data management, February 2019. arXiv e-prints. arXiv:1902.09857. https://arxiv.org/abs/1902.09857
2. Begy, V., Barisits, M., Lassnig, M., Schikuta, E.: Forecasting network throughput of remote data access in computing grids. J. Comput. Sci. **44**, 101158 (2020). https://doi.org/10.1016/j.jocs.2020.101158. http://www.sciencedirect.com/science/article/pii/S1877750320304592
3. Bogado, J., Monticelli, F., Diaz, J., Lassnig, M., Vukotic, I.: Modelling high-energy physics data transfers. In: 2018 IEEE 14th International Conference on e-Science (e-Science), pp. 334–335 (2018). https://doi.org/10.1109/eScience.2018.00081
4. Bogado, J., Lassnig, M., Monticelli, F., Díaz, J., Beermann, T.: Atlas rucio transfers dataset. Zenodo, December 2020. https://doi.org/10.5281/zenodo.4320937
5. Kiryanov, A., Álvarez Ayllón, A., Salichos, M., Keeble, O.: FTS3 - a file transfer service for grids, HPCs and clouds. In: International Symposium on Grids and Clouds 2015, p. 028, March 2016. https://doi.org/10.22323/1.239.0028
6. Lassnig, M., et al.: Rucio beyond ATLAS: experiences from Belle II, CMS, DUNE, EISCAT3D, LIGO/VIRGO, SKA, XENON. Technical report, ATL-SOFT-PROC-2020-017, CERN, Geneva, March 2020. https://doi.org/10.1051/epjconf/202024511006. https://cds.cern.ch/record/2711755
7. Lassnig, M., Toler, W., Vamosi, R., Bogado, J.: Machine learning of network metrics in atlas distributed data management. J. Phys. Conf. Ser. **898**, 062009 (2017). https://doi.org/10.1088/1742-6596/898/6/062009
8. Zheng, A.: Evaluating Machine Learning Models. O'Reilly Media, Inc., Sebastopol (2015)

Web and Mobile Computing

LOBD: Linked Data Dashboard
for Marine Biodiversity

Marcos Zárate[1,2]([✉])[iD] and Carlos Buckle[2][iD]

[1] Centre for the Study of Marine Systems, Patagonian National Research Centre
(CESIMAR-CENPAT-CONICET), Puerto Madryn, Argentina
zarate@cenpat-conicet.gob.ar
[2] Laboratorio de Investigaciones en Informática (LINVI) - Facultad de Ingeniería,
Universidad Nacional de la Patagonia San Juan Bosco (UNPSJB),
Puerto Madryn, Argentina
cbuckle@unpata.edu.ar

Abstract. In this paper we describe new features and data visualization
components of *Linked Open Biodiversity Data* (*LOBD*), an application
that uses Linked Data to link information extracted from Global Biodiversity Information Facility (GBIF) with different linked open datasets
such as *Wikidata, NCBI Taxonomy* and *OpenCitation*, to visually present
the information as a scientific dashboard. The application allows to complement information about marine Biodiversity with information not initially available. To demonstrate this, a use case is presented.

Keywords: Linked data · Wikidata · Semantic interoperability ·
Marine biodiversity

1 Introduction

Researchers accumulate mountains of data every year, and the only way to effectively manage and analyze it is with scalable cloud computing systems and big
data analytics applications [1]. By applying computer techniques to Biodiversity
data (taxonomic, biogeographic and ecological information), scientists can generate detailed biological models that allow them to better forecast the outcome of
events such as the spread of invasive species or the impact of climate change. Biodiversity is one of the areas with greatest volume and variety of historical data.
Research in big data analysis is fostering a new profile of a biologist scientist,
who from his desk, generates findings and produces new knowledge from other
people's data [2]. To make this a reality, some computer scientist researchers
are working to solve the bottleneck presented by cloud storage and processing.
Complementary, another branch of science works on how to integrate the vast
diversity and heterogeneity of data, under common vocabularies and concepts,
aiming to represent a body of common knowledge.

One of the most prominent technologies that attracted interest from the
scientific community, not only in Biodiversity but also in various areas is Linked

© Springer Nature Switzerland AG 2021
M. Naiouf et al. (Eds.): JCC-BD&ET 2021, CCIS 1444, pp. 151–164, 2021.
https://doi.org/10.1007/978-3-030-84825-5_11

Data [3], a web-based technology that enables describe, model, store, publish, and interconnect data from different sources in a uniform way across the Internet. In essence, LD has two elements: Uniform Resource Identifiers (URIs) and the use of controlled vocabularies. URIs make data accessible and reusable for a global audience on the Internet, and controlled vocabularies help add the correct semantics, metadata, and provenance information to this data. Individuals and organizations can better understand what their data means, how it can be reused, and what meaningful new connections can be made with other datasets. With LD, different datasets become more compatible, more interoperable, and easily extensible across different environments and domains. Working in this way, data silo problems [4] can be solved by removing semantic and technical barriers to facilitate data sharing and exchange [5,6].

In recent years, the community working on Biodiversity informatics has made great efforts creating specific vocabularies such as Darwin Core (DwC) [7], and publishing mechanisms such as Integrated Publishing Toolkit (IPT) [8]. However, datasets published in this kind of system are stored in isolated silos, which limits its analysis in an integrated way with context information. Hence, coordinating, integrating, and performing effective use of the vast amount of environmental data, which are generated from many different providers and across research domains, remain challenging [9].

These considerations provide strong motivations to formulate a web application considering the semantic interoperability that may provide answers to questions such as the following: **(Q1)** *Is it possible to complement information of a particular species without relying on proprietary APIs?* **(Q2)** *How are the species distributed in a certain region?* **(Q3)** *Given a species, what is the bibliography associated with it?* **(Q4)** *How to relate occurrences of species with environmental variables within a specific region?*. Aiming to this purpose, in 2020 a prototype application was presented in [10], this application uses LD to complement information extracted and converted to Resource Description Framework (RDF) [11] from GBIF with different RDF datasets such as Wikidata [12], NCBI Taxonomy [13] and OpenCitation corpus [14] to demonstrate the benefits of publishing Biodiversity content as LD. To achieve semantic interoperability we use SPARQL query language [15], which allows us not to depend on proprietary APIs to retrieve information. After obtaining feedback from specialized users, we developed SPARQL queries which are presented in this paper, and incorporated as soon as possible into *LOBD* interface.

The remainder of this paper is organized as follows: Sect. 2 introduce the required components for data modeling and details the provenance of information. Section 3, describes the methodology used to create LD and the proposed architecture. In Sect. 4, the application is briefly described. Section 5, presents the use case, its limitations and new queries that were developed, while in Sect. 6, the related works are presented. Finally, Sect. 7 presents the conclusions.

2   Background

This section explains how the information is represented according to the domain to which it belongs. In our case, standard ontologies and vocabularies are used to guarantee reusability and interoperability. We also explain the provenance of information that were used to build the application.

2.1   Ontologies and Datasets Used

BiGe-Onto [16]: provides an ontology and RDF dataset designed for modeling Biodiversity and Marine Biogeography data. The main concept of *BiGe-Onto* is the *occurrence*. Given that the CESIMAR data are occurrences at a specific time and place, we consider *BiGe-Onto* fits the nature of our data. At the same time, it reuses different vocabularies such as DwC [7], which is the core one in *BiGe-Onto*. Its main classes are: *dwc:Occurrence*, *dwc:Event*, *dwc:Taxon* and *dwc:Organism*. Moreover, *BiGe-Onto* reuses *foaf:Person void:Dataset* and *dc:Location*, among others. To consult documentation of classes and relationships, see the link: http://www.w3id.org/cenpat-gilia/bigeonto/1.0.0.

Wikidata [12]: is the linked database of the Wikimedia Foundation. Like Wikipedia it is open to humans and machines. Initially primarily intended as a central repository of structured data for the approximately 200 language versions of Wikipedia, Wikidata currently also serves many other use cases. It is an open, Semantic Web-compatible database that anyone can edit.

NCBI Taxonomy [13]: National Center for Biotechnology Information (NCBI) database is a curated classification and nomenclature for all of the organisms in the public sequence databases. This currently represents about 10% of the described species of life on the planet. All information is LD compliant and makes its data available through a SPARQL endpoint.

OpenCitations [14]: is an independent infrastructure organization for open scholarship dedicated to the publication of open bibliographic and citation data by the use of Semantic Web technologies. It complies with the FAIR data principles [17] (data should be findable, accessible, interoperable and re-usable) and it complies with the recommendations of Initiative for Open Citations (I4OC)[1] that citation data in particular should be structured, separable, and open.

All previously described datasets are available as LD, through SPARQL endpoints. Table 1 presents the URLs to access each one.

2.2   Data Provenance

Marine Biodiversity datasets previously published in GBIF[2] belong to *Centre for the Study of Marine Systems* hosted in Puerto Madryn, Patagonia Argentina

---

[1] https://i4oc.org/.
[2] https://www.gbif.org/.

Table 1. SPARQL endpoints used by LOBD.

Dataset	URL
BiGe-Onto	http://web.cenpat-conicet.gob.ar:7200/sparql
Wikidata	https://query.wikidata.org/
OpenCitations	https://opencitations.net/sparql
NCBI Taxonomy	https://bio2rdf.org/sparql

(CESIMAR-CENPAT-CONICET)[3]. The institute is engaged in oceanographic and marine research activities, monitoring information management and data acquisition activities on different platforms. Datasets extracted from GBIF are aligned according to the model proposed in *BiGe-Onto* to become instances of different classes. Table 2 shows the Digital Object Identifiers (DOIs) associated with each dataset that was used in this paper, as well the corresponding URI in *BiGe-Onto*. To access the *BiGe-Onto* dataset, the user must authenticate with the following credentials: user: **bigeonto** pass: **bigeonto.**

Table 2. Dataset used and DOIs provided by GBIF.

BiGe-Onto URI	DOI
dwca-argentina-cenpat-fishes-v1.11	10.15468/zhifkw
dwca-arobis-sealsi-v1.3	10.15468/qcwa73
dwca-inv_nem_sacsb-v3.1	10.15468/bwgjkd
dwca-sjnem-v4.0	10.15468/mibuwi
dwca-arobis-sealsi-v1.4	10.15468/qcwa73
dwca-arobis-radiolaria-v1.5	10.15468/48bsyj
dwca-sao2009-v2.1	10.3897/zookeys.574.7222
dwca-argentina-ecocentro-whales-v1.6	10.15468/2ftsfs

3 Methods

This section presents the methodology used to develop the application following good practices for publishing LD [18]. In particular, with special emphasis on how external links are used.

3.1 Linked Data Generation and Interlinking

The LD generation was done following the methodology described in detail in [16], where the species data are modeled using the *BiGe-Onto* ontology, which

---

[3] https://cenpat.conicet.gov.ar/cesimar/.

fits adequately to the datasets coming from GBIF. Links between URIs were defined using the `owl:sameAs`[4] property to indicate that two resources represent the same thing. Figure 1, shows an example of this property that links the URI of *BiGe-Onto* with the URI of the same species in Wikidata whose identifier is http://www.wikidata.org/entity/Q215343, the ovals represent URIs and the rectangles are literals. This relationship of equality between URIs allows that through the use of federated queries [19] included in SPARQL through the `SERVICE` clause. In this way we can consult all the properties that the resource has in the Wikidata.

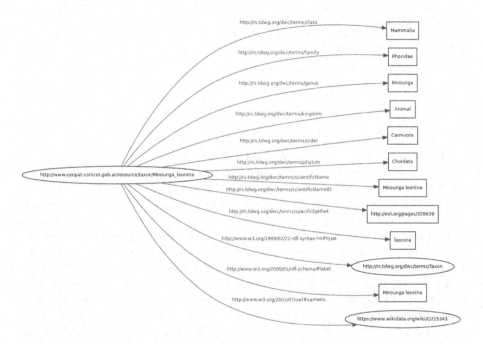

Fig. 1. URI visual representation and its links to Wikidata through `owl:sameAs` property. To access the URI content, use the link: http://www.cenpat-conicet.gob.ar/resource/taxon/Mirounga_leonina

After having defined the corresponding link, we can retrieve information that initially does not exist in our dataset. To do this, we define a set of SPARQL queries that are embedded within the dashboard. An example of this can be seen in Table 3. The SPARQL query allows consulting Wikidata endpoint (line 9), after this we must choose which properties we are interested in, in particular we are interested in knowing the state of conservation and its distribution map, among others.

---

[4] https://www.w3.org/TR/owl-ref/#sameAs-def.

Table 3. Federated query used in LOBD.

```
1 PREFIX owl: <http://www.w3.org/2002/07/owl#>
2 PREFIX wdt: <http://wikidata.org/prop/direct/>
3
4 SELECT DISTINCT ?item ?scientific_name ?common_name
5                 ?status ?rangemap ?length
6                 ?life_expectency ?height
7 WHERE {
8     <http://www.cenpat-conicet.gob.ar/resource/taxon/Mirounga_leonina> owl:sameAs ?item
9     SERVICE <https://query.wikidata.org/> {
10        ?item wdt:P225 ?scientific_name;
11              wdt:P1843 ?common_name.
12        OPTIONAL { ?item wdt:P2043 ?length. }
13        OPTIONAL { ?item wdt:P2250 ?life_expectency. }
14        OPTIONAL { ?item wdt:P2048 ?height. }
15        OPTIONAL { ?item wdt:P141 ?status.}
16        OPTIONAL { ?item wdt:P181 ?rangemap.}
17    }
18 }
```

In the same way, we can consult NCBI Taxonomy and OpenCitations using the owl:sameAs links to each one and using the URLs of each endpoint shown in Table 1. It is important to note that the links were made semi-automatically using *SILK Framework*[5]. In cases where it was not possible to generate the links automatically, the resource was searched manually in the corresponding dataset; if available, the link was created manually. For interlinking species between Wikidata and our dataset, we used *Levenshtein distance* a comparison operator that evaluates two inputs and computes the similarity based on a user-defined distance measure and a user-defined threshold. This comparator receives as input two strings wdt:P225 (scientific name in Wikidata) and dwc:scientificName. The Levenshtein distance comparator was set up with <Thresholds = "0.0" and Weight = "1">. After the execution, SILK discovered 150 links to Wikidata with an accuracy of 100% and 85 link with an accuracy between 65% and 75%. In this case, we permit only one outgoing owl:sameAs link from each resource.

3.2   Overview of the System Architecture

The system architecture of our application it is based on the classic and well known client/server model [20], where the first side (Client) performs requests that are processed by the second part (Server) to provide suitable responses (see Fig. 2). The server side was developed using Shiny [21] which is a powerful R package allowing create interactive web applications using the R programming language. Shiny applications have two components. The front-end builds the webpage that is actually shown to the user and includes layout, appearance,

---

[5] http://silkframework.org/.

and design features. In Shiny terminology, this is called the *ui*, which stands for user interface. The *ui* file contains R functions that are then translated into an HTML file. The other component is the back-end, which includes the code for producing the app's contents (e.g. functions or data import, management, and analysis). Here, we create the objects that are later shown on the front-end. In Shiny terminology this is called *server*.

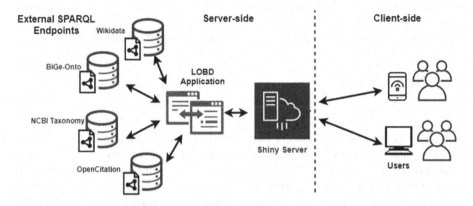

Fig. 2. Simplified system architecture of *LOBD*

4   Dashboard Development and Hosting

One crucial aspect is how to access and analyze data, and especially how to get only that part of data which is of interest for a given research question. SPARQL solves the access part and allows to query only a subset of the data.

4.1   General Structure and Components

To show the exploitation of the dataset, we developed a dashboard that allows to consult the general and specific information of an specie. To query our endpoint we use the SPARQL package for R [22] that allows to import directly results of SELECT queries into the statistical environment of R as a data frame. Next, we describe the modules that *LOBD* presents.

- **General information:** this module uses Wikidata endpoint to retrieve additional information about the selected species, including links to other databases and information about the species extracted from NCBI.
- **Bibliography:** all publications related to the species are retrieved and extracted from OpenCitation.
- **Environment:** this module allows users to plot species on a map and add layers related to marine regions as well as environmental layers (e.g., temperature, salinity, etc.). Leaflet [23] were used to set up the presentation and

Web-GIS interfaces, marine regions are obtained from Marineregions.org[6] and environmental layers are extracted from Bio-ORACLE [24].

4.2 Hosting

To host the application we decided to use the hosting service provided by *Shinyapps.io*[7] for its simplicity, security and scalability, in addition to that it does not require hardware, installation or annual purchase contract. The application runs in its own protected environment and access is always SSL encrypted. To access the application, use the link:: https://cesimar.shinyapps.io/lobd/.

5 Discussion

5.1 Case-Study

Interoperability and links among data sources would allow integration of information that is otherwise disconnected, enabling scientists to answer broader questions. In this use case, we will show how *LOBD* can be used to study a certain species and answer the questions raised in Sect. 1. In our case we will focus specially on one of the marine mammals that can be used as an oceanographic sampling platform and is known as Southern elephant seal, *Mirounga leonina (Linnaeus, 1758)*. These mammals make it possible to collect information from areas difficult to access by oceanographic vessels, with excellent temporal and spatial resolution at low cost.

Data from Wikidata: Figure 3 shows information extracted from *Bige-Onto* endpoint, in this case *Mirounga leonina* and shows how the information is complemented with data from Wikidata, which uses identifiers for each resource, in this case Q215343 represents *Mirounga leonina* identifier. It can also be seen in the column range map, the map of the distribution of the species, the conservation status, the length, life expectancy, weight and average mass columns are also retrieved if that information exists in Wikidata. In addition, you can see how in the section *Links to biodiversity databases* you can see the same species in different databases. Each one focuses on a specific domain, for example, the link to World Register of Marine Species (WoRMS)[8] (row number 27) allows to explore the taxonomic classification of the species, information that is not initially available. On the other hand, using the NCBI Taxonomy endpoint, it is possible to recover the genetic code of the species for a later analysis.

In this way, question **Q1** is answered, since it is not necessary to have any proprietary API to retrieve the information.

---

[6] https://marineregions.org/.

[7] https://www.shinyapps.io/.

[8] https://www.marinespecies.org/index.php.

Fig. 3. General information extracted from Wikidata and NCBI to complement the information on the Mirounga leonina species.

Data from OpenCitations: Complementing information about the species chosen for this study is essential, since many times there is a vast amount of bibliography on the web, this task is not trivial. To provide the bibliography associated with *Mirounga leonina*, we use links to OpenCitations to perform a federated query that retrieves the related bibliography. Figure 4 shows the screen where the bibliography is observed. It is important to note that response times can be on the order of 50 s in some cases.

In this way we show that it is possible to complement the information of the species with related bibliography. So, we fully answer the question **Q3**.

Environmental Data: Linking data on the occurrence of a species with the physical and biotic environment provides us a framework to formulate hypothesis about the ecological processes that govern the spatial and temporal patterns of biological diversity. This is useful for the management and conservation of marine ecosystems. Figure 5 shows a simple analysis where the occurrences of *Mirounga leonina* are obtained from *BiGe-Onto* (points on the map), furthermore, it can be seen that the region under study is the Exclusive Economic Zone (EEZ) of Argentina[9] and we overlap the layer contains the bathymetry (depths of the sea) to understand the relationship between locations and depths within the EEZ of

---

[9] http://marineregions.org/mrgid/8466.

Fig. 4. Bibliography related to the species, retrieved from OpenCitations endpoint.

study. Temperature and salinity layers are also available for studies involving these environmental variables.

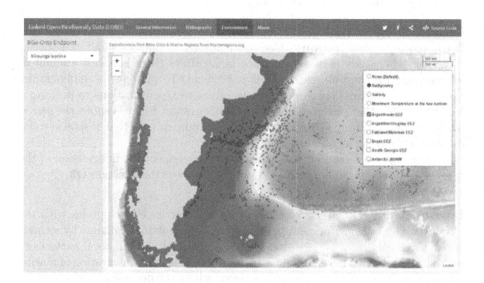

Fig. 5. Information of the species (points) together with the marine region of study and the bathymetry layer.

In this way, we fully answer questions **Q2** and **Q4**. Although in this case we partially answer question **Q1**, since the information necessary to answer **Q2** and **Q4** is not available as LD, so we need to use R libraries developed by Marineregions.org and Bio-Oracle.

5.2   Case-Study Limitations

We have presented an application that allows us to partially answer the questions raised in Sect. 1. However, there are some limitations that we will discuss below:

1. **Availability of environmental data:** Currently and as far as we understand, environmental data such as temperature, depth, salinity, etc., are not always available as LD, there is only metadata that is not useful for developing a detailed map. That is why to answer questions such as **Q2**, we need to use data sources that provide information in raster format, standard for scientists who work with geographic information systems. While exist proposals as described in [25], at present we did not perform all the necessary tests to convert our raster files to LD.
2. **Endpoints availability:** As discussed in [26], the availability of datasets is limited to the maintenance and availability of the SPARQL endpoints, so the correct operation of the application not only depends on us, also depends on third parties for proper operation.
3. **Changes in data model:** Another limitation that arises is due to the fact that in the future there may be changes in the data models that were used (for example Wikidata could decide to use another semantics to represent species) this would force to check each part of the application to ensure that that change does not affect the correct operation.

5.3   New Features of *LOBD*

We are currently working on develop SPARQL queries to answer new questions and improve the work of scientists to perform more complex analyzes. One of the most relevant efforts made was to include information related to censuses, dives and hydrographic data collected by sensors attached to *Mirounga leonina* collected during 1990 to 2017. Initially, this information was isolated in a relational database belonging to (CESIMAR-CENPAT-CONICET). The work done was based on the transformation of a relational model (MySQL database) to an RDF graph model to make it accessible through a SPARQL endpoint. The whole conversion process can be consulted in [27]. The SPARQL endpoint is available online at the following link: http://linkeddata.cenpat-conicet.gob.ar/snorql/.

Finally, new queries are summarized in Table 4 with their respective links to be tested. We hope to incorporate these queries into *LOBD* interface during 2021.

Table 4. New queries developed in LOBD.

Query	Link
Sensors associated with each Mirounga leonina	Query 1
Number of dives made by each Mirounga leonina	Query 2
Temperatures sampled	Query 3
Locations, depths and dates registered	Query 4
1990 census grouped by categories	Query 6

6   Related Work

To provide the bases for our dashboard, we conducted a literature review to find systems that manage marine Biodiversity data. In particular, we did not find a specific one of the marine domain, instead we found three systems related to general Biodiversity.

Two systems base their data model on LD principles [18], while the third does not use these principles. *OpenBiodiv Knowledge Graph* [28], presented at the annual conference of the Biodiversity Information Standards (TDWG) in 2016 its based mainly on data from Pensoft[10] and Plazi[11], this means that the coverage of this work is mainly the bibliography associated with the taxa. *Ozymandias Knowledge Graph* [29], winner of the GBIF Ebbe Nielsen Challenge 2018, its based on data from the Atlas of Living Australia (ALA)[12] and Australian Faunal Directory (AFD)[13]. This knowledge graph combines information about taxa, publications, authors of those publications along with their interrelationships. *Biologer* [30], a simple and free system designed to collect data on biological diversity of Eastern Europe. This system does not provide bibliographic information associated with species.

All projects manage taxa, persons and institutions and have practical applications. Nevertheless, only [29] and [28] make use of LD principles, for this reason we discard [30], because we consider that developing a system that does not use LD as a backend can be considered a disadvantage when it comes to interoperating and complying with the FAIR principles. However, in contrast to our approach, *Ozymandias Knowledge Graph* and *OpenBiodiv Knowledge Graph* do not provide visual components (such as maps) for studies involving species and environmental variables.

7   Conclusion

In this work we have presented latest efforts carried out in *LOBD*, a dashboard that facilitates the analysis of marine Biodiversity data for scientists who need

---

[10] https://pensoft.net/.
[11] http://plazi.org/.
[12] https://www.ala.org.au.
[13] https://biodiversity.org.au/afd/home.

to complement information about species with external sources. We recognize that there is still a long way to go in terms of publishing 100% LD compliant Biodiversity data. Nevertheless, promoting the use of LD as a tool for scientists is crucial to generate new approaches to Biodiversity informatics. From the Biodiversity informatics point of view, *LOBD* addresses many challenges that have affected interoperability between repositories and services within and across domains that are highly heterogeneous in nature. The Biology community adopted international formats and extensions that avoid the loss of complementary information. With the use of LD it is possible to keep the system distributed along several nodes, from the technical point of view, LD facilitate the realization of many of the FAIR principles, reducing human intervention. Therefore, we hope that our modest development on this paper will help advance conversations about the challenges we face in managing and using LD on Biodiversity.

Acknowledgments. This paper was supported by project *Linked Open Data Platform for Management and Visualization of Primary Data in Marine Science.* Project No. PI-1562. Financed by Secretariat of Science and Technology of the National University of Patagonia San Juan Bosco (UNPSJB).

References

1. Devictor, V., Bensaude-Vincent, B.: From ecological records to big data: the invention of global biodiversity. Hist. Philos. Life Sci. **38**(4), 1–23 (2016)
2. Marx, V.: The big challenges of big data. Nature **498**(7453), 255–260 (2013)
3. Heath, T., Bizer, C.: Linked data: evolving the web into a global data space. Synth. Lect. Semantic Web Theory Technol. **1**(1), 1–136 (2011)
4. Patel, J.: Bridging data silos using big data integration. Int. J. Database Manag. Syst. **11**, 01–06 (2019)
5. Franklin, J., Serra-Diaz, J.M., Syphard, A.D., Regan, H.M.: Big data for forecasting the impacts of global change on plant communities. Global Ecol. Biogeogr. **26**(1), 6–17 (2017)
6. Soltis, D.E., Soltis, P.S.: Mobilizing and integrating big data in studies of spatial and phylogenetic patterns of biodiversity. Plant Divers. **38**(6), 264–270 (2016)
7. Wieczorek, J., et al.: Darwin core: an evolving community-developed biodiversity data standard. PLoS ONE **7**, e29715 (2012)
8. Robertson, T., et al.: The GBIF integrated publishing toolkit: facilitating the efficient publishing of biodiversity data on the internet. PLoS ONE **9**, e102623 (2014)
9. Walls, R.L., et al.: Semantics in support of biodiversity knowledge discovery: an introduction to the biological collections ontology and related ontologies. PLoS ONE **9**(3), e89606 (2014)
10. Zárate, M., Zermoglio, P., Wieczorek, J., Plos, A., Mazzanti, R.: Linked open biodiversity data (LOBD): a semantic application for integrating biodiversity information. Biodivers. Inf. Sci. Stand. **4**, e58975 (2020)
11. RDF 1.1 concepts and abstract syntax. W3C recommendation, 25 February 2014 (2014). https://www.w3.org/TR/rdf11-concepts/. Accessed 15 Mar 2021
12. Vrandečić, D., Krötzsch, M.: Wikidata: a free collaborative knowledgebase. Commun. ACM **57**(10), 78–85 (2014)

13. Federhen, S.: The NCBI taxonomy database. Nucleic Acids Res. **40**(D1), D136–D143 (2012)
14. Peroni, S., Shotton, D.: Opencitations, an infrastructure organization for open scholarship. Quant. Sci. Stud. **1**(1), 428–444 (2020)
15. SPARQL 1.1 overview. W3C recommendation, 21 March 2013 (2013). https://www.w3.org/TR/sparql11-overview/. Accessed 16 Mar 2021
16. Zárate, M., Braun, G., Fillottrani, P.R., Delrieux, C., Lewis, M.: BiGe-Onto: an ontology-based system for managing biodiversity and biogeography data. Appl. Ontol. J. **15**, 411–437 (2020)
17. Wilkinson, M.D., et al.: The fair guiding principles for scientific data management and stewardship. Sci. Data **3**(1), 1–9 (2016)
18. Janowicz, K., Hitzler, P., Adams, B., Kolas, D., Vardeman, C., II., et al.: Five stars of linked data vocabulary use. Semantic Web **5**(3), 173–176 (2014)
19. SPARQL 1.1 federated query. W3C recommendation, 21 March 2013 (2013). https://www.w3.org/TR/2013/REC-sparql11-federated-query-20130321/. Accessed 11 Mar 2021
20. Adler, R.M.: Distributed coordination models for client/server computing. Computer **28**(4), 14–22 (1995)
21. Shiny: Web application framework for R (2021). https://cran.r-project.org/web/packages/shiny/index.html. Accessed 12 Mar 2021
22. SPARQL: SPARQL client (2013). https://cran.r-project.org/web/packages/SPARQL/index.html. Accessed 12 Mar 2021
23. Leaflet for R (2014). https://rstudio.github.io/leaflet/. Accessed 17 Mar 2021
24. Assis, J., Tyberghein, L., Bosch, S., Verbruggen, H., Serrão, E.A., De Clerck, O.: Bio-Oracle v2. 0: extending marine data layers for bioclimatic modelling. Global Ecol. Biogeogr. **27**(3), 277–284 (2018)
25. Tran, B.-H., Aussenac-Gilles, N., Comparot, C., Trojahn, C.: Semantic integration of raster data for earth observation: an RDF dataset of territorial unit versions with their land cover. ISPRS Int. J. Geo Inf. **9**(9), 503 (2020)
26. Buil-Aranda, C., Hogan, A., Umbrich, J., Vandenbussche, P.-Y.: SPARQL web-querying infrastructure: ready for action? In: Alani, H., et al. (eds.) ISWC 2013. LNCS, vol. 8219, pp. 277–293. Springer, Heidelberg (2013). https://doi.org/10.1007/978-3-642-41338-4_18
27. Zárate, M., Braun, G., Lewis, M., Fillottrani, P.: Observational/hydrographic data of the South Atlantic Ocean published as LOD. Semantic Web (2021, prepress). http://dx.doi.org/10.3233/SW-210426
28. Penev, L., et al.: OpenBiodiv: a knowledge graph for literature-extracted linked open data in biodiversity science. Publications **7**(2), 38 (2019)
29. Page, R.D.M.: Ozymandias: a biodiversity knowledge graph. PeerJ **7**, e6739 (2019)
30. Popović, M., et al.: Biologer: an open platform for collecting biodiversity data. Biodivers. Data J. **8**, e53014 (2020)

3D-Domotic: A 3D Mobile Application for Domotic Control

Sebastián Dapoto$^{(\boxtimes)}$ ⓘ, Diego Encinas ⓘ, Federico Cristina ⓘ, Cristian Iglesias, Federico Arias, Pablo Thomas ⓘ, and Patricia Pesado ⓘ

III-LIDI, Universidad Nacional de La Plata, La Plata, Buenos Aires, Argentina
{sdapoto,dencinas,fcristina,pthomas,
ppesado}@lidi.info.unlp.edu.ar

Abstract. Domotics integrates a set of systems for home or office automation in order to improve comfort, security, energy savings, communication facilities and entertainment possibilities for the user. In turn, Domotics is closely related to the most recent concept of the Internet of Things, which proposes the interconnection of everyday objects in a home or office through the Internet. In this work, a 3D mobile application called *3D-Domotic* is presented. This application allows to recreating the three-dimensional structure of a house and remotely control the electronic devices in it. These devices are located in their actual physical location, and are controlled directly on the model of the house, in a simple and completely visual way. Device status is monitored in real time, simplifying the control of the house.

Keywords: Mobile devices · 3D applications · Unity · Domotics · Smart sensors · IoT

1 Introduction

Domotics, or home automation, is the combination of information technology, electrical engineering and communications used to make homes become *smart*. Domotics allows controlling systems, devices and automations with the goal of improving the quality of life, comfort, energy savings, and security of homes. A smart or automated home is characterized by technological integration and by how technologies are able to meet constantly evolving needs [1].

A home automation system allows the control or monitoring of various household features, such as temperature, lighting, climate, curtains, electrical appliances, security systems, and so forth. In addition, every house has routine processes with repetitive habits or similar situations that can be easily automated. Illuminating sectors of a house on preset times, turning lights and AC units on and off depending on whether or not there are people in a room, turning lights or other devices on and off to simulate occupation, controlling cameras and security devices are some examples of what it is possible with a domotic system.

© Springer Nature Switzerland AG 2021
M. Naiouf et al. (Eds.): JCC-BD&ET 2021, CCIS 1444, pp. 165–176, 2021.
https://doi.org/10.1007/978-3-030-84825-5_12

Domotics focuses on two key points: the user and the technical aspect. From the user's point of view, an automated home offers a better quality of life through new technologies, allowing a reduction in household chores, improved well-being, better consumption control (energy efficiency), and other benefits. From a technological point of view, the ability of the various objects in the home to communicating with each other is available.

The Internet of Things (IoT) is a concept that refers to the digital interconnection of everyday objects with the Internet. Already in 2009, the number of electronic devices connected to the Internet exceeded the number of people connected to it [2].

The IoT constitutes a radical change in the quality of life of people within any society, offering new and greater opportunities to access data and specific services in different areas, such as education, security, healthcare, transportation, among others.

There are numerous applications for devices connected to the Internet, and these can be divided into three categories of use – consumer, business, and infrastructure. Embedded systems with limited CPU, memory and power capabilities can be connected, meaning that the IoT has potential applications in any area.

At present, a large part of the IoT devices that are created are included in most of today's household appliances, and in particular, they are intended for applications for home automation.

This work presents a 3D mobile application, called 3D-Domotic, which allows to recreate the three-dimensional structure of a house and remotely control the electronic devices it contains. The paper is organized as follows: in Sect. 2 the related works are presented, and then, the reasons that motivated this work are discussed. Section 3 details how the 3D mobile application was developed. Followed by this, Sect. 4 presents a discussion of the experiments carried out. Finally, our conclusions and future work are presented in Sect. 5.

2   Related Works

The beginnings of Domotics date back to the early 1970s, when the first prototypes of automated devices began to be installed in buildings. Commercial use did not begin until a decade later. Comprehensive communication within homes became an aspect of interest as well as a priority, and in the 1990s this type of technology was gradually adapted for use in houses. Advances in computer communication networks, Wi-Fi and the evolution of communication protocols have allowed a great variety of possibilities to be offered nowadays to create smart homes.

Some of the commercial products currently available for the automated management of a home involve the use of dedicated hardware, special keys and switches, custom panels and specific touch screens for managing and controlling home devices. Products offered by Orvibo [3], for instance, include smart panels to lighting control, HVAC, curtains and other appliances to replace traditional switches. Iddero [4], Basalte [5] and Zennio [6] offer programmable touch screens that allow creating scenes and include controls for the automation of the different rooms.

Other systems allow local or remote control of the house from a mobile application. This type of application usually includes a number of modules, menus and drop-down lists, and, by navigating through them, the desired configuration for each connected device can be selected. In general, in order to control a given electronic device, the user needs to navigate to a specific module, find the desired device in a list, select it, and finally access its configuration options. Fibaro [7], Sophia [8] and Gira [9] are some companies that offer an application with these characteristics.

There are also prototypes and research work related to domotic control through the use of mobile devices. In [10], a mobile domotic system that operates via Bluetooth is presented; in [11], a framework is detailed that allows integrating new classes of devices and sensors to existing systems; and in [12], an architecture for a domotic control system consisting of a console for each environment but which also allows control through a mobile device is proposed. In [13], a domotic control system based on mobile devices that allows controlling blinds and curtains is presented. In [14], a mobile application with manual and voice commands is proposed to control the devices of a domotic network. In [15], an embedded home domotic system for room temperature control that allows remote control using mobile devices is presented. In [16], a home automation prototype is exposed that allows users with motor disabilities to control their home appliances by using a mobile device with a touch screen. In [17], an automation system based on gloves that recognize gestures is presented, which is designed to help people with specific accessibility problems within their homes.

As regards works related to 3D applications that can be used for domotic control, [18] shows a software system that uses a three-dimensional environment (which is fixed and previously created using the 3DStudio Max tool) where, by means of traditional drop-down lists and menus, connected devices can be controlled.

In the survey carried out in this section, different ways of controlling connected home devices have been identified. Most of those propose traditional interaction methods, such as menus and drop-down lists. Others use special hardware, such as virtual reality gloves, since they are aimed at users with specific accessibility problems.

However, no product alternatives have been found that meet the following characteristics:

- The design of a virtual 3D model of the different environments of the home or office to be controlled.
- The control of the devices visually, interacting directly with said model.
- The monitoring of the status of the devices directly on the model and in real time.
- Being an open-source product.

This originated the idea of developing *3D-Domotic*, an open-source 3D mobile application for domotic control that is attractive and places priority on visual control over traditional navigation; an application that provides quick and simple access to the different rooms in the building, that is easy to configure and user friendly, and that allows checking in real time the status of each connected device.

3   Developing 3D-Domotic

This section describes in detail the different components of the domotic control software developed. The project source code can be found in the following repository [19].

3.1   System Architecture

The architecture of the system consists of a client application that sends control messages through a communications medium to a server application. These messages have as final recipients the control nodes used in the physical medium.

The server is in charge of distributing the messages to the control nodes, which receive the orders from the client and perform a set of actions associated with each order on the device or appliance they control. In this work, the server was deployed on Amazon Web Services [20].

Figure 1 depicts the different components of the system.

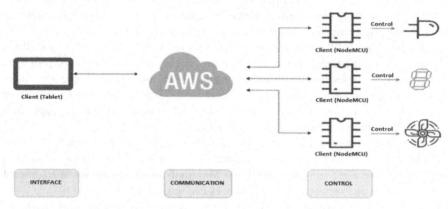

Fig. 1. System components.

3.2   Communication

In terms of communication between the client and the control nodes, requests and messages need to be processed: this is done using an MQTT (Message Queuing Telemetry Transport) broker [21].

MQTT is a light and simple network protocol of the publication-subscription type that can be used by devices with limited resources that do not have a large bandwidth. This protocol is typically mounted on TCP/IP and is one of the most widely used in IoT fields [22].

MQTT defines two network entities – a Server or Broker and a number of Clients connected to said Broker. The communication protocol works as follows:

- Messages are organized by topic.
- When a client wants to publish something, a topic must be selected.
- The broker will be in charge of distributing the message sent to all those who have subscribed to said topic.
- A topic can contain several subtopics using the character "/" as a separator, for example "Room0/Lamp-1".

Based on this, a hierarchy was made where each home has a set of rooms, and each room has a number of devices. The data sent by the client application contains the information necessary for the receiving node to analyze and perform the corresponding action on the physical device it controls.

The structure of a topic is the following: *BUILDING/ROOM/DEVICE*. For example, let's say we have a building called *SmithResidence* with only one room defined where a lighting device is set up. If you want to turn on the lighting device, the generated topic will be *SmithResidence/Room-0/Light-1*. In addition, there will be another topic that will be used for the node to send the status of the device, which allows knowing if it has been manipulated externally to the application (using, for example, a physical switch).

Each physical device is matched to a control node, and the said node only controls that physical device, so it has a topic that identifies it. When the client application is launched, the topics from each device are sent to the Broker. The broker then identifies the devices and subscribes them to the topics. In turn, the application must subscribe to each topic in which the nodes will publish their status.

Thus, communication is bidirectional through two topics, one that sends information from the client application to the control node, and the other that sends information from the control node back to the client application. This allows displaying in the application in real time the changes produced in the devices.

3.3   Server

A cloud-based server was used; namely Amazon Web Services, with the Ubuntu free software and open source operating system. Mosquitto [23], an open source message agent that implements the MQTT protocol, was installed for communications.

3.4   Client Application

The client is a 3D mobile application developed in Unity [24]. Unity is a 3D application development framework that stands out for the volume of available documentation, a large and very active user community, a wide variety of pre-developed components (assets) and plugins that facilitate integration with other tools. In addition, Unity offers a variety of publishing platform options.

The client application allows creating a virtual three-dimensional model that represents the physical space that the user wants to control. Thus, the different rooms in the building can be modeled and then representations of the electrical appliances can be placed within that virtual model, mirroring the position of the real devices in the real world. By manipulating the 3D model, orders can be sent to the components and actions can be triggered in the physical system.

When using the application for the first time, the models for the different rooms to be controlled in the house need to be created. For this, the model of the house must be created first, and then the relevant rooms have to be added to it. In Fig. 2, the home screen of the application is shown. As it can be seen, a name can be assigned to the new house, which is created by pressing the *Construir Casa* (Build House) button. When pressing this button, an empty house is generated and any relevant rooms can be added to it. Figure 3 shows how a room is created. Once all rooms have been created, the layout of the house is stored and it will appear on the list of available houses, where it can be selected and loaded using the *Cargar Casa* (Load House) button (see Fig. 2). It should be noted that currently the application offers a single language available: Spanish. Given this, all the figures that involve screenshots of the application are in that language.

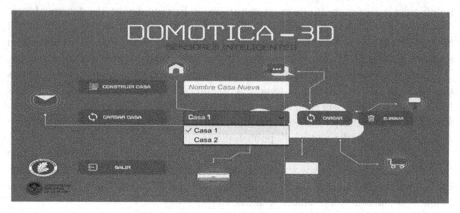

Fig. 2. Client application home screen.

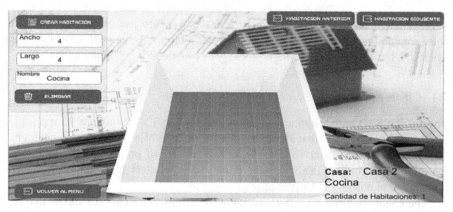

Fig. 3. Creation of a room for a house.

Once the house is loaded, the devices to be controlled in each room must be added and configured. This process needs to be carried out only once. Figure 4 shows the house configuration and control screen. The *Editar Habitaciones* (Edit Rooms) button is found on this screen, which allows editing the rooms in the house.

In order to locate the devices in the house, the *Colocar Objetos* (Place Objects) button is used. When this button is pressed, a new screen opens that allows selecting a position on the wall, floor or ceiling of a room simply by touching on the desired location. Figure 5 shows a selected floor space (highlighted in green) and the options to choose the type of device to be located in that position in the room. Depending on whether a space is selected on the wall, floor or ceiling, a number of different devices are displayed. For example, if a wall space is selected, the *Aire acondicionado* (AC Unit) device type will be available, but it will not be available if a ceiling space is selected.

Fig. 4. House setup and control screen.

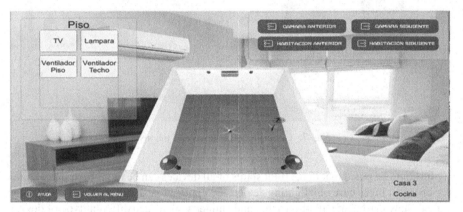

Fig. 5. Placement of devices in a room.

Using the *Cámara Anterior* (Previous Camera) and *Cámara Siguiente* (Next Camera) buttons, the room can be rotated to facilitate device positioning. The *Habitación Anterior* (Previous Room) and *Habitación Siguiente* (Next Room) buttons are used to navigate through the different rooms in the house.

Once all devices have been placed, each of them has to be associated to their controlling sensor. This is done through the configuration module, as shown in Fig. 6. This is also a one-time task.

To be able to use the devices in a house, the *Usar* (Use) button is pressed to enter the house use module. In this module, when a device is touched, a menu with all available device functions appears. Figure 7 shows that a device of the type *Ventilador* (Fan) has been selected, and the functions corresponding to it are now showing.

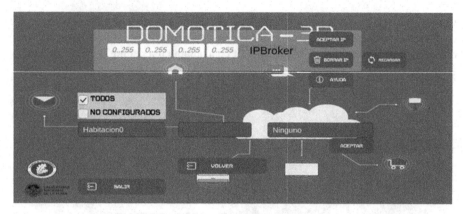

Fig. 6. Setting up the devices in a house.

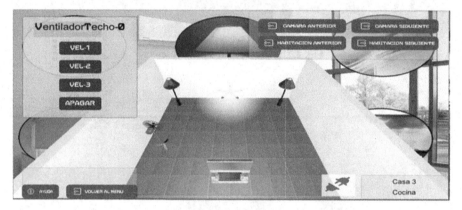

Fig. 7. Controlling the devices in a house.

It should be noted that the current status of all devices can be monitored in real time. For instance, in the case of a lighting device, the application shows if it is on or off, a fan will be shown as being still or moving, and similarly with each different type of device.

4 Experimentation

To validate the operation of all system modules, a set of tests was carried out using a scale model with basic representations of the possible types of devices. Table 1 details how each type of device was represented. Some of the representations in operation can be seen in Fig. 8 and Fig. 9.

Other types of tests, focused on checking the proper operation of the two-way communication feature of the system, were also carried out. For this, a series of devices were defined in the mobile application, but these devices could also be controlled by means of a physical switch. Then, the status of the devices was monitored using the application to check if changes were reflected in real time, whether they are controlled from their physical switch or from the mobile application.

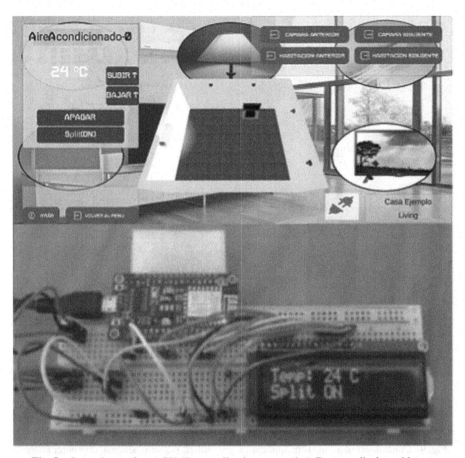

Fig. 8. Control test of an ACU. Top: application screenshot. Bottom: display with text.

Table 1. Representation of the different types of devices on the model.

Type of device	Representation
Air-conditioning unit	Display with text. The temperature set and the ON/OFF status is shown (see Fig. 8)
TV set	Display with 7 segments. The selected channel is shown
Lighting	Led. The ON/OFF status of the led is shown
Fans (floor and ceiling)	Personal computer cooler. There are four possible statuses: 3 speeds and OFF (see Fig. 9)

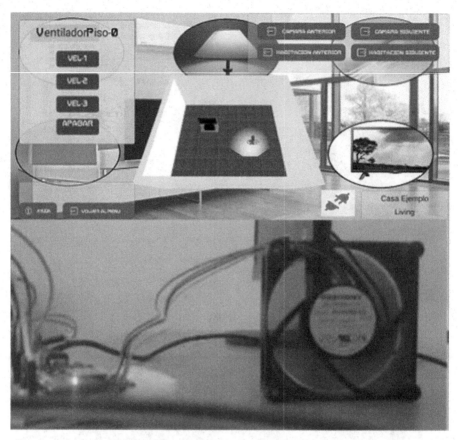

Fig. 9. Control test of a fan. Top: application screenshot. Bottom: personal computer cooler.

5   Conclusions and Future Works

An exhaustive study of commercially available products and research work related to domotic control systems through mobile applications has been carried out. As a result, no mobile applications have been found that allow remote electronic devices to be controlled visually, interacting directly with a virtual 3D model of a home or office.

With the idea of contributing to this area, a 3D mobile application for domotic control has been developed, which we called *3D-Domotic*. This application allows visually and remotely controlling electronic devices, which is an improvement over the traditional navigation through menus and drop-down lists.

3D-Domotic allows the creation of a virtual three-dimensional model that represents the physical space whose appliances the user wants to control. To that end, models of the electrical appliances are placed in the 3D representation of the house, mirroring the position of their real-world counterparts.

The application communicates with a server deployed in Amazon Web Services, which is responsible for distributing the messages to the control nodes that act on home devices. Therefore, devices can be controlled remotely.

3D-Domotic is an attractive application, since it provides quick and easy access to the different rooms in the house, and it is easy to set up and use. The application also allows monitoring the status of each connected device in real time, since it receives information from the control nodes.

In addition, a series of experimental tests has been carried out to validate the correct operation of the application.

In the future, our goal consists of adding security and reliability components for message exchange, as well as developing new functionalities and new types of controllable devices.

It is also planned to carry out an evaluation by the users of the proposed 3D interface, in order to contrast it against a traditional interface.

Additionally, a performance analysis of the existing cloud computing infrastructures used for communications between 3D applications and sensors in different rooms would be of interest.

References

1. CEDOM: Asociación Española de Domótica a Inmótica. http://www.cedom.es/es
2. Evans, D.: Internet de las cosas: cómo la próxima evolución de Internet lo cambia todo. Cisco Internet Business Solutions Group, April 2011
3. Orvibo: https://www.orvibo.com/en/product/productList_index.html
4. Iddero: http://www.iddero.com/es/products
5. Basalte: https://www.basalte.be/es/productos
6. Zennio: https://www.zennio.com/productos
7. Fibaro: https://life2better.com/fibaro-home-center-2
8. Sophia: https://www.sophia-intelligence.com
9. Gira: https://www.gira.com/en/en/products
10. Leite, E., Várela, L., Pires, V.F., Cardoso, F.D., Pires, A.J., Martins, J.F.: A ZigBee wireless domotic system with Bluetooth interface. In: IECON 2014 - 40th Annual Conference of the IEEE Industrial Electronics Society, Dallas, TX, USA, pp. 2506–2511 (2014). https://doi.org/10.1109/IECON.2014.7048858
11. Frontoni, E., Liciotti, D., Paolanti, M., Pollini, R., Zingaretti, P.: Design of an interoperable framework with domotic sensors network integration. In: 2017 IEEE 7th International Conference on Consumer Electronics - Berlin (ICCE-Berlin), Berlin, pp. 49–50 (2017). https://doi.org/10.1109/ICCE-Berlin.2017.8210586
12. Monteiro, P., Tomé, P., Albuquerque, D.: Domotics control system architecture. In: 2015 10th Iberian Conference on Information Systems and Technologies (CISTI), Aveiro, Portugal, pp. 1–6 (2015). https://doi.org/10.1109/CISTI.2015.7170403
13. Gutierrez, S., Acero, C., Rodrigo, P.M.: Domotic control system for blinds with zigbee communication mobile device. In: 2018 International Conference on Research in Intelligent and Computing in Engineering (RICE), San Salvador, El Salvador, pp. 1–4 (2018). https://doi.org/10.1109/RICE.2018.8627899
14. Montesdeoca Contreras, J.C., Avila Campoverde, R.S., Cabrera Hidalgo, J.C., Vintimilla Tapia, P.E.: Mobile applications using TCP/IP-GSM protocols applied to domotic. In: 2015 XVI Workshop on Information Processing and Control (RPIC), Cordoba, Argentina, pp. 1–4 (2015). https://doi.org/10.1109/RPIC.2015.7497085

15. Dobrescu, L.: Domotic embedded system. In: Proceedings of the 2014 6th International Conference on Electronics, Computers and Artificial Intelligence (ECAI), Bucharest, Romania, pp. 55–58 (2014). https://doi.org/10.1109/ECAI.2014.7090180
16. Cofre, J.P., Moraga, G., Rusu, C., Mercado, I., Inostroza, R., Jimenez, C.: Developing a touchscreen-based domotic tool for users with motor disabilities. In: 2012 Ninth International Conference on Information Technology - New Generations, Las Vegas, NV, USA, pp. 696–701 (2012). https://doi.org/10.1109/ITNG.2012.139
17. Kshirsagar, S., Sachdev, S., Singh, N., Tiwari, A., Sahu, S.: IoT enabled gesture-controlled home automation for disabled and elderly. In: 2020 Fourth International Conference on Computing Methodologies and Communication (ICCMC), Erode, India, pp. 821–826 (2020). https://doi.org/10.1109/ICCMC48092.2020.ICCMC-000152
18. Redondo, C.L., Cañones, F.J.L., Oostrom, F.P.L., Guitard, I.G., Galdón, A.S.: Virtual domotic systems: a new 3D multi-user, highly immersive and intuitive interface for residential gateways. In: IADIS Web Virtual Reality and 3D Worlds 2009 (Web3DW 2009) Conference. Portugal, 19–22 June 2009. ISBN/ISSN: ISBN: 978-972-8924-84-3
19. 3D-Domotic: Project source code. https://github.com/cristianniglesias/3D-Domotic-A-3D-Mobile-Application-for-Domotic-Control.git
20. Amazon Web Services. https://aws.amazon.com/
21. MQTT: The Standard for IoT Messaging. https://mqtt.org
22. Light, R.: Mosquitto: server and client implementation of the MQTT protocol. J. Open Source Softw. 2(13), 265 (2017). https://doi.org/10.21105/joss.00265
23. Eclipse Mosquitto: An open source MQTT broker. https://mosquitto.org
24. Unity: https://unity.com

Visualization

Visualization Technique for Comparison of Time-Based Large Data Sets

Martín L. Larrea[1,2,3]($\boxtimes$) ⓘ and Dana K. Urribarri[1,2,3] ⓘ

[1] Department of Computer Science and Engineering, Universidad Nacional del Sur (UNS), Bahía Blanca, Argentina
{mll,dku}@cs.uns.edu.ar
[2] Computer Graphics and Visualization R&D Laboratory, Universidad Nacional del Sur (UNS) - CIC Prov. Buenos Aires, Bahía Blanca, Argentina
[3] Institute for Computer Science and Engineering, Universidad Nacional del Sur (UNS) - CONICET, Bahía Blanca, Argentina

Abstract. Comparison is one of the essential tasks that motivate a data set exploration, and it is particularly arduous when it involves large data sets. The objective of information visualization is to help gain insight into the data, and in this context, it should assist the user in the task of comparison. However, few visualization techniques have been specifically developed to support the comparison process, even less for large data sets. In this paper, we present a visualization technique, with its corresponding set of interactions, designed to assist in time-based large data sets comparison. The proposed solution is based on Dynamic Time Warping and presents a visual comparison of the misalignment between a set of time series. The proposal includes an overview of the misalignment between the data and a by-demand detailed view focusing on the comparison between any two of them. As a validation of the technique, we also introduce a case study on the historical meteorological data from Bahía Blanca city.

Keywords: Visualization · Comparison task · Time-based data

1 Introduction

Information visualization is the process that represents data in a visual and meaningful way so that the user can gain a better understanding of it. Through visual representations, information visualization allows users to extract information from data efficiently and effectively. In the context of information visualization, we can identify two large sets of tasks or goals that motivate the construction or creation of a visualization. On the one hand, we have the *why*, which motivates the user to look for a visualization; on the other, we have the *how*, how the user manages to satisfy those motivations. Brehmer and Munzne [2] provided a task topology that identifies abstract tasks linked to *why* and *how*.

M. Naiouf et al. (Eds.): JCC-BD&ET 2021, CCIS 1444, pp. 179–187, 2021.
https://doi.org/10.1007/978-3-030-84825-5_13

One of the motivations detected is that of comparison. However, few visualization techniques are thought of in terms of this task and even less for big data sets.

In 2019 we developed and published [11,12] a new visualization technique that originated in the visualization of karate movements. That work, designed to facilitate the comparison between two people's movements, allowed us to start testing this technique on large data sets in other application domains. Due to the satisfactory results found, we carried out this work, where we introduced the visualization technique and its interactions in the context of large data sets. The proposed technique is an overview+detail visual analysis tool, where the overview visualization shows a quantitative summary of the misalignment between every two data sets. The detailed visualization, based on Dynamic Time Warping, mainly shows how a *reference* data set should be transformed to match a *target* one. We also provide a case study of the technique using historical meteorological data from Bahía Blanca city [15], in Buenos Aires province.

This paper continues with a discussion of the previous work in Sect. 2 and a summary of the visualization technique proposed for meteorological data in Sect. 3. Section 4 presents the meteorological data to visualize, and analyze the achieved visualization. Finally, Sect. 5 draws some conclusions and presents possible future work.

2   Previous Work

A first approach to visualize the comparison between time-based data is using the raw data itself without any processing [7,8,10,13]. These techniques are straightforward in their implementations but do not scale properly to large data sets.

Zhao et al. [14] investigated visualization techniques for comparative analysis of multiple event sequence data sets. They designed MatrixWave, a matrix-based representation that allows analysts to get an overview of differences in traffic patterns and interactively explore paths through a website. They used color to encode differences and size to offer context over traffic volume. Figure 1 shows a screenshot of the visualization, the result is a visual representation loaded with detail, which does not make it especially adaptable to large data sets.

Jekic et al. [6] introduced an interactive visual data analysis solution called ADAM (Aluminum production Data Analysis and Monitoring). Among other goals, this tool was designed to create a visual representation of the comparison of process data that were recorded and/or calculated from the casting of aluminum pieces. The compared dimensions are translated into circles on coordinate axes. The color and radius attributes are used to represent comparison results. Although the article mentions large data sets, the included examples do not mention exact amounts of data. The system does not integrate the comparison process in a single visualization but forces the user to carry out the visual comparison by himself, as can be seen in Fig. 2.

Gotz et al. [4] presented a new visual analytic approach for dynamic hierarchical dimension aggregation on temporal event data. They allow the user to

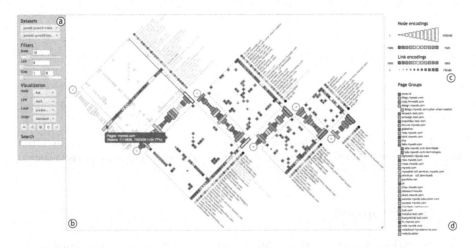

Fig. 1. A MatrixWave screenshot shows the GUI interfaces and the visual representations for the data comparison. It is a is a visual representation very heavy on the details, which does not make it especially adaptable to large data sets. The image was taken from the original article [14].

define group type aggregations as part of the analysis workflow rather than as a pre-processing. This means that the visualization presented to the user does not necessarily allow them to answer their questions, but rather requires the user to explore and modify the visual representation until an answer can be found.

Gleicher et al. [3] provided a survey of works in information visualization related to comparisons. The authors proposed three categories of visual comparison, which can be distinguished by the principal mechanism used to make connections between objects: juxtaposition uses the viewer's memory, superposition uses the visual system and explicit encoding uses computation to determine the relationships. The three categories can also be distinguished by how the correspondences between parts are encoded: in juxtaposition, they are not; in superposition, proximity is used to encode connections; and explicit encoding uses some other visual encoding. Although the authors acknowledge the notable increase in size and complexity of the data sets that are being handled today; none of the techniques reviewed throughout the work fit the context of large data sets.

Heim [5] acknowledges that the comparison task is typically cognitively demanding, time-consuming, and thus error-prone; because of these problems, she proposes a comparative visualization framework. She used an approach very similar to our own, an overview visualization first and detail on-demand later. However, his proposal does not include the time dimension, nor does it mention how the technique scales in the case of large data sets.

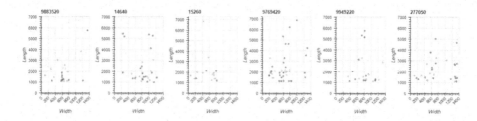

Fig. 2. In Jekic et al. work, the user is responsible from making the comparison itself because the system does not integrate the comparison process in a single visualization. Image taken from the original article [6].

3 Our Proposal

In this section, we summarize a previously presented time-series visualization conceived to compare motion capture information [11,12]. In this work, we state that this visualization can also be used to analyze big temporal data, for example, meteorological data.

We based our comparative analysis on a visual comparison of the misalignment between a set of time series. We present an overview of the misalignment between the data corresponding to n different data sets. A detailed view focusing on the comparison between two of them can be obtained on demand. The proposed solution comes from a combination of signal processing and data visualization techniques. All misalignment is pre-calculated based on Dynamic Time Warping, which we describe below.

Unlike previous works [7,8,10,13], our proposal does not visualize the raw data itself without any processing. The presentation of information carried out by our comparison tool hierarchizes the information into two levels of detail, where the first works as an overview and the next one offers more information. In this way, information overload such as that seen in Fig. 1 is reduced, which makes it easy to handle large data sets. Both levels of detail integrate the comparison process in a single visualization reducing the cognitive load required of the user, making a difference with Fig. 2 where the user must carry out the visual comparison by himself. Our proposal removes the possibility of exploring the data as allowed in [4]; however, we believe this allows for a clearer and more user-friendly display.

3.1 Dynamic Time Warping

To measure the similarity or dissimilarity between two temporal sequences a technique called Dynamic Time Warping (DTW) was introduced [1,9]. This method provides a mapping between the series and induces a warping function. This function transforms one of the sequences to obtain two time-aligned sequences, representing misalignment function.

DTW compares all the records from two sequences to compute an accumulated-distance matrix $M \in R^N \times R^L$, where N and L are the lengths of both sequences. Any distance function can be used to calculate the distance between records; in this particular implementation and just for time alignment, every attribute of the data set was normalized between 0 and 1, and the distance between records was calculated using Euclidean distance. $M_{1,1}$ is the distance between the two first records of the sequences, while $M_{N,L}$ is the accumulated distance for the two last records. The accumulated distance for every pair of records is the distance between those two records plus the minimum between the accumulated distances for the three immediately preceding pairs of records.

3.2   The Misalignment Function

The *warping path* is a list of pairs of records defined by the minimal accumulated-distance path from $M_{1,1}$ to $M_{N,L}$. This warping path can define a function F such as given a record n in data set R, the function $F(n)$ returns the record number in T that matches the best. The distance from $F(n)$ to n is the misalignment function $G(n)$, and is given by Eq. 1:

$$G(n) = F(n) - n \tag{1}$$

The relation between $G(n-1)$ and $G(n)$ indicates whether record n of R is late, on-time, or early with respect to the one corresponding in T. If $G(n-1) = G(n)$, then R is on-time and G has a flat slope. If $G(n-1) < G(n)$, then R is early and the slope of G is positive. Finally, if $G(n-1) > G(n)$, then R is late and the slope of G is negative.

4   Case Study: Historical Weather Data of Bahía Blanca

The data set consists of meteorological information gathered from the years 2009 to 2019. In addition to the date, each record has ten meteorological measures, described in Table 1.

4.1   Color Scales

This visualization uses various colors to encode information. The misalignment function is encoded using the colors red, yellow, and blue (see Fig. 3), and different measurements use a specific color scale depending on the measuring unit, as shown in Table 2.

Fig. 3. Color coding for the misalignment information.

Table 1. Meteorological measures gathered throughout each year.

Name	Description	Units
Tmáx	Maximum temperature	°C
Tmed	Average temperature	°C
Tmin	Minimum temperature	°C
Td	Dewpoint temperature	°C
STP	Pressure at station	hPa
Vis	Visibility	km
Vmed	Average wind velocity	km/h
Vmáx	Maximum wind velocity	km/h
Prec	Precipitation	mm
Rad	Incident solar radiation	W/m^2

Table 2. Color scale for each type of measure.

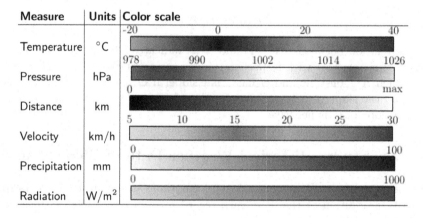

4.2   Overview

The overview consists of a matrix that displays a comparison between each sequence against all others. The comparison shows the percentage of days of the reference year in which the weather matches early, on-time, or late the weather of the target year. Figure 4 shows the overview of the 11-years comparison of weather information; the year 2009 stands out for having a persistent misalignment compared to the others.

4.3   Detailed View

The detailed view consists of three graphs (see Fig. 5). The upper one shows the difference between every record of the reference data set and the correspondent in the target (represented by the height of the curve), plus the time alignment

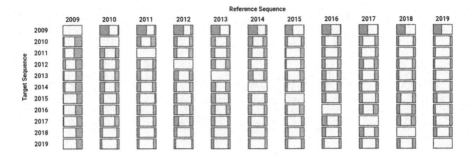

Fig. 4. Overview matrix displaying the comparison of meteorological data between every pair of years.

between the two data sets (represented by the color of the area under the curve). The middle graph is a representation of the misalignment function G described in Subsect. 3.2. The bottom one is a *parallel heat-map visualization* [11]. A parallel heat-map visualization consists of two *heat maps* and a *parallel time-relationship visualization*. Each heat-map visualization represents a whole sequence, where the color of each pixel encodes a meteorological measure following the color scales in Table 2. The width of the image represents the timeline in days, and the height, the collected measures. The parallel time-relationship visualization connects the two heat maps to visualize the misalignment between the sequences. The heat maps serve as the temporal axes, which are connected to represent the warping, i.e. the misalignment, between the sequences. The color of the connections emphasizes the temporal relationship following the color scale in Fig. 3.

4.4 Visualizing Large Datasets

The overview is a visualization that allows a quick comparison of how similar the behavior of the climate is over the different years. This matrix form is suitable for approximately a 20 time-series, even more for smaller boxes. The detailed view presents two graphs aimed at detecting trends in the data. In addition, the heatmap representation of the compared years allows visualizing the climate of the whole year in a single image. Since the first two visualizations are suitable for continuous data and the heatmaps are image-based visualizations, the detailed view scale easily to longer time series.

4.5 Implementation Notes

A prototype of the comparison tool presented in this work is available at https://cs.uns.edu.ar/~dku/vis/vis-temp-datos-meteorologicos/. The prototype was implemented using Javascript and the D3.js library. The input sequences for the application are the original data set, and the warping function (Subsect. 3.1) for each possible pair of sequences was computed offline.

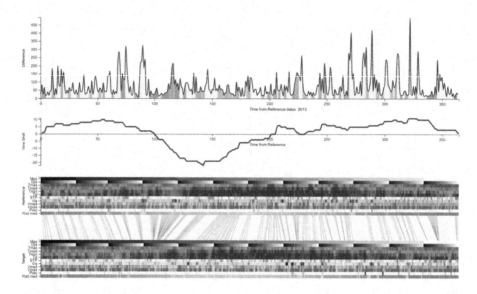

Fig. 5. Detailed view showing more information about the misalignment between two years.

5   Conclusions and Future Work

All information visualization intends to assist the user in the detection of patterns, the transmission of ideas, or the verification of hypotheses. In essence, there is always a goal or reason that motivates such creation. Comparison is one of the goals that motivate the exploration of any data set and is an especially arduous task when it comes to large ones.

Few visualization techniques specifically assist the information comparison process. Those that allow it usually requires the user extra cognitive processing to solve the comparison. In this work, we present a technique developed by us, which has already proven to be effective for the comparison of karate movements, and that, in this opportunity, we demonstrate its value as a tool for the comparison of large data sets.

Although the technique is limited to time-based large data sets, this does not mean a narrow scope. For this article, we have used a meteorological data set that contains 10-years climate measures from Bahía Blanca city. We hope that this work will allow us to take the technique to new application fields and obtain new requirements to improve its capacity.

In future work, we will push the limits in the amount of information that the technique can display while still allowing the user to resolve the comparison. Meteorological data has turned out to be a field of application very rich in opportunities and, we will look forward to expanding the technique with new representations and interactions.

Acknowledgments. This work was partially supported by the following research projects: PGI 25/N050, PGI 24/ZN29 and PGI 24/ZN35 from the Secretaría General de Ciencia y Tecnología, Universidad Nacional del Sur, Argentina.

References

1. Berndt, D.J., Clifford, J.: Using dynamic time warping to find patterns in time series. In: Proceedings of the 3rd International Conference on Knowledge Discovery and Data Mining, AAAIWS 1994, pp. 359–370. AAAI Press (1994)
2. Brehmer, M., Munzner, T.: A multi-level typology of abstract visualization tasks. IEEE Trans. Vis. Comput. Graph. **19**(12), 2376–2385 (2013)
3. Gleicher, M., Albers, D., Walker, R., Jusufi, I., Hansen, C.D., Roberts, J.C.: Visual comparison for information visualization. Inf. Vis. **10**(4), 289–309 (2011)
4. Gotz, D., Zhang, J., Wang, W., Shrestha, J., Borland, D.: Visual analysis of high-dimensional event sequence data via dynamic hierarchical aggregation. IEEE Trans. Visual Comput. Graph. **26**(1), 440–450 (2019)
5. Heim, A.: Visual comparison of multivariate data ensembles. Ph.D. thesis, Wien (2021)
6. Jekic, N., Mutlu, B., Schreyer, M., Neubert, S., Schreck, T.: Similarity measures for visual comparison and retrieval of test data in aluminum production. In: VISI-GRAPP 2021. 16th International Joint Conference on Computer Vision, Imaging and Computer Graphics Theory and Applications (2021)
7. Krstajic, M., Bertini, E., Keim, D.: Cloudlines: compact display of event episodes in multiple time-series. IEEE Trans. Vis. Comput. Graph. **17**(12), 2432–2439 (2011)
8. Plaisant, C., Milash, B., Rose, A., Widoff, S., Shneiderman, B.: LifeLines: visualizing personal histories. In: Proceedings of the SIGCHI Conference on Human Factors in Computing Systems, pp. 221–227 (1996)
9. Rabiner, L., Juang, B.H.: Fundamentals of Speech Recognition. Prentice Hall, Inc., Upper Saddle River (1993)
10. Shin, M., et al.: Attentionflow: visualising influence in networks of time series. In: Proceedings of the 14th ACM International Conference on Web Search and Data Mining, pp. 1085–1088 (2021)
11. Urribarri, D.K., Larrea, M.L., Castro, S.M., Puppo, E.: Overview+Detail visual comparison of karate motion captures. In: Pesado, P., Arroyo, M. (eds.) CACIC 2019. CCIS, vol. 1184, pp. 139–154. Springer, Cham (2020). https://doi.org/10.1007/978-3-030-48325-8_10
12. Urribarri, D.K., Larrea, M.L., Castro, S.M., Puppo, E.: Visualization to compare karate motion captures. In: XXV Congreso Argentino de Ciencias de la Computación (CACIC 2019, Universidad Nacional de Río Cuarto) (2019)
13. Zhao, J., Drucker, S.M., Fisher, D., Brinkman, D.: Timeslice: interactive faceted browsing of timeline data. In: Proceedings of the International Working Conference on Advanced Visual Interfaces, pp. 433–436 (2012)
14. Zhao, J., Liu, Z., Dontcheva, M., Hertzmann, A., Wilson, A.: Matrixwave: visual comparison of event sequence data. In: Proceedings of the 33rd Annual ACM Conference on Human Factors in Computing Systems, pp. 259–268 (2015)
15. Zotelo, C., Martín, E.: Meteobahia. datos meteorológicos (2014). https://meteobahia.com.ar/. Accessed 10 Mar 2021

npGLC-Vis Library for Multidimensional Data Visualization

Leandro E. Luque[1,2]([✉]) [iD], María Luján Ganuza[1,2] [iD],
Antonella S. Antonini[1,2] [iD], and Silvia M. Castro[1,2] [iD]

[1] VyGLab Research Laboratory (UNS-CICPBA), Department of Computer Science
and Engineering, Universidad Nacional del Sur, Bahía Blanca, Argentina
{leandro.luque,mlg,antonella.antonini,smc}@cs.uns.edu.ar
[2] Institute for Computer Science and Engineering (UNS-CONICET),
Universidad Nacional del Sur, Bahía Blanca, Argentina
http://vyglab.cs.uns.edu.ar/, https://icic.conicet.gov.ar/

Abstract. While information is growing exponentially, datasets are getting bigger and bigger containing valuable information that can expand human knowledge. To extract meaningful information from these dense datasets, the need for effective graphical representations that take advantage of the human's visual perception capabilities is revealed. The visualization of this kind of data is a complex task. These big datasets are in general inherently multidimensional (n-D), facing the challenge of finding suitable mappings from the n-D space to a 2D or 3D space. Even though multiple visualization methods have been developed for n-D data, many of them do not allow the complete restoration of the data from its reduced representation and/or do not represent the complete n-D dataset. The General Lines Coordinates (*GLC*) are reversible visual representations that preserve n-D information for knowledge discovery. In this paper, we present the *npGLC-Vis* Library, a data visualization library supporting Non-Paired General Line Coordinates (*npGLC*) with associated traditional interactions like brushing, zooming, and panning. *npGLC-Vis* is a collection of visualization methods, designed for experimenting with *npGLC* techniques in the development of visualization applications. We present the library design and implementation, exemplifying it through the representation of different datasets.

Keywords: General line coordinates · Multidimensional data · Data visualization · Big-data

1 Introduction

As datasets grow, a combination of visual and analytical elements offers a powerful opportunity to gain insights from them. Through the use of data visualization, the perceptual and cognitive capabilities, that are unique to humans, can be exploited into the process of analysis and discovery. Undoubtedly, this motivates the use and evolution of data visualization methods. In general, these

© Springer Nature Switzerland AG 2021
M. Naiouf et al. (Eds.): JCC-BD&ET 2021, CCIS 1444, pp. 188–202, 2021.
https://doi.org/10.1007/978-3-030-84825-5_14

datasets are inherently multidimensional (n-D), a feature that represents a major challenge to our cognitive and perceptual capabilities, which are reduced to the 2-D or 3-D space. Moreover, not only is the visualization of these datasets a difficult task, but to enable users to intuitively and interactively explore them and discriminate individual dimensions makes it even more challenging.

Even though multiple visualization methods have been developed for n-D data, many of them are not reversible and/or lossy, i.e. they do not allow restoring the n-D data completely from its reduced representation and/or do not represent the complete n-D dataset. Although data reduction techniques can be applied for big datasets analysis, they should be as lossless as possible to preserve the information present in the original data. The representation of this complete information is very important because our ability to visually analyze n-D data from incomplete 2-D or 3-D representations is limited and could potentially be erroneous. The loss of significant n-D information in visualizations and the difficulties in finding visual representations that evidence clear and meaningful patterns are essential challenges in visualizing n-D data.

These challenges have been addressed, in the area of visualization, by developing reversible and lossless visual representations. However, the number of available approaches is quite limited, being those of Parallel and Radial Coordinates two of the most valuable ones. Both Parallel and Radial Coordinates have been used for many years, and have been very useful in obtaining information from various datasets, demonstrating their advantages. This has marked their evolution and improvement, allowing their use in various application areas. However, both suffer from occlusion. Given the advantages of reversible and lossless methods for visualizing n-D data, there is a definite need to focus on reversible and lossless visual representations of n-D data that allow its visual analysis.

In recent years a new class of such representations, called General Line Coordinates (*GLC*), has emerged [9,10,12]. These are a set of visual representations for visualizing multidimensional data in 2-D and 3-D in a reversible and lossless way. While new approaches are explored, both theoretically and experimentally, we believe that having a large new class of coordinates increases the likelihood that they will allow humans to discover hidden n-D patterns in the data through visualization. Kovalerchuck [10] describes *GLC* and their advantages and includes analysis of several datasets. However, considering that this is a new concept, there is still a lot of work to be done.

To the best of our knowledge, although some graphics and references corresponding to the *GLC* types defined by Kovalerchuk (N-Gon, In-Line, Bush, and Circular) can be found in different non-academic sources, there are no implementations yet published in the literature. In this context, we consider that a valuable contribution is the design and development of a library that allows the above methods to be used for the analysis of big datasets. We focus on *npGLC*, which generalize the Radial and Parallel Coordinates that have shown to be highly suitable for visualizing multi-dimensional data.

In this paper, we present *npGLC-Vis*, a library for Non-Paired General Line Coordinates Visualization. *npGLC-Vis* allows the representation of different datasets with all the $npGLC$ methods defined by Kovalerchuck [10]. In addition, it supports traditional brushing, zooming, and panning interactions that will allow the user to iteratively and interactively explore the space of their data.

This paper continues with a brief introduction of the General Lines Coordinates concept, its main characteristics, and the GLC classification adopted for the library design in Sect. 2. Then, in Sect. 3.2, we describe the basic principles of the $npGLC$-Vis library, including the performance measurements for our implementation. In Sect. 4, the software modules, their methods, and their interfaces are detailed. In Sect. 5, usage examples of the techniques are given. Finally, Sect. 6 draws some conclusions and presents possible future work.

2   General Lines Coordinates (GLC)

The General Line Coordinates or GLC refer to different alternatives for the visualization of n-D data items in 2D or 3D reversibly and without loss of information [9–12]. Two types of GLC are defined, the *Non-Paired General Line Coordinates* ($npGLC$) and the *Paired General Line Coordinates* ($pGLC$). The $npGLC$ generalize Parallel and Radial Coordinates, including N-Gon, Circular, In-Line, Dynamic, and Bush Coordinates. The $pGLC$ generalize Cartesian Coordinates, including Paired Orthogonal, Non-orthogonal, Collocated, Partially Collocated, Shifted, Radial, Elliptic, and Crown Coordinates.

Today, the most valuable methods for visualization of reversible and lossless n-D data are Parallel and Radial Coordinates. For this reason, we focus on the $npGLC$ which are more suitable for representing n-D data. Besides, we chose to work on a 2D version of the $npGLC$ instead of a 3D version. The main reason for our decision is that while the choice of using 2D or 3D for data visualization depends on diverse factors (like the data complexity, the visualization technology, the tasks or application context), in general, when possible, the use of 2D space for representation is preferred for information visualization [14,16].

From now on we use $X_1 - X_n$ to notate the coordinate axes, $\mathbf{x}$ for a n-D data item, and x_i for the *i-th* attribute value of $\mathbf{x}$ corresponding to the X_i axis.

2.1   Non-paired General Line Coordinates ($npGLC$)

In the Radial Coordinates [6], the axes are arranged radially and laid out in equal angles from a common origin. On the other hand, in the Parallel Coordinates [8], the axes are arranged parallel to each other and are separated by equal distances. Every data item $\mathbf{x}$ is represented by a polygonal line intersecting each axis X_i at the point corresponding to x_i. Each of the n axes is scaled individually for each attribute (Fig. 1).

The $npGLC$ generalize the Parallel and Radial Coordinates. Considering different layouts for the axes and different ways of drawing the data items, we can distinguish various GLC representations. According to Kovalerchuk [12], in $npGLC$, the polyline can be curvilinear or straight. In addition, the axes can have different lengths, scales, and ranges, and they can be oriented in any direction, all of which determines the multiple layouts defined in [12].

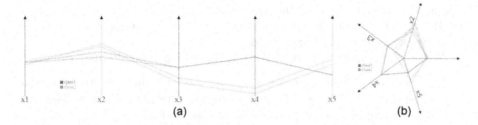

Fig. 1. Using the *npGLC-Vis* library to represent a small dataset with (a) Parallel Coordinates and (b) Radial Coordinates.

3   *npGLC-Vis* Library Design

For the library design, we considered and supported all the representations proposed by Kovalerchuk [10] for *npGLC*. However, we designed our own *npGLC* classification that we adopted for the library design. Next, we describe the proposed classification and provide details of the design decisions followed in the implementation of the library.

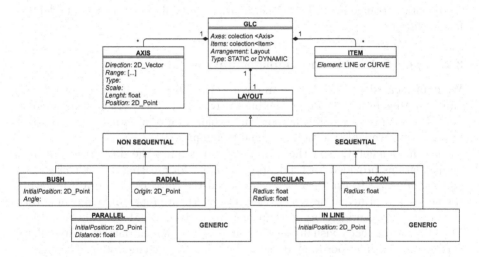

Fig. 2. *npGLC* Classification adopted for the library design.

3.1   Non-paired General Line Coordinates Classification

Figure 2 shows the designed classification. Each *GLC* representation has an associated collection of axes along with its arrangement, a collection of data items, and an attribute that describes if the data items will be drawn statically or dynamically. The axes are arranged according to a layout, detailed above. Each axis in the **axes collection** has associated its direction, range, type, scale, length, and position attributes. Each data item in the **items collection** can be drawn with curves or straight lines.

Concerning how to represent a data item, there are two alternatives.

- Static mapping. Given an axes layout, the location p_i for each attribute value x_i of an n-D data item **x** is located on the corresponding X_i axes. The data item is represented by the polyline joining the positions p_i, $i = 1, ..., n$.
- Dynamic mapping. Given an axes layout, an n-D data item is represented by a dynamically constructed polyline. The location p_1 of x_1 is on the X_1 axis. The location of the next values x_i, $i = 2, ..., n$ depends on the location of x_{i-1} and the orientation of the corresponding X_i axes. Then, the polyline is constructed in the following way. The first point of the polyline is p_1. Each i-th segment, $i = 1, ..., n - 1$, is oriented parallel to the corresponding X_{i+1} axis and is drawn between each position pairs p_i and p_{i+1}, $i = 1, ..., n - 1$.

Axes Layout. We group layouts into two basic classes, the *sequential* layouts the *non-sequential* layouts. In a *sequential* layout, the coordinate axes are placed one after the other to form a shape. They can be arranged clockwise or counter-clockwise. In a *non-sequential* layout, the axes are freely oriented, not following a sequential arrangement. Table 1 summarizes the different axes layouts defined for our library.

3.2 *npGLC-Vis* Library Implementation

We implemented *npGLC-Vis* as an open-source library built on top of D3js [3] and ES6, to get the benefits of the data-driven and object-oriented paradigms. Our library aims to visually support the exploration of a dataset using a set of lossless and reversible multidimensional techniques.

The implementation of the proposed work applies the directrices and recommendations provided for the D3js community for creating reusable charts [4] and modules [5]. In that sense, we developed the *npGLC-Vis* library following the next set of principal design choices. The charts are repeatable, meaning that they can be instantiated more than once in a given DOM (Document Object Model) selector, each visualizing the same or a different dataset. This allows supporting multiple coordinated views. The charts are configurable. Through an API, we provide a simple interface to interact with the chart in real-time. In this way, the user can create more elaborate behaviors to manipulate the chart. Finally, the charts are extensible due to the hierarchical structure of the design (Fig. 2).

As web browsers are gaining popularity for data exploration and analysis steps in data science, we focus the development on a platform-independent approach. However, it is important to notice that when the number of data is large (in order of GB), the capabilities of the browser decrease rather than a desktop application. Keep in mind that, we achieved a complexity order of O(n) for small and medium datasets, but for larger datasets, our implementation does

Table 1. Summary of the main characteristics of the different *GLC* representations.

Type	Characteristics
Non-sequential	
Parallel	Set of equidistant vertical axes arranged from left to right (Fig. 3(a))
Bush	This layout is a modification of the Parallel Coordinate, where only the middle coordinate axis is vertically oriented. All other coordinates axes are tilted increasingly from the middle axis to shape a bush (Fig. 3(e))
Radial	The axes radiate at equal angles from a common origin (Fig. 3(f))
Generic	The axes are oriented in any direction, spaced apart, and arranged consecutively in the plane from left to right (Fig. 3(c))
Sequential	
Circular	The coordinate axes are curved segments arranged to form a circle (Fig. 3(g))
N-Gon	The coordinate axes are arranged to form a polygon (triangle, square, pentagon, and so on). Each edge of the polygon corresponds to a coordinate axis and all of them are oriented clockwise or counterclockwise (Fig. 3(h))
In-Line	All axes are horizontal, collinear and oriented in the same direction; however they may or may not overlap (Fig. 3(d))
Generic	The axes are arranged consecutively in the plane one after the other, clockwise or counterclockwise, and each axis is oriented in any direction (Fig. 3(b))

not scale well. A possible solution for this issue (that is out of our scope) is to take advantage of the GPU cards using parallel computing through web API.

4   *npGLC-Vis* Library

To install the library, is necessary to download the latest release[1]. Once installed, to generate a new *GLC* plot, the following function must be invoked:

```
var chart = glc.newChart({data, width, height, selector, type,
dimensions, target, dynamic});
chart.draw();
```

Where *data* is the input data array, *width* and *height* are the width and height of the SVG, *select* corresponds to the ID of the DOM element container, *type* indicates the type of *npGLC* to be display ('radial', 'parallel', 'circular', 'bush', 'inline', 'polygon', 'seq-generic', or 'nseq-generic'), *dimensions* is an array containing the names of the dimensions, *target* corresponds to the field name of the

---

[1] https://github.com/visualprojects/npGLC-Vis/tree/main/dist.

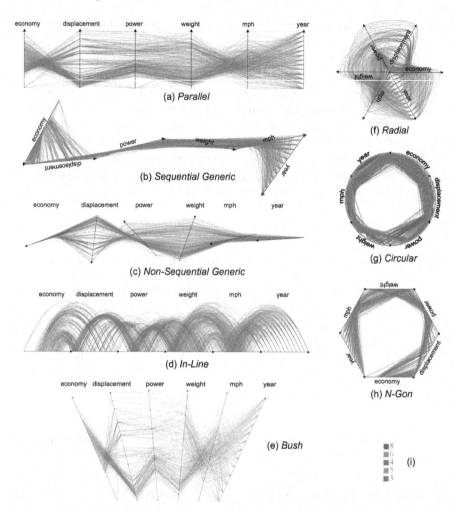

Fig. 3. Several representations of the Cars (Auto MPG) dataset [1] generated with *npGLC-Vis* library. In each case, static mapping of data items was used. The representations include (a) Parallel, (b) Sequential Generic, (c) Non-Sequential Generic, (d) In-Line, (e) Bush, (f) Radial, (g) Circular, and (h) N-Gon Coordinates. (i) An ordinal color scale was applied according to the "cylinders" attribute.

target dimension, and *dynamic* specifies if the data item is drawn statically or dynamically.

The library offers the set of functions defined in Table 2.

Table 2. *npGLC-Vis* Library Functions.

Scope	Function	Functionality
General	setOpacity(value)	The opacity of the items is modified according to the specified *value*, which must be in the range of [0, 1]
	colorize(boolean)	The items are colorized follow by the target field or colorized using black color depending on whether *boolean* is true or false
	getAxis()	Returns a collection containing all the axes in the *GLC* chart
	getItems()	Returns a collection containing all the items in the data
Radial	setCurve(value)	Specifies if the items are drawn with curves or straight lines (*value* must be <'CURVE' | 'LINE'>)
Radial Circular	setRadius(value)	The axes are arranged at distance *value* from the origin
In Line	compareClasses(c1, c2)	The items corresponding to the class *c1* are drawn above and the items corresponding to the class *c2* are drawn below
	focusClass(class)	The items corresponding to *class* are drawn above and items of the rest of the classes are drawn below
	setLine(value)	Specifies if the items are drawn with curves or straight lines (*value* must be <'CURVE' | 'TRIANGULAR'>)
Sequential Generic	setOrientations(value)	The orientation of each axis is configured according to *value*, that is an array of integers between [0, 360] with length L (where L is the number of dimensions). By default, the orientations are calculated randomly

5   Using the npGLC-Vis Library

The methods implemented in the *npGLC-Vis* library allow the visualization of multidimensional data using the *GLC* methods detailed in Sect. 2. In this Section, we show some of the library capabilities by detailing several stand-alone examples.

5.1   Visual Analysis: Cars Dataset

We use our library to generate a variety of charts (Fig. 3), with static mapping of items, using the Cars (Auto MPG) dataset from the UCI Machine Learning repository [1]. These plots prove their usefulness to reveal insights. In some cases, the hidden structure is not trivial to see due to the nature of the method. In this situation, it is possible to employ the concept of the dynamic mapping of items as an alternative to represent the data items and to work as a complement in the analysis phase. Figure 4 and 5 are examples of how the spatial limitations of the technique in its static version can be minimized using dynamic mapping of items. This enables a better division of similar items from the rest. As the occlusion due to crossing lines is often a consequence of a poor choice of the orientations of the axis, we use the Sequential Generic representation to analyze this effect. As shown in Fig. 5, the dynamic mapping of the items solves the occlusion problem in most cases because the polylines have fewer chances of crossing with others polylines. A similar result can also be seen in Fig. 4, where particularly in the case of the Polygon Chart, the visual clutter is handled better compared to its static version.

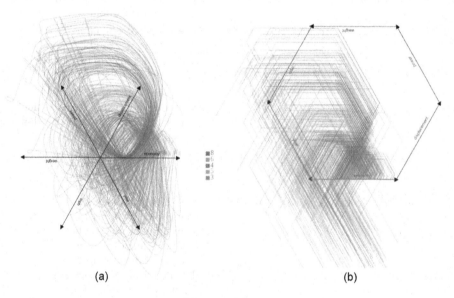

(a)   (b)

Fig. 4. The Cars (Auto MPG) dataset [1] represented with (a) the Radial and (b) N-Gon Coordinates using dynamic mapping of items.

Re-ordering Strategies. *npGLC-Vis* allows changing the orientation and the order of the axes. In this section, we analyze how these factors influence the chosen *npGLC* representation. For this purpose, we employ the tool Dimension Reordering for Parallel Coordinates mentioned in Blumenschein et al. [2], to generate different configurations of axes arrangement according to three algorithmic:

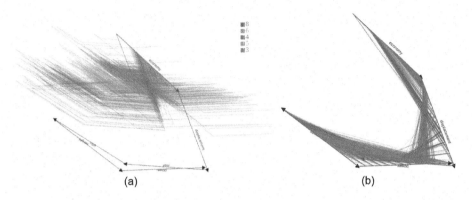

(a)   (b)

Fig. 5. Difference between using (a) dynamic and (b) static mapping of items applied on a Sequential Generic representation.

similarity-based [13], contribution-based [13], and clutter-based [15]. It is important to remark that these techniques were designed for Parallel Coordinates, and their use has not been studied for *GLC*. However, for a better comprehension of how data can be distributed in visual space, it is crucial to analyze the effect of the re-ordering strategies in *GLC*, in particular, over the dynamic charts.

In Fig. 6, we explore how these different reordering strategies impact the visual patterns in Sequential Generic charts using dynamic mapping of items. Figure 6(a) shows the default ordering, exposing the initial patterns. For the default ordering the following orientations are applied: [192°, 38°, 341°, 143°, 233°, 76°]. In this case, the more prominent colors indicate the three clusters corresponding to the more used cylinders in the cars. As a result, the blue cluster is emphasized over the rest. To verify this, we tried to improve this separation by employing other configurations of the axes while preserving the original orientations. Figure 6(b) depicts the same division of classes using the clutter-based technique. Figures 6(c) and (d) are the result to apply the arrangement based on contribution and similarity respectively. Both arrangements present a similar structure, however, a small difference shows up in Fig. 6(d), where the red cluster has more preponderance.

Interactions. Our library provides three traditional interactions to manipulate the generated chars: panning, zooming, and brushing. The brushing allows to select dimensions and/or items to filter. Figure 7 shows the result of brushing on a particular attribute that examines the influence it on the data. The user can perform more complex selections involving more dimensions in order to explore the possible hidden relationships between them.

Another interaction is implemented for the In-Line chart, through which is possible to easily compare different classes in a dataset choosing which class is plotted above and which class is plotted below the axes. Figure 8 shows how two classes can be compared to analyze which dimensions are more/less important for each one. This interaction can be very useful to analyze two very similar classes, and eventually detect if any dimension separates the data. It can also help to examine disjoint groups. Besides, it is also possible to compare one class

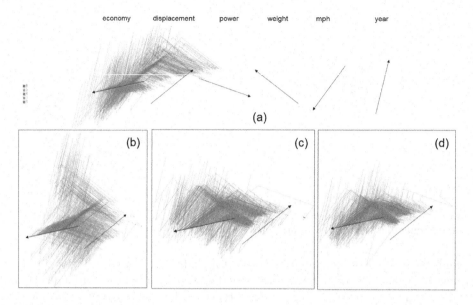

Fig. 6. Different re-ordering strategies of the axes produce different visual patters. The image shows the result of applying (a) the default ordering, (b) clutter-based ordering with a threshold of 0.5, (c) contribution-based ordering, and (d) similarity-based ordering.

with the rest of the dataset, being useful to characterize a subset of data in the context of the whole dataset.

5.2   Cluster and Outlier Detection

Another possible use of *npGLC-Vis* is for performing analysis on datasets without a ground label to perform clustering detection. In an early stage of the clustering analysis, visual inspection often allows a first understanding of the data and finds insights, that must be later verified using other methods. To test if *npGLC-Vis* techniques are useful for detecting clusters and outliers, we create a synthetic dataset using MDCGEN [7] (Multidimensional Dataset for Clustering Generator) that is a tool for testing clustering algorithmic in a wide range of use cases. We use a minimal configuration to generate the artificial data, with 3000 items, 10 features, 3 clusters, Gaussian and Uniform probabilistic distribution, and 100 outliers.

A first step in attempting to detect clusters is to employ a multi-dimensional approach such as Parallel Coordinates (Fig. 9), wherein in most cases the hidden patterns emerged. In this case, we see that there are some subsets of items that have the same properties but there is some degree of occlusion in the middle part of the chart. The same situation occurs in In-Line Coordinates, but the possible clusters are not as clear as in Parallel Coordinates. A minor change in the orientations of the axis in Parallel Coordinates generates a Bush Coordinates

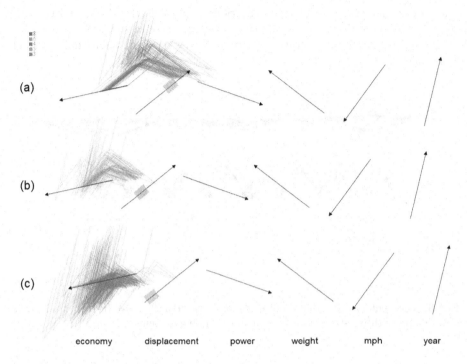

Fig. 7. Brushing on the *displacement* attribute allows to detect the three majority clusters, the cars with (a) eight cylinders, (b) six cylinders, and (c) four cylinders.

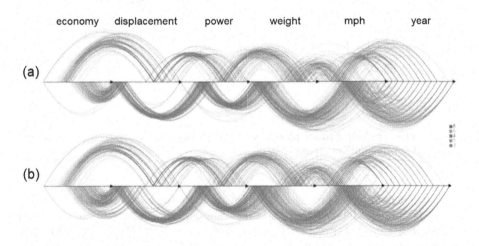

Fig. 8. Comparison between two different clusters using In Line Coordinates. The corresponding classes are analyzed at the same time. In (a) the eight cylinder class is plotted above the axes and the four cylinder class is plotted below the axes. In (b) the eight cylinder class is plotted above the axes and the rest of the dataset is plotted below them.

that depicts a better visual representation of the clusters. As we notice, the groups of polylines are farther apart from each other in some dimensions (6, 7, and 8 for example), generating an even better representation than Parallel Coordinates.

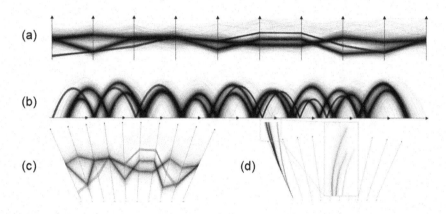

Fig. 9. The synthetic dataset represented with (a) Parallel, (b) In-Line, and Bush Coordinates with (c) static and (d) dynamic mapping of items.

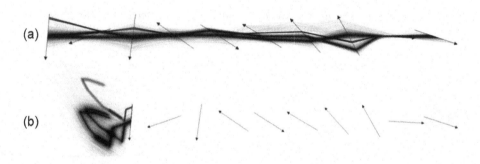

Fig. 10. The synthetic dataset plotted with Non-Sequential representations using (a) static and (b) dynamic mapping of items.

Another possible approach consists of rotating the axes of Parallel Coordinates to minimize the occluded zones. For this experiment, we choose a random initialization of orientations (265°, 199°, 262°, 146°, 328°, 150°, 133°, 120) that we preserved for both Sequential and Non-Sequential Generic techniques for avoiding the introduction of visual artifacts. As shown in Fig. 10, this initialization does not seem to be convenient as we get an occluded representation of the data. However, when the items are drawn dynamically the three clusters defined in our synthetic dataset emerge clearly. This phenomenon also happens in Sequential Generic and Polygonal Chart (Fig. 11), which leads to conclude

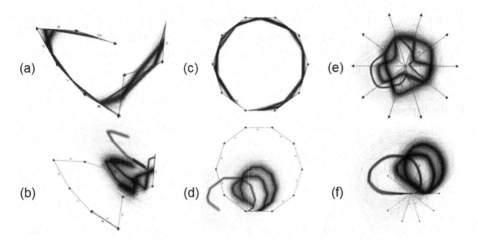

Fig. 11. The synthetic dataset plotted using static mapping of items with (a) the Sequential Generic representation, (c) the N-Gon, and (e) the Radial Coordinates; and dynamic mapping of items with (b) Sequential Generic representation, (d) N-Gon and (f) Radial Coordinates.

that, for these representations, the dynamic mapping option is not affected by the axis arrangement. Finally, the Radial chart exhibits the more distinguished clusters in both versions, where is possible to analyze how each dimension contributes to a particular cluster (static) and get a global understanding of the behavior of the data (dynamic).

6   Conclusions

In this paper, we present *npGLC-Vis*, a library for *npGLC* Visualization. Our proposal supports sequential and non-sequential layouts, integrating all the *npGLC* methods defined by Kovalerchuck [10]. In this work, as in [10], it is apparent how for some datasets, some *GLC* reveal particular patterns better than others. For some particular layouts (e.g. non-sequential and sequential generic) the emerging patterns depend on the chosen orientations of the axes and the expertise of the user to interpret the visual findings. Besides, the interactions associated with these visualizations are an essential factor that enhances the techniques in revealing patterns.

The library presented in this paper is a comprehensive library for experimenting with *npGLC* techniques and incorporates a state-of-the-art implementation of them. We consider it a very valuable tool for building visualizations for multidimensional data exploration to obtain information for discovery. However, even though our implementation achieved a complexity order of $O(n)$ for small and medium datasets, it presents scalability problems for larger datasets. The presented implementation does not scale well for datasets in the order of GBs. In this context, we propose as future work to modify the implementation taking advantage of the GPU cards using parallel computing through web API. Finally, also as future work, we aim to integrate to *npGLC-Vis* the implementation of all the *pGLC* in order to provide a tool that supports all the *GLC* representations defined by Kovalerchuk [10].

References

1. Asuncion, A., Newman, D.: UCI machine learning repository (2007). http://archive.ics.uci.edu/ml
2. Blumenschein, M., Zhang, X., Pomerenke, D., Keim, D.A., Fuchs, J.: Evaluating reordering strategies for cluster identification in parallel coordinates. In: Computer Graphics Forum, vol. 39, pp. 537–549. Wiley Online Library (2020). https://doi.org/10.1111/cgf.14000
3. Bostock, M., Ogievetsky, V., Heer, J.: D^3 data-driven documents. IEEE Trans. Vis. Comput. Graph. **17**(12), 2301–2309 (2011)
4. Bostock, M.: Towards reusable charts (2012). https://bost.ocks.org/mike/chart/
5. Bostock, M.: Let's make a (D3) plugin (2015). https://bost.ocks.org/mike/d3-plugin/
6. Draper, G.M., Livnat, Y., Riesenfeld, R.F.: A survey of radial methods for information visualization. IEEE Trans. Vis. Comput. Graph. **15**(5), 759–776 (2009). https://doi.org/10.1109/TVCG.2009.23
7. Iglesias, F., Zseby, T., Ferreira, D., Zimek, A.: MDCGen: multidimensional dataset generator for clustering. J. Classif. **36**(3), 599–618 (2019)
8. Inselberg, A.: A survey of parallel coordinates. In: Hege, H.C., Polthier, K. (eds.) Mathematical Visualization, pp. 167–179. Springer, Heidelberg (1998). https://doi.org/10.1007/978-3-662-03567-2_13
9. Kovalerchuk, B.: Visualization of multidimensional data with collocated paired coordinates and general line coordinates. In: Visualization and Data Analysis 2014, vol. 9017, p. 90170I. International Society for Optics and Photonics (2014). https://doi.org/10.1117/12.2042427
10. Kovalerchuk, B.: Visual Knowledge Discovery and Machine Learning, p. 144. Springer, Heidelberg (2018). https://doi.org/10.1007/978-3-319-73040-0
11. Kovalerchuk, B.: GLC case studies. In: Kovalerchuk, B. (ed.) Visual Knowledge Discovery and Machine Learning. ISRL, vol. 144, pp. 101–140. Springer, Cham (2018). https://doi.org/10.1007/978-3-319-73040-0_5
12. Kovalerchuk, B., Grishin, V.: Adjustable general line coordinates for visual knowledge discovery in nd data. Inf. Vis. **18**(1), 3–32 (2019)
13. Lu, L.F., Huang, M.L., Zhang, J.: Two axes re-ordering methods in parallel coordinates plots. J. Vis. Lang. Comput. **33**(C), 3–12 (2016). https://doi.org/10.1016/j.jvlc.2015.12.001
14. Munzner, T.: Visualization Analysis and Design. CRC Press (2014). https://doi.org/10.1201/b17511
15. Peng, W., Ward, M.O., Rundensteiner, E.A.: Clutter reduction in multidimensional data visualization using dimension reordering. In: IEEE Symposium on Information Visualization, pp. 89–96. IEEE (2004)
16. Tominski, C., Schumann, H.: Interactive Visual Data Analysis. CRC Press (2020). https://doi.org/10.1201/9781315152707

Author Index

Printed in the United States
by Baker & Taylor Publisher Services